Dirty Glory is a powerful, personal, and honest story from a prayer warrior I love and admire.

BEAR GRYLLS
Adventurer and chief scout, UK, from the foreword

I must admit that I was skeptical of reviewing a book entitled *Dirty Glory*, but from page one I was captivated by the many fascinating personal stories, the extraordinary answers to prayer, the accounts of historic prayer meetings, and Pete Greig's amazing journey with God. Reading about God's redemptive work in response to the 24/7 prayer movement challenged and summoned me to become a "walking, talking prayer room, a carrier of his presence," and a willing, worthy field hand who falls on her knees digging in and cultivating the soil in order to reap souls—thus the convicting and profound title, *Dirty Glory*.

CYNTHIA HEALD
Author of *Becoming a Woman* Bible study series

This is a story of the remarkable adventure of a group of people who sought the presence of God and said yes to the Holy Spirit. Pete Greig is a master storyteller, but don't be fooled: These are more than stories. They are a living theology because they are the result of a lived theology. Pete lives out of the deep and joyful belief that God is present in his world. This book will surely awaken your heart to love the Father, to join Jesus in his prayer, and to follow the Spirit in his wild and wonderful work. I know, because that is what Pete's life and friendship have done for me.

GLENN PACKIAM
Pastor, New Life Downtown, Colorado Springs; and author of *Discover the Mystery of Faith*, *Lucky*, and *Secondhand Jesus*

Pete Greig is a unique voice in the church, and this is a unique book. His words cut through any unnecessary religiosity but always remain reverent. Pete argues that the pressing need today is not for greater spiritual activity but for greater spiritual authority—and that the key to this is prayer. Nothing is sanitized here—this is a call to get your hands gloriously dirty in the service of God and to cry out in prayer for the world he so loves.

MATT REDMAN
Songwriter

I have had the privilege of working closely with Pete Greig for a number of years. We've found ourselves leading together all over the world, from churches to palaces to open fields. Time with Pete is always massive amounts of fun, brilliantly inspiring, and deeply profound. *Dirty Glory* is no different. I couldn't put it down. It was like an adrenaline shot in my arm. This book will challenge you to think bigger, risk more, and love recklessly. It's a reminder that we are invited into the adventure of a lifetime: knowing God and making him known.

TIM HUGHES
Songwriter and pioneer of Worship Central

Pete Greig has again shared for us God's dreams for a new monasticism, in the real life story unfolding around the global church. For me, Pete has been one of the huge inspirations in my life of prayer and leadership. For the church, the 24/7 prayer movement is perhaps one of the most important unifying forces under heaven.

REV GRAHAM SINGH
Executive director of Church Planting Canada, and Pasteur of St. James Montreal

How do I weave the adventure of a real friendship with God into my daily life? Pete Greig in *Dirty Glory* captures the wit and grit of normal people swept into some incredible situations just because they prayed. These stories don't offer us a foolproof formula but rather some real-world examples—often entertaining ones—of what might happen if we joined in. A great read for those who are open to more of God's mystery and mischief in their lives.

TIM DAY
Author of *God Enters Stage Left*

Few people stir my heart and challenge my faith like Pete Greig. In *Red Moon Rising* and now with *Dirty Glory*, Pete steps into my walk with Jesus and calls me to a journey of prayer that is raw and challenges the status quo at every turn. Before I was even through the introduction of *Dirty Glory*, I could feel my heart coming alive to what Jesus calls every believer to. That is a life lived with radical abandonment and childlike faith. A passion to see others experience the real and authentic touch of God in their lives. We were never meant to settle for a safe Christian existence; we were always meant to live on the edge, in the middle of the chaos, lifting up our hearts in prayer. We are to reach out to the broken and destitute. I am so grateful for the voice that Pete has been in my life, calling me out of the mundane and into the radical life of following Jesus and praying as he prayed.

BANNING LIEBSCHER
Pastor and founder of Jesus Culture

DIRTY**GLORY**

GO WHERE YOUR BEST PRAYERS TAKE YOU

• • • • • • • **RED MOON CHRONICLES #2** • • • • • •

PETE GREIG

NAVPRESS

*A NavPress resource published in alliance
with Tyndale House Publishers, Inc.*

NavPress is the publishing ministry of The Navigators, an international Christian organization and leader in personal spiritual development. NavPress is committed to helping people grow spiritually and enjoy lives of meaning and hope through personal and group resources that are biblically rooted, culturally relevant, and highly practical.

For more information, visit www.NavPress.com.

Dirty Glory: Go Where Your Best Prayers Take You

Copyright © 2016 by Pete Greig. All rights reserved.

Study Guide copyright © 2016 by Hannah Heather. All rights reserved.

A NavPress resource published in alliance with Tyndale House Publishers, Inc.

NAVPRESS and the NAVPRESS logo are registered trademarks of NavPress, The Navigators, Colorado Springs, CO. *TYNDALE* is a registered trademark of Tyndale House Publishers, Inc. Absence of ® in connection with marks of NavPress or other parties does not indicate an absence of registration of those marks.

Cover illustration of praying hands copyright © Prixel Creative/Lightstock. All rights reserved.

Author photo by Jim McNeish, copyright © 2016. All rights reserved.

Illustrations by Ben Connolly. Copyright © Pete Greig. All rights reserved.

The Team:
Don Pape, Publisher
David A. Zimmerman, Developmental Editor
Melissa Myers, Managing Editor
Dean Renninger, Designer

All Scripture quotations, unless otherwise indicated, are taken from the Holy Bible, *New International Version,*® *NIV.*® Copyright © 1973, 1978, 1984, 2011 by Biblica, Inc.® Used by permission. All rights reserved worldwide. Scripture quotations marked KJV are taken from the *Holy Bible*, King James Version. Scripture quotations marked MSG are taken from *THE MESSAGE* by Eugene H. Peterson, copyright © 1993, 1994, 1995, 1996, 2000, 2001, 2002. Used by permission of NavPress Publishing Group. All rights reserved. Scripture quotations marked NASB are taken from the New American Standard Bible,® copyright © 1960, 1962, 1963, 1968, 1971, 1972, 1973, 1975, 1977, 1995 by The Lockman Foundation. Used by permission. Scripture quotations marked NKJV are taken from the New King James Version,® copyright © 1982 by Thomas Nelson, Inc. Used by permission. All rights reserved. Scripture quotations marked NLT are taken from the *Holy Bible*, New Living Translation, copyright © 1996, 2004, 2015 by Tyndale House Foundation. Used by permission of Tyndale House Publishers, Inc., Carol Stream, Illinois 60188. All rights reserved. Scripture verses marked *Phillips* are taken from *The New Testament in Modern English* by J. B. Phillips, copyright © J. B. Phillips, 1958, 1959, 1960, 1972. All rights reserved.

Some of the anecdotal illustrations in this book are true to life and are included with the permission of the persons involved. All other illustrations are composites of real situations, and any resemblance to people living or dead is purely coincidental.

Cataloging-in-Publication Data is available.

ISBN 978-1-63146-615-1

Printed in the United States of America

22	21	20	19	18	17	16
7	6	5	4	3	2	1

The Word became flesh
and made his dwelling among us.
We have seen his glory . . .

JOHN 1:14

Go where your best prayers take you.
Unclench the fists of your spirit and take it easy.
Breathe deep of the glad air, and live one day at a time.
Know that you are precious.

FREDERICK BUECHNER

People often ask me what's happening with 24-7 these days, and whether that whole crazy, non-stop prayer thing is finally running out of steam.

Well, we spent the first few years expecting it to slow down and sometimes secretly hoping that it might stop altogether so that we could get on with the things we'd been doing before it kicked off. But that first unsuspecting prayer room has self-seeded into the lives of more than 2 million people, in more than 12,000 locations, most denominations, and more than half the nations on earth. Along the way, to my constant surprise, churches have experienced renewal, new ministries have been born, radical young firebrands have been propelled out of prayer rooms to fight injustice, journalists (from *Rolling Stone* to *Reader's Digest*) have taken note, and countless people have encountered Jesus—many for the first time. All accidentally. All because of prayer.

We only started praying because we had nowhere else to go. But then, when we did, we somehow stumbled into a story worth telling. I began recounting our adventures in *Red Moon Rising*. But that, as it turned out, was just the beginning of the journey. That was before a terrifying encounter set me down four thousand miles from home on Christmas Day in a forgotten graveyard at a place they call Blue Camp 20.

Here, then, is the next chapter of our story . . .

Pete

For Gill Greig-Allen,
who taught me to pray,
and prays as I teach.

• • •

With particular thanks to:
Brian and Tracy Heasley,
Jon and Mindy Petersen,
Kelly and Zach Tietsort.

• • •

You that would judge me, do not judge alone
This book or that, come to this hallowed place
Where my friends' portraits hang and look thereon;
Ireland's history in their lineaments trace;
Think where man's glory most begins and ends,
And say my glory was I had such friends.

WILLIAM BUTLER YEATS

CONTENTS

JUSTICE—GOD'S PRESENCE IN THE POOR

". . . but you have made it a den of robbers"

JOY—GOD'S PRESENCE IN US

"I will give you joy in my house of prayer"

FOREWORD

BEAR GRYLLS

I was about sixteen when I remember praying one of my first real prayers. I didn't grow up going to church, but I'd always had faith. Then my godfather, who was like a second dad to me, died, and I was devastated. I remember climbing a tree and saying a very simple prayer: "If you're there, will you please be beside me. Be my friend." That was the start of something that has grown to become the backbone of my life.

Six years later, when my parachute ripped and I fell thousands of feet to earth, you'd better believe I was crying out to God—you don't get many atheists in a situation like that! And maybe my prayers were answered, because the surgeon later said I came "within a whisker" of total paralysis.

Eighteen months later, as I stood on top of Everest mesmerised by the incredible curvature of the earth from the top of the world's highest mountain, it was just natural to feel, "Wow, God, you made all this?" I guess that is worship. And what a privilege to climb mountains with the One who made them.

My Christian faith has so often been a quiet backbone to our life as a family and through my work. When I took President Obama into the Alaskan wilderness for an episode of *Running Wild*, it was a special moment to finish the adventure by praying together. Out in the wild you discover pretty quickly that even the most famous, extraordinary people are asking the same questions and looking for the same things in life as all the rest of us. It was another president—Abraham Lincoln—who once confessed, "I have been driven to my knees many times by the overwhelming conviction that I had no place else to go." Smart and humble man.

I probably don't go to church as much as I should, but I do start every day on my knees, praying by my bed, asking God for strength and wisdom for the day ahead. That is the grounding for my day. Christianity isn't about religion. It's about a real relationship with God—being held, being forgiven, finding joy, finding home. And at the heart of that kind of relationship is the conversation we call prayer: asking God for help when life is tough, thanking him for the good things, and trying to listen out for that still, small voice of his guidance.

Although I know that prayer is important, I don't find it particularly easy. I am pretty impatient and struggle to sit still for long. That's one of the reasons I love this book. My friend Pete Greig has written it to inspire and help ordinary, "dirty" people like me find a bit more of God's glory. *Dirty Glory* is a powerful, personal, and honest story about life's most important adventure. It comes from the heart and from the hand of a prayer warrior whom I love and admire.

INTRODUCTION

I will tell of the kindnesses of the LORD,
the deeds for which he is to be praised,
according to all the LORD has done for us.

ISAIAH 63:7

I found myself travelling around England with Justin Welby in the week prior to his enthronement as 105th Archbishop of Canterbury. Wherever he stopped, crowds converged for a day of prayer at the local cathedral. And quite by chance, the final day of this tour was to be in Chichester, the picturesque Roman city where the 24-7 prayer movement had begun more than a decade earlier. It was to be a particularly poignant day.

The local police clearly hadn't expected anything more than a few old ladies with interesting hats, but the crowds outside Chichester Cathedral that day were large enough to stop the traffic. We were surprised too. Kneeling on a cold stone floor in a Gothic barn beside a man in a long black dress is hardly a compelling prospect. And yet thousands of normal-looking people—only a few of them with interesting hats—had turned up, just as they had at previous locations, merely to pray.

Who could possibly have foreseen any of this ten years earlier, when we had begun our quest just down the road, in a pop-up prayer space in a faceless warehouse on a dead-end street at the edge of town? Back then the cathedral authorities had viewed us suspiciously as the lunatic fringe: fire-breathing zealots, radicalised youngsters taking it all a bit too seriously. But a decade of non-stop prayer in more than half the nations on earth had carried us a mile and a half across town, from that first peripheral prayer room cocooned in clumsy graffiti to this fan-vaulted temple, built a millennium ago, at the geographical and psychological centre of the city.

Attempting to walk through the crowd outside the cathedral, Justin Welby paused by a Costa Coffee delivery van. Its driver was sitting in his cabin, helplessly adrift in a sea of pilgrims. "Saving the Nation from Bad Coffee" boasted the slogan immediately above the new archbishop's head.

Wherever we stopped on our Prayer Tour, we began the day by sharing a hearty breakfast with the local bishop. Justin Welby would always make a powerful speech, between mouthfuls of porridge, about his three great priorities. The primary objective, he would say, is *a renewal of prayer and the religious life*, and he would then point out that there has never, to the best of his knowledge, been a revival in the church that did not begin with a renewal of prayer. His second priority, he would continue, is *reconciliation*, because relationships are broken at every level in society: within families, between nations, and even in the church. We would all nod at this, of course—the bishop, the dean, the canons, and me. And then the archbishop would progress to his third priority: *evangelism*, because the nation needs the good news of Jesus. "We're not just the Rotary Club with a pointy roof," he would say, munching his toast and fixing a beady eye on the local hierarchy. "That's why prayer must come first. Without prayer there will be no renewal of the church, and without a renewal of the church, there is very little hope for the world."

> "Without prayer there will be no renewal of the church, and without a renewal of the church, there is very little hope for the world."
> —JUSTIN WELBY

It was quite a moment. For a decade members of the 24-7 movement had been scurrying around back-street clubs, independent coffee shops, and university campuses, banging a drum for "prayer, mission, and justice." We aren't used to palaces and pontiffs. Men in dresses tended, in our world, to be transvestite clubbers in Ibiza, not venerable clerics presiding over ancient ecclesiastical institutions. And yet here I was with the leader of the third largest denomination on earth as he declared prayer, mission, and justice to be his top three aims. It was a head-mash. I nearly shouted "Amen, brother!" and "Hallelujah!"—but that's not the sort of thing you do over breakfast in a bishop's palace with a man who is about to be enthroned as the leader of 80 million people.

Arresting Thunderbolts

Of course, the archbishop was right. The Bible teaches that prayer is the most powerful transformational force in the lives of individuals, churches, and even nations. Whenever and wherever God's people truly rediscover their purpose, their peculiarity, and their power, they do so through prayer. And the result of any such renewal, if it truly is a renewal of the Spirit, is first that the church is revived and then that the prevailing culture is rewired for the glory of God. There isn't a single example of a transformational Christian renewal that did not begin in prayer.

Church attendance may be declining throughout much of the Western world, but the proportion of the population that prays has remained consistently high,[1] with 75 to 97 per cent of Americans claiming to do so at least once per week, and 57 per cent praying daily.[2] In Britain, a government survey of beliefs discovered that a quarter of those who describe themselves as "nonreligious" still "take part in some spiritual activity each month, typically prayer."[3] We have often been surprised at the number of non-Christians who don't want to be preached at, yet still want to be prayed for. Prayer, it seems, is bigger than the church—a wide-open space for missional connection with a post-Christian culture that

> **Prayer, it seems, is bigger than the church—a wide-open space for missional connection with a post-Christian culture that remains surprisingly spiritually open.**

remains surprisingly spiritually open. But this is not a new phenom-enon. Christ's first apostles prioritised prayer before all other leadership tasks, in spite of the demands of spectacular church growth (see Acts 6:4). They understood that their calling, as the renewed people of God, was to be "a house of prayer for all nations," a theme we shall explore throughout this book. Christians today, who disagree about so many important things, tend to agree about the absolute priority of Christ's call to be a people dedicated wholeheartedly to prayer.

It was in the fourth century that John Chrysostom wrote an effusive hymn acknowledging prayer to be "the root, the fountain, the mother of a thousand blessings":

> The potency of prayer hath subdued the strength of fire, it
> hath bridled the rage of lions . . . extinguished wars, appeased
> the elements, expelled demons, burst the chains of death, . . .
> rescued cities from destruction, stayed the sun in its course and
> arrested the progress of the thunderbolt.[4]

It is tempting to downgrade Chrysostom's rhetoric. Our own experi-ences of prayer probably fall a little short of "extinguishing wars" and "arresting the thunderbolt." Yet every one of his examples has been drawn directly from the Bible. It was Shadrach, Meshach, and Abednego who "subdued the strength of fire." It was Daniel who "bridled the rage of lions." It was Moses, Joshua, Jehoshaphat, and Hezekiah who har-nessed prayer to "extinguish wars." And so on.

Prayer, Mission, and Justice

Of course, prayer alone won't get the job done. There is a gritty prag-matism to most of the great biblical prayer warriors. Daniel prayed diligently three times every day, but he also made astute political choices. Moses raised his hands in protracted intercession against the Amalekite army, but all the while Joshua was wielding his sword in the valley below. The great abolitionist William Wilberforce urged against "neglecting God in the secret place of prayer," but in fact he spent most of his life writing letters, making speeches in the Houses of Parliament, and building a consensus against slavery.

There's a lovely old Russian proverb: "Pray to God but continue to row for the shore." Prayer must outwork itself in action, and so this book is about more than prayer and presence. It is also about mission and justice. It is about the *saying* of prayers, for sure, but also about the *becoming* of prayers in a thousand practical ways.

• • •

Ever since that first prayer room in Chichester went viral, we've been Forrest Gumping our way around the world, praying through 9/11 and the financial crash, the war on terror, presidential elections, and the rise of Taylor Swift. Having never intended to start a movement, we don't feel particularly responsible to maintain it. To this day we don't advertise or try to persuade anyone to start prayer rooms or Boiler Rooms.[5] People just seem to want to do these things, and so we try to help them. We have become a little more organised and efficient over the years, but there still isn't any kind of plan for marketing or global domination.

For more than fifteen years we have lived in a fairly constant state of bewilderment at the places God takes us, the surprising new things the movement becomes. I am aware, therefore, as I sit down to write this book, that my part of the 24-7 story is merely one perspective, a fraction of the whole. Just last night I was told by a publisher that the impetus to start her new business had come from a divine commission received in a prayer room. A nationally renowned professor of psychology recently told me that many of his most formative experiences have taken place in prayer rooms. One of my best friends confessed that he only finally found the courage to marry his beautiful girlfriend after a succession of prayer vigils, wrestling with God until he finally overcame his terror of commitment. God is weaving a million stories together, creating a narrative far bigger than us all.

This book cannot possibly, therefore, be *the* 24-7 Prayer story. It is just my experience of the thing, woven in with that of three particular friends: Brian Heasley, the Irish ex-con who pioneered our work on the Mediterranean island of Ibiza; Kelly Tietsort, who moved from the buckle of the American Bible Belt to work with prostitutes in a walled city run by the Mexican mafia; and Jon Petersen, who grew up in Japan, raised his family in the red-light district of Amsterdam, and now lives at the foot of the Rocky Mountains in Denver, Colorado. I am indebted to them for allowing me to share their remarkable stories alongside mine.

• • •

Dirty Glory is a sequel to my earlier book *Red Moon Rising*, but I have tried to write it for new readers, too. It explores four overarching themes:

1. *Incarnation.* As its title implies, *Dirty Glory* is a celebration of the Incarnation, the "Word made flesh." That's why there are so many stories of God's glory working in unlikely places, through ordinary, dirty people like you and me. It is, I hope, a message of grace for us all.

2. *The presence paradigm.* The presence paradigm, unpacked in this book, is an exciting way of viewing the message of the Bible and the purpose of life itself through the lens of God's primary desire for friendship, family, and partnership. It shapes the way we pray, the way we preach the gospel, and the way we seek to love the poor.

3. *The house of prayer.* This book also explores what it really means to be a "house of prayer for all nations" (Isaiah 56:7), perhaps one of the most important, most misappropriated phrases in the Bible. Why is the house of prayer such a priority for Isaiah, for Jesus, and for us today? You'll find that each section of *Dirty Glory* explores a different facet of this theme.

4. *The life of prayer.* Perhaps inevitably, the most important topic explored in this book is prayer itself. Drawing on the lessons we've learned through fifteen years of continual intercession, these stories have been compiled in order, I hope, to *equip* and *inspire* you in prayer.

It is disheartening to observe how rarely anyone teaches thoughtfully about prayer, in spite of the fact that it features, in one way or another, on almost every page of the Bible, and that it was the one area in which the disciples explicitly asked Jesus for training.

You probably remember that embarrassing occasion when the disciples prayed for a boy afflicted by terrible epileptic seizures, but it didn't work. Presumably he suffered a seizure right there in front of them as they were praying—how else could they have known that he hadn't been healed? It would have been a humiliating moment for the disciples, and heartbreaking for the boy and his dad. But then Jesus returned from the Mount of Transfiguration and healed the son immediately, explaining to his red-faced followers that "this kind can come out only by prayer" (Mark 9:29). It's easy to imagine their indignation. What did he think they'd been doing out there? Hadn't they been praying too? Didn't their prayers count?

In this dramatic encounter we see that some people's prayers at certain times can be more powerful than others. Not all prayers carry the same weight. We may recoil from such an apparent grading of intercession, and yet we know this difference to be true in our own experience. Who hasn't found their faith levels heightened after a particular time of spiritual retreat or blessing? Who doesn't know at least one faithful old saint whose whispered prayers can shift things that entire stadia of young zealots can merely tickle?

We are living at a remarkable time of vast, global mobilisation in the realm of intercession. Prayer initiatives proliferate in the West and especially in the developing world. Crowds gather in auditoriums or online, just to pray. At such a time it is important to remember that God's hand is not overpowered by a certain critical mass. Revival is not awaiting one more stadium rally, or one million more hours of intercession, or—dare I say it?—one more 24-7 prayer room. The pressing need in an age like our own, when so many people are praying so much, is not for greater *activity* but for greater spiritual *authority*.

It is urgently important that we learn to partner with God in prayer, yet our pulpits and platforms remain predominantly silent about how to pray and why. Contemporary seekers are therefore still coming to Jesus with that ancient request: "Lord, teach us to pray" (Luke 11:1).

That is why—if our mission to this culture is to be more than a marketing campaign; if our acts of Christian mercy are to be anything more than well-meaning social work; if our churches are to be something other than religious clubs; if our voice is to ring out with the authority of prophetic dissonance in contemporary culture; if miracles are to multiply; if the gospel is to be preached "with signs following" (Mark 16:20, KJV); if the kingdom of God is truly to be "not a matter of talk but of power" (1 Corinthians 4:20); if our faith is to be a real, deepening, conversational relationship with the living God—we must discover how to pray.

My other reason for telling these stories is to inspire you to seek God with renewed passion. *Knowing how* to pray is less important than *wanting* to do it. My aim, therefore, is to recount our experiences in such a way as to remind you that prayer works and that it is worth it in the end. That's why I set out to describe the first five years of the 24-7 journey in *Red Moon Rising*, which has had such an unexpected impact. But our thinking has inevitably moved on since I wrote that book, and so have the stories of answered prayer which have, if anything, been even more amazing than those we experienced during those first five years. We have often been left shaking our heads in utter wonder at the miraculous ways God answers prayer.

But if this is a glory story, it is a peculiar kind of glory, mostly touching down in broken places and messed-up people who rarely feel as spiritual as the story makes them sound. I've tried to be honest, therefore, about the wonder of the journey as we've prayed nonstop since the start of this century, but also about the struggles, the simple, bare-knuckle questions with which we have often been forced to wrestle.

And so I'm here now, pulling up a chair, grinning like a maniac, saying, "You'll never believe what's been happening." And I'm planning to keep right on yarning at you, telling you tales, throwing you thoughts, until eventually you beg me to stop. Until you throw up your hands and cry, "OK, OK! I get the point. I hear you, Pete. Quit talking about it and let's start doing it. Cut out the middleman! Let's pray!"

God my Father,
  you love us too much to leave us as we are;
Jesus my Lord,
  you live to intercede for us;
Holy Spirit,
  you are praying for us now with groans beyond talking;
  so lead us out onto the wild frontiers of faith.

May this book sow a little mischief in our lives.
May these simple stories wake us up,
May they rub salt on our lips and defibrillate our hearts.
May our desire for your presence begin to erupt beyond the
    predilections of current circumstance.
May the frameworks of normality begin to feel intolerable.
Compel us to wonder again, inspire us to innovate, provoke us to rage
    against injustice.

Pete Greig
Guildford
Pentecost, 2016

1

PUNK MESSIAH

The Word became flesh and made his dwelling among us.
We have seen his glory . . .

JOHN 1:14

God's story from beginning to end describes glory getting dirty and dirt getting blessed. The Creator made humanity out of the dust, and if on that day we left a little dirt behind in the creases of his hands, it was surely a sign of things to come.

When God made us again, he came first to a teenage girl, and then to unwashed shepherds and later to pagan astrologers. God spoke the gospel as a dirty word into a religious culture. "The Word," we are told by John at the start of his Gospel, became "flesh." The Latin used here is *caro*, from which we get "carnivore," "incarnation," "carnival," and even "carnal."[1] God became a lump of meat, a street circus, a man like every man.

John is messing with our minds. He knew perfectly well that this opening salvo was a shocking, seemingly blasphemous way to start his Gospel. Like Malcolm McLaren, Alexander McQueen, or Quentin Tarantino, he is grabbing attention, insisting upon an audience, demanding a response. "In the beginning," he says, echoing the opening line of the Bible, lulling us all into a false sense of religious security.

At this point, I imagine John pausing mischievously, just long enough for every son of Abraham to fill in the blank incorrectly.

"In the beginning," he continues, "was the Word, and the Word was with God, and the Word was God." It's the familiar creation narrative outrageously remixed, featuring a mysterious new aspect of the divinity named, like some kind of superhero in a Marvel comic, *The Word*.

And yet for John's Greek readers—the vast majority of Christians by the time the Gospel was written[2]—the Word was not a new concept at all. For them this was the familiar *Logos* of domestic philosophy, that divine animating principle pervading the cosmos. The bewildering thing for their ears would have been John's emphatic conflation of this pagan Greek notion of divinity with the Creator God of Jewish monotheism: "The Word," he says unambiguously, "was God."

And so, in just these first thirty words of his Gospel, John has effectively both affirmed and alienated his entire audience, Greek and Jew alike. And then, like a prizefighter in the ring, while we are all still reeling from this first theological onslaught, John lands his body blow: "The Word," he says, "became *flesh*."

It's a breathtaking statement, equally appalling for the Jews, who had an elaborate set of 613 rules to help segregate holiness from worldliness, and for the Greeks, who despised the flesh with its malodorous suppurations and embarrassing, base instincts. "The Word became flesh." Imagine the intake of breath, the furrowed brows, the wives looking at their husbands silently asking, "Did he just say what I think he said?" and the husbands glancing towards their elders wondering, "Is this OK?" It's punk-rock theology. It's a screaming "hello."

"The Word became flesh and made his dwelling among us and we have seen his glory." One scholar says that this is "possibly the greatest single verse in the New Testament and certainly the sentence for which John wrote his gospel."[3] God's infinite glory has moved, as Eugene Peterson says, "into the neighbourhood" (John 1:14, MSG). He has affirmed our humanity fully. He has identified with us completely, both in our joy and in our pain.

"God made him who had no sin to be sin for us," explains the apostle Paul. The Word didn't just pretend to become flesh. He wasn't fraternising with humanity from a morally superior plane. Jesus *became* sin for us, "so that in him we might become the righteousness of God" (2 Corinthians 5:21). This is the staggering message of Christ's incarnation: God's glory became dirt so that we—the scum of the earth—might become the very glory of God.

This then is our creed. We believe in the blasphemous glory of Immanuel; "infinity dwindled to infancy," as the poet once said.[4] We believe in omnipotence surrendering to incontinence, the name above every other name rumoured to be illegitimate. We believe that God's eternal Word once squealed like a baby and, when eventually he learned to speak, it was with a regional accent. The Creator of the cosmos made tables, and presumably he made them badly at first. The Holy One of Israel got dirt in the creases of his hands.

Here is our God—the Sovereign who "emptied himself out into the nature of a man," as one popular first-century hymn put it (see Philippians 2:7). The Omniscience who "learned obedience," as the book of Hebrews says (5:8). The King born in a barn. The Christ whose first official miracle took place at a party involving the conversion of more than a hundred gallons of water into really decent wine. Two thousand years on, and some religious people are still trying to turn it back again. And of course it was these same people who accused him at the time of partying too hard. Rumours followed him all the days of his life, and he did little enough to make them go away.

Perfect Dirt

You probably remember the story about Jesus asking a Samaritan woman with a dubious reputation for a drink (as if he didn't know how that would look). And how he recruited zealots, harlots, fishermen, despised tax-collectors, and Sons of Thunder. And how he enjoyed a perfumed foot-rub at a respectable dinner party. One scholar says of the woman in this particular encounter, "Her actions would have been regarded (at least by men) as erotic. Letting her hair down in this setting would have been on a par with appearing topless in public. It is no wonder that Simon [the host] entertains serious reservations about Jesus' status as a holy man."[5] Jesus made himself unclean again and again, touching the untouchables: lepers, menstruating women, and even corpses. He got down on his knees and washed between the toes of men who'd been walking dusty roads in sandals behind donkeys.

And while the dirt lingered in the creases of his hands, he accused those whose hands were clean of sin. Did you hear the one about the whitewashed tombs (Matthew 23:27)? Or about the dutiful son who despised the prodigal brother staggering home penniless and covered in pig (Luke 15:30)? Or the story about the dirty low-life tax-collector whose snivelling apologies were heard by God while the precise intercessions of a righteous Pharisee merely bounced off the ceiling (Luke 18:9-14)? The Word told dirty stories, and the stories told the Word.

Offended, they washed their hands of him—Pontius Pilate, the Chief Priest, even Simon Peter—and they hung him out to die: a cursed cadaver, a carpenter pinned to clumsy carpentry in the flies of that Middle Eastern sun. Eventually it was extinguished: the sun and the Son. Ashes to ashes. Dust to dust. Glory gone the way of all flesh.

But the dirt could not contain him for long. Three days later the sun rose and the Son rose. And now that he could do anything, go anywhere, what would he do and where would he go? Out of the whole realm of creation, the entire populace of humanity, Jesus chose to appear first to a woman. A woman in a chauvinistic culture that refused to teach women the Torah and discounted their testimony in a court of law. Mary Magdalene was a colourful woman, a woman with a questionable reputation from whom seven demons had been cast. It was the biggest moment of her life. And yet at first, embarrassingly, she mistook the resurrected Jesus for an ordinary gardener, a man with the earth ingrained in the creases of his hands at the start of a working day. Yet he had chosen her quite deliberately, another Mary for another birth, another Eve in another garden, to be his first apostle.[6] This, too, is offensive to some to this day.

Yes, we believe in the Word made flesh who dwelt among us as a kind of prayer and sends us out to speak the "Amen" in every dark corner of his creation. He handpicks dim-witted people like us: "the foolish things of the world to shame the wise" (1 Corinthians 1:27). Bewildered by grace we go wherever he sends us, eat whatever is put before us, kneel in the gutter, make the unlikeliest locations places of prayer. We participate fervidly in a morally ambiguous world, carrying the knowledge of his glory "in jars of clay to show that this all-surpassing power is from God and not from us" (2 Corinthians 4:7).

And so, with angels, archangels, and that great company of gnarly old saints, we believe that someday soon this whole dirty world will finally be filled with the knowledge of God's glory. He will breathe once more into the dust of the earth. And on that day, every knee will bow. Every blaspheming tongue will cry, "Oh my God!" Every hand will be raised in surrender. And he will choose the ones with dirt in the creases of their hands, just as he always did. Flesh will become Word, and dwell with him in glory.

SELAH

Although the word *selah* occurs seventy-four times in the Hebrew Bible, no one really knows exactly what it means. Featuring mostly in the Psalms, it may have been a note to the choirmaster marking a change of verse, rhythm, or melody. *Selah* probably meant "pause."

But there's more to it than that. Its Hebrew root seems to be the word *calah*, meaning "to hang" or "to weigh." *Selah* may also, therefore, have been a reminder to the worshippers to weigh the words they had just sung or heard.

At the end of every chapter of this book you will find an invitation to *selah*—to pause and to weigh the words you have just read. Not to rush ahead to the next chapter, but to stop and reflect. It's a reminder to be still, so that this book about prayer can become your own living conversation with God.

PRESENCE

ENCOUNTERING GOD

My Father's house . . .

JOHN 2:16

If your Presence does not go with us, do not send us up from here.
How will anyone know that you are pleased with me and with your
people unless you go with us? What else will distinguish me and
your people from all the other people on the face of the earth?

MOSES, EXODUS 33:15-16

2
THE TIME OF OUR LIVES

PORTUGAL · NEW YORK CITY · ENGLAND

It is a strange glory, the glory of this God.

DIETRICH BONHOEFFER

It was breakfast time in New York City and well past midnight in Tokyo. Throughout the Middle East the shadows were lengthening, offices closing, preparing for *Maghrib*—the evening call to prayer. On the cliffs of Cape St. Vincent, that arid Portuguese headland where the Mediterranean and Atlantic oceans collide, it was 3:46 p.m. You probably remember where you were when it happened too.

There is a symmetry to life: the shape of a tree; the mirror image of a beautiful face; the cadence of a melody; the pattern of breathing, in and out; the tender way a mother cares for her daughter when she is little, and then the daughter cares for her mother when she is old; the daily constellation of coincidences attributed to luck, genetics, God, or the stars.

In the symmetry of my own life, Cape St. Vincent has become a Bethel, a fulcrum, the sort of unlikely location where you wake up blinking one day and say, "Surely the LORD is in this place, and I was not aware of it. . . . How awesome is this place!" (Genesis 28:16, 17). On my only previous visit, several years earlier, I had been a long-haired student, hitch-hiking around Europe with a friend. We were having the time of our lives, camping wild, cooking fish on open fires, drinking cheap red wine under the brightest stars you ever saw, relentlessly travelling west, traversing the golden coves and rugged battlements of the Portuguese Algarve. Eventually the ocean on our left began to appear on the right as well. The land gradually tapered, rising steadily, becoming more desolate, until we found ourselves standing alone on the vast natural ramparts of Cape St. Vincent. Laughing that we were to be the most southwesterly people in Europe for a night, we had pitched our tent and fallen asleep. But I had woken and climbed quietly out of the tent. Standing there on those cliffs, commanding the prow of a sleeping continent, I'd lifted my hands to pray, first for Africa to the south, then for America to the west, and finally, turning my back to the seas and staring at our little tent and the scrubland beyond, I'd begun to pray for Europe. And that was when I had witnessed the thing that would, I suppose, change the course of my life; the thing that had finally drawn me back here, after all these years, for this strange day of all the days there'd been.

Waves of electrical power had begun pulsing through my body, and I'd found myself looking out at an army, a multitude as far as the eye could see. Thousands of ghostly young people seemed to be rising up out of a vast map superimposed—like a scene from *The Lord of the Rings*—on the physical landscape. There was an eerie hush, a sense of expectancy, as if they were preparing for something portentous, solemnly awaiting orders. I was trembling, blinking in disbelief at the scene, barely daring to breathe. If you're going to start shaking uncontrollably while hallucinating, a cliff top at night is pretty much the worst place and time to do it.

I didn't speak about that experience for several years. Partly because I didn't know what to do about it, but mainly because I didn't want anyone thinking I was insane. But then eventually, by the time that I finally managed to convince myself that Cape St. Vincent might never have happened, it started coming true in ways that bewilder me to this day, ways that had compelled me now to return.

• • •

After that first visit to Cape St. Vincent ten years earlier, I had returned to England, graduated from university, cut my hair, and landed myself a job working with disabled adults on the south coast of England. Inevitably I fell in love with Sammy, the flirtatious lead singer of a covers band, who was relentlessly fun and wide-eyed with wonder about her newfound faith in Jesus. She didn't yet know how respectable Christian girls were supposed to conduct themselves and, better still, how they were supposed to dress, and I was not in any kind of hurry to put her right.

Sammy's life had, I discovered, changed dramatically three years earlier at the age of seventeen, when her newly converted sister, Andrea, took her along to a Christian music festival. A man had preached, inviting people to come to the

> "I prophesied . . . and breath entered them; they came to life and stood up on their feet—a vast army."
> —EZEKIEL 37:10

front if they wanted to become followers of Jesus. Sammy wasn't used to the religious protocol and hadn't really been concentrating during the talk and so, when she saw people streaming forward, she assumed that they wanted autographs or further details, and innocently joined the happy throng.

She was ushered enthusiastically into a side room, allocated a personal "counsellor," and handed a fistful of literature. Realising that she was now expected to pray some kind of prayer committing herself to being as mad about religion as her sister, Sammy rushed out of the building, lit a cigarette, and tried to gather her thoughts. But Andrea came bouncing round the corner, screamed, "Hallelujah!" and pulled the cigarette from her sister's lips. "You won't be needing these any more! Not now you're a Christian!"

Sammy didn't have the heart to explain that the whole thing was just an excruciating, toe-curlingly embarrassing mistake. Nodding that she had indeed given her life to Jesus Christ, she heard herself promising to attend a particular local church every single Sunday, come rain or shine, hell and high water, henceforth and forever more.

Faking Faith

For several months Sammy pretended to be a Christian quite successfully, lying dexterously about the church she was now supposedly attending. But then Andrea announced that she would be coming to visit one Sunday and that she couldn't wait to worship together, side by side, for the first time.

The church was meeting in a school hall. Sammy smiled a lot and pointed things out as if she was a regular member: "See that table with all the cups on it? That's where you get coffee. Those chairs? That's where we sit." She greeted perfect strangers like long-lost relatives, leaving them blinking, and moving on swiftly before they could ask her name. Sammy chose seats near the back and breathed a sigh of relief as the service started. There was a band and screens with words about Jesus, a kind of soft-rock karaoke singalong but without the big hits. She pretended to know all the songs, joining in as best she could, and drawing the line only at waving her hands around in the air. Surprisingly, each song was repeated again and again, until eventually a sweet little lady moved to the front. "The Lord has shown me," she said, "that there's someone here who is actually only pretending to be a Christian." Sammy froze. "If it's you," the lady continued, "why don't you just come to the front right now, because I'd love to pray with you."

I'm not doing that again, thought Sammy, gripping the sides of her seat and staring resolutely at the karaoke screen. But no one else moved. There was a long silence. "Does that relate to anyone?" asked the lady hopefully. "Anyone at all?" Another awkward silence. Sammy's hands were sweating. She felt sure that everyone was looking at her. But then, with a slight shrug, the prophetess shuffled back to her seat and Sammy sighed with relief. It had been the narrowest of escapes.

The service continued, Sammy began to relax, but then—with a tenacity to which we owe our entire family tree—that determined little lady returned to the microphone. "God really is telling me this," she insisted. "Someone here—you've been saying you're a Christian, but you don't know Jesus. Please, if that's you, just come to the front."

Clearly this woman was not about to surrender without a fight. And so, with a sigh of resignation, Sammy left her seat and walked dutifully, once again, to the front. What was it, she wondered, with these Christians and "coming to the front"?

The woman smiled kindly, introduced herself as Anona, and suggested that they move to a quieter place to talk. Sammy explained how and why she had been faking faith for several months. The older woman listened, laughed, and admitted that the confusing evangelist at the concert had in fact been her husband. Then she explained very simply just how easy it is to become a Christian for real.

"So let me see if I've got this right," said Sammy eventually. "You just face up to the fact that you've messed your life up and apologise to God for everything?" Anona smiled, paused, and nodded.

"And you turn your back on all the wrong stuff and make a decision to start putting Jesus first instead?" Anona smiled again and said something about the cross and a relationship with God.

"Well, that's a no-brainer. I mean, I've definitely messed things up. Badly." Sammy paused and decided not to reveal the tangled state of her love life, the seven boys she was dating simultaneously, and the broken relationships within her own family. "Yep, I definitely need a fresh start. And I think I would like to know God in a way that's real, the way my sister does. But, um, just one last question."

> "When a great moment knocks on the door of your life, its sound is often no louder than the beating of your heart. It's easy to miss."
> —BORIS PASTERNAK

"Sure. What is it?"

"Why didn't anyone explain this to me before?"

Sammy bowed her head and prayed a prayer of repentance, surrendering her life to Jesus. No more pretending. It was a simple choice—just a few words—that would change her life for ever in ways she could never have imagined. She whispered, "Amen," and the fractals of grace began spiralling out from that small prayer to touch every single member of her extended family. In the months to come, Sammy's mother, her father, both her grandparents, and her aunt, uncle, and cousins would all give their lives to Jesus. A little later, her decision that day would begin to touch me and the members of my family too. It now shapes our children and impacts the lives of those we lead. It may well impact a thousand others down decades to come.

Unaware of any of this, but feeling as if a weight had lifted from her shoulders, Sammy walked back to her seat beaming with joy. She caught her sister's quizzical expression and laughed. "I guess I owe you an explanation!"

· · ·

Sammy said yes to my proposal one night on the Isle of Skye in Scotland, and we married eight months later on a wet day in May at Goodwood Racecourse, on the South Downs of England. Our wedding was filled with family and friends, kids from the local housing estate wearing their dads' ill-fitting suits, a DJ, a barbershop choir, and a couple of hippie jugglers. Sammy's band—she in her wedding dress—belted out golden oldies from ABBA, R.E.M., and the Beatles. To this day the opening bars of "Jumpin' Jack Flash" and "Losing My Religion" conjure in my mind a blonde girl with blue eyes like a summer sky.

We didn't have a lot of money and we didn't care. Long before we had furniture, we filled our new home with the weirdest people we could find. A local drug dealer came to live with us for a few weeks while he withdrew from his own dangerous addictions. Somehow he wound up staying for three and a half years and remains part of our family to this day, with a key to our front door.

Around this time we were asked to pioneer a new church for local students. I quit my job working in the care home in order to pastor full-time. God blessed us. Life became furiously full and fun. The church grew quite quickly. We rarely had an evening to ourselves, but we really didn't mind.

But gradually, as if by some osmotic transfer, over years not weeks, the excitement of pioneering began to wear off. The colours began to bleed from my mornings. I found that I was becoming frustrated with my own superficiality, dissatisfied with pop-faith, increasingly hungry for a truer Christian experience. I became tired of talking more about Jesus in public than I talked *with* him in private. Why didn't I know God the way other people seemed to know him? Surely there had to be more?

> **"Do your friends know that you're a fraud yet?"**

The epic vision of an army of young people which I'd seen at Cape St. Vincent had somehow faded into the running of programmes which barely required God to exist. The church was attracting attention, and I was increasingly being invited to travel and teach. But as life got busier and my profile increased, so did my inner sense of dissonance. I began to realise that it would now be possible to live the rest of my life as a minor entity on a Christian production line, busy and occasionally even applauded, peddling religious experiences without ever really nurturing the kind of inner garden that I admired in others, and which could make it all mean something in the end.

It dawned on me, but only very slowly, that my inner turmoil could not be dismissed as a quarter-life crisis. It wasn't boredom, nor could it be attributed to a besetting sin from the predictable checklist. Worryingly, nothing was wrong. Everything was right and yet I felt hollow. "Within me," confessed St. Augustine, "was a famine of that inward food: Thyself, my God."[1] This hunger in my soul, I began to realise, was not bad. In fact it was good: a gift of dissatisfaction directly from the Holy Spirit.

Tentatively, I emptied my schedule of speaking engagements and persuaded the church that my prayer problem was in fact theirs as well. We converted part of a warehouse into a night-and-day prayer room, just to see what would happen. I wasn't thinking about Cape St. Vincent, trying to start a movement, or aspiring to get into *Guinness World Records*. I was simply hoping that we might learn to pray, because prayer seemed to me to be the key to pretty much everything else in life, and yet we were just utterly terrible at it. I was terrible at it. If our continuous prayer vigil ran out of steam after the first week, we would still have prayed more than ever before.

Making Room for God

Legendary record producer Quincy Jones said that, when making music, "you've got to leave space for God to walk through the room."[2] That was, I guess, what our non-stop prayer room was all about: a busy church finally exhaling, making a little space for God. And much to our surprise, when we eventually did make that space, he accepted the invitation almost immediately. The Word became flesh and moved into a warehouse on an industrial estate in a back street of a nowhere place on the south coast of England. Instinctively people felt they could talk to him in our pop-up prayer space in ways they couldn't elsewhere. Creative expressions of intercession—not just words but music, movement, and art—began to fill the room and spider across the walls until it resembled a giant family fridge covered in a blizzard of shopping lists, special offers, and clumsy children's paintings.

When your journey to the prayer room leads you through sniper fire, you know that you are desperate for God.

A few visitors came to the prayer room as non-Christians and un-expectedly encountered God. They surrendered their lives to his love without anyone saying anything to them. Others claimed to have seen or heard angels. Half-smoked cigarette packets were discarded, pornographic addictions were broken, marriages were restored, and sicknesses were healed. Sometimes in those days I wondered just how long the Lord had been standing on the church doorstep, ringing the bell, before we stopped doing Christianity long enough to let him in.

And then God sneezed.

How else could we explain the fever of new life that suddenly, unexpectedly began to spread out from our anonymous little prayer space to infect people we'd never met in nations we couldn't even spell? Complete strangers somehow started hearing about what we were doing and decided to join in, rising to pray night after night. Our prayer vigil had gone viral. It was exciting and weird. I began to wonder if this might be the beginning of that mysterious army I'd seen at Cape St. Vincent.

We were discovering that prayer didn't have to be boring and benign, the gentle pursuit of sweet ladies in their autumn years. It could be militant, defiant, catalytic, even violent. In prayer Ezekiel summoned a mighty army in the valley of dry bones (Ezekiel 37:1-14). In prayer Moses overcame the Amalekite forces (Exodus 17). In defiant worship, King Jehoshaphat won a famous military victory (2 Chronicles 20:21). Hadn't the apostle Paul described a spiritual battle raging all around us (Ephesians 6)? Hadn't Jesus begun his ministry with forty days of intense spiritual combat (Matthew 4)? And hadn't the kingdom always taken great leaps forward whenever he returned from one of his all-night prayer vigils? Maybe the army I'd seen at Cape St. Vincent was meant to march on its knees?

As the 24-7 movement began to spread out from that first prayer room, we were deluged with exciting reports from all around the world.

- "I saw an angel in our prayer room," reported one bewildered Australian Baptist pastor. "The presence of God is now so intense that many people can't stand in there. I've never experienced anything like this before. In the forty-eight hours since that visitation, there have been healings. I think we just saw a glimpse of 'thy kingdom come.'"

- We received a photograph of Syrian believers using a prayer room near Damascus. It wasn't an exceptional picture—it looked like hundreds of other prayer spaces I'd seen—but it came with a chilling message. Muslim extremists, they said, had moved into their neighbourhood. Christians were being systematically slaughtered. Bombs were exploding as they prayed, and their journey to the prayer room passed through sniper fire. What kind of courage must it take, I wondered, to pray at a time and place like that?

- Elderly ladies gathered to pray at a Salvation Army citadel in England, asking God to send young people because they didn't have any children or teenagers in their church. Suddenly, as they prayed for young people, there was a loud thud at the door. A group of teenagers was playing football outside. What, they asked, were the old ladies doing inside? "Well, why don't you come in and find out?" said one of the ladies bravely. And so, within seconds of asking God to send young people, a new youth group was born.

I suppose we shouldn't really be surprised by the power of prayer. Jesus promised explicitly to do anything we ask in his name (John 14:13-14). The church itself was born in a 24-7 prayer room, where the Spirit first fell on the day of Pentecost. When the authorities later commanded Peter and John to stop preaching the gospel, all the Christians immediately, instinctively, "raised their voices together in prayer to God. . . . After they prayed, the place where they were meeting was shaken. And they were all filled with the Holy Spirit and spoke the word of God boldly" (Acts 4:23-31). It was during a time of prayer that the apostle Peter experienced the shocking shift of paradigm which propelled the gospel out from the Jews to the Gentiles. And its next great leap, from Asia to Europe, occurred when Paul met Lydia in the place of prayer. Such places, we realised, have been established and used by God throughout history to catalyse the advancement of his kingdom.

And so, as we began to pray, we found ourselves caught up in something bigger than we'd ever known. God seemed to be building a circuit board, connecting us with new friends who shared our simple yearning to revive the church and rewire the culture. In fact, we discovered that there were thousands and thousands of like-minded souls, churches, even entire denominations hungering for more of God's power and presence. Like us, they were dissatisfied with business as usual, disillusioned with those preachers and programmes promising breakthrough for the price of a product and a ticket to the latest conference. Our earnest desire was simply, truly beyond cliché and pretence, to know Jesus.

"I saw an angel in our prayer room. I'm sure I'm not going crazy. The presence of God is now so intense that many people can't stand in there."

•　•　•

We were a year or so into the prayer movement, our church community had rediscovered its purpose in prayer, life was wildly exciting, and our second child was just seven weeks old when Sammy had the first seizure. They rushed her to hospital, where an Irish brain surgeon identified a tumour the size of an orange.

We were traumatised and terrified, but the surgery was a success. The surgeon told us later that he'd never known so much pressure in someone's skull. I've never since quite managed to shake the thought of the hissing noise you hear when you open a can of Coke.

The hospital staff removed the bandages to reveal dreadlocked hair dyed red by iodine from the operation. Sammy looked amazing! There were many setbacks, but gradually she began to recover. Her blonde hair re-emerged. We started to relax. But then came the storms.

Sammy began to experience countless conscious seizures. Sometimes they came several times a week. I watched her, deathly pale and gasping for air, trapped within her contorted body again and again, feeling as if the bones in her wrists were splintering. I cried out to God to please make them stop, but the deepest, most desperate prayers of my life didn't seem to work.

Up until then, I guess we'd believed that our prayers were going to save the world, but now I began to wonder whether they could even save my wife.

Sitting by her hospital bed during those long, grey months, reading coffee-stained copies of *Hello!* magazine and exciting e-mails from prayer rooms around the world, I had plenty of time to ponder the years since Cape St. Vincent. I watched Sammy sleeping and remembered the girl singing in a cover band, the beautiful woman walking down the aisle, the joy of becoming parents, the churches we had planted, the bewildering explosion of 24-7 Prayer. I worried about our children and found myself wrestling with unfamiliar questions.

Slowly a tantalising idea began to crystallise in my imagination. Perhaps it was merely the thought of blue skies and sunshine on those grey winter days, or perhaps it was a strange migratory urge, a homing instinct, triggered in a creature that had been confronted with its own mortality. Maybe it was the gentle whisper of God. Something seemed to be beckoning me back to the place of my call, to reconnect with that mysterious vision of an army and try to process the ensuing years, which had been the most thrilling and terrifying of our lives. Cape St. Vincent had a lot to answer for.

So I made God a quiet promise: If Sammy ever got out of the hospital, I would take her there. We would stay in a white villa, swim in the Mediterranean Sea, and barbecue tuna steaks under the stars. And then on one of the days we would drive west in an open-top jeep along the Portuguese Algarve, and when we reached the end, I would show my bride the place where a long-haired student saw something that had changed the course of our lives.

• • •

It's a risky business, revisiting holy places. Lightning rarely strikes in the same place twice. God's not big on nostalgia. But I couldn't deny how good it felt to be back at Cape St. Vincent that afternoon with Sammy by my side, several months after her successful surgery, with that distant vision of an army of young people finally beginning to materialise before our eyes.

Cape St. Vincent was pretty much as I remembered it except that, on this second visit, it seemed utterly unremarkable. There were no glowing strangers, no epiphanies, no Instagram filters that could make it anything more than a barren coastline by a mirror-ball sea on a sunny afternoon. Wanting to make the day memorable even if it wasn't to be meaningful, I bought a cheap Celtic cross pendant from one of the souvenir stalls. It leaves grey marks on my skin to this day.

The shadows were lengthening, and eventually, reluctantly, we climbed into the jeep and began the long drive back to our villa. Sammy reached for the radio, looking for some lazy Balearic beats to match the mood. Tanned and smiling, she was beautiful with her blonde hair tied back loosely under a straw hat to protect the long, curved scar on her head from the sun.

There were no blinding lights, no booming voices, no sign at all that by some strange twist of fate, we had returned to Cape St. Vincent of all places on the very day, and at the precise moment, that would define the landscape of our times.

• • •

If you're old enough you probably know where you were when you heard the news. We were driving along the Portuguese coast, listening to music on the radio, celebrating Sammy surviving a brain tumour, remembering the vision of an army of young people from my only previous visit many years before, rejoicing at the explosion of 24-7 Prayer, and quietly wondering "Why?" "What for?" and "Where do we go from here?"

The answer could not have come more clearly.

Suddenly the music on the radio stopped.

We strained to hear the voice of the US president beneath the frenetic Portuguese translation.

It had been breakfast time in New York City, past midnight in Tokyo, and 3:46 p.m. on the cliffs of Cape St. Vincent when the first plane hit the first of the Twin Towers.

The date was 9/11.

This, then, was to be our time.

SELAH

I trust in you, LORD . . .
My times are in your hands.
PSALM 31:14, 15

Eternal Love, teach me to trust your timing. Set me free from the fear of missing out. It's such a relief to remember that you believe in me more than I believe in either of us. Thank you that my destiny is safe in your hands. Amen.

If you had felt yourself sufficient, it would have been proof that you were not.
ASLAN TO PRINCE CASPIAN, C. S. LEWIS, *PRINCE CASPIAN*

3

ENCOUNTER CULTURE

NETHERLANDS · USA · UK

Let us set out on the street of love together, making for Him
of whom it is said, "Seek his face always."
ST AUGUSTINE

God plays chess. Mindful of a million variables, he carefully positions the pieces that are his. He bluffs and double-bluffs his opponent, even allowing apparent mistakes. On my first visit to Cape St. Vincent as a student, I believe that he allowed me to glimpse a move that he was planning: a generation awakening in prayer. I was speechless when I saw it and speechless when it all began to come true.

But my return visit to Cape St. Vincent had proven even more momentous. I don't know for sure whether it was mere coincidence or divine choreography that positioned us there, of all places, on that particular day, but as Sammy and I stood on those cliffs gazing out across the Atlantic Ocean and praying about God's purposes for our lives now that we knew she was going to live, the earth began to shake three thousand miles away in America, and the aftershocks continue to this day. The world was changing. America was suddenly grieving. We didn't know it at the time, but the next chapter of the 24-7 story was to carry us west.

• • •

In the long, dark shadow of 9/11 we gathered with friends in Amsterdam to seek God in prayer. The whole world seemed to be rumbling ominously. America was mourning the sudden, violent loss of 2,996 citizens. Europe was wired, a-jitter with bomb threats. The Middle East and North Africa—a landmass tagged by intercessors as "the 10-40 Window"—had suddenly become everyone's greatest concern.

In this supercharged atmosphere, the call to prayer was resounding with some urgency. Thousands were suddenly responding, rising up to intercede. But as we gathered in Europe I found myself worrying privately about lesser developments on another continent. My book *Red Moon Rising* was due to be released in America. I knew that the publisher had taken a significant risk backing a new book about a chaotic, accidental prayer movement by an unknown British author who claimed to have received a vision on a bunch of cliffs somewhere in Europe. Not unreasonably, they were expecting me to do my bit to promote it by touring American churches and conferences.

I wanted to help, but Sammy was still too unwell to be left alone even for a night, and I was still the primary caregiver for our two young children. I was barely coping with all the competing demands. The ministry was exploding around Europe, my family seemed to be imploding at home, and I was standing in the middle of it all hyperventilating.

The ministry was exploding, my family was imploding, and I was standing in the middle hyperventilating.

"There has to be another way," I said a little desperately to the group of friends gathered in Amsterdam. "Would you please pray that God gets the word out about *Red Moon Rising* in America without me having to leave Sammy and tour the conference circuit?"

Everyone duly lifted their voices, crying out to God at the same time in different languages. A Californian raised his tattooed arms and prayed, "Lord, Pete's kinda fried right now, and it seems to me that this is your project, not his. So I'd like to propose you a little deal." I opened one eye, but everyone else was earnestly agreeing. "Lord, we'll give you all the glory if the book flies in America, and all the blame if it bombs. It's your job to promote your own book, Lord, and we just wanna lift all the pressure off of Pete."

I laughed a little nervously—it was an audacious prayer—but everyone else just said "Amen."

Within ten minutes my phone rang.

"Hi, is this Peter Greeg?"

An American accent. A woman.

"Yep, this is me. But it's pronounced 'Greg.' It's Scottish."

"Peter," she said—and no one calls me that except sometimes my mother when I'm in trouble—"I'm phoning on behalf of *Rolling Stone* magazine. We'd like to do a five-thousand-word feature about the 24-7 movement. Could I perhaps fly out to interview you?"

For a moment I was speechless. Was it a joke? I looked at my friends suspiciously, anticipating the inevitable guffaw. Silence.

"OK, hi there," I said cautiously, still scanning faces for a trace of mischief. "Can I just check that you realise we just, erm, pray? It's not very cool. No leather pants. No drugs. We're not rock'n'roll. It's just Christianity, really."

Rolling Stone confirmed that they knew how uncool we were, and then they assured me that they were simply interested in our approach to spirituality, which they considered fresh and innovative. The call ended and we all just freaked out, thanking the Lord and joking about what to wear for our fleeting moments of rock'n'roll glory.

There wasn't a PR company anywhere in the world that could have achieved in a year what God had just done in five minutes. Certainly not for a penniless organisation, an obscure Christian ministry, dedicated merely to prayer.[1]

It was exhilarating to find ourselves caught up in a movement that the Holy Spirit was so clearly orchestrating. Some people make waves, but we were getting to surf them, which is way more fun. We were amazed to discover that Mike Bickle had launched a house of prayer in Kansas City on exactly the same day that we had started ours in England. What, we wondered, were the statistical chances of two global 24-7 prayer movements beginning on precisely the same day on different continents without any human coordination? But the level of coincidence moved even further into the realms of improbability when we later learned that many Indonesian churches had also launched night-and-day prayer at that particular time, and so had many Catholics under the leadership of a Texan nun, Sister Kim Marie Kollins.

Don't try to make waves. Surf waves. It's easier and way more fun.

Within a period of just a few weeks around the turn of the millennium, God seemed to have sounded a trumpet, calling millions of people to pray without ceasing. Our tentative little experiment had somehow lifted us onto the crest of a great global wave of intercession, and we were determined to surf it wherever it went—from Cape St. Vincent to the UK to Amsterdam, and now perhaps even into the hallowed pages of *Rolling Stone*.

• • •

Unsolicited media interest was encouraging, but the sudden deluge of answered prayers was the most exciting thing of all. Many reports from prayer rooms around the world sounded to us a bit like footnotes from the book of Acts. Others just made us smile.

- In Brazil a couple in their eighties gave their lives to Christ: "He is blind, they are totally illiterate and poor," wrote the local 24-7 leader, "but they immediately volunteered to pray, and did so very loudly indeed, for an entire hour!"
- In Australia, an Aboriginal lady received a dream in which she was guided by a moving light to a particular building in

town. When she awoke she wasted no time in seeking out the mysterious venue, accompanied by her three children. It was a 24-7 prayer room run by the Salvation Army, and she immediately gave her life to the Lord.

- In England a couple of particularly wild teenagers arrived at a prayer room, "and when it was time to write names of people we wanted to see become Christians, they wrote their own names on the wall!"

Every single story was encouraging in its own right, but when they were taken together with all the other reports from prayer rooms around the world, we could see that the Holy Spirit was doing something on a massive scale, far bigger than any of us. It was a thrilling realisation, but also a sobering one. Whenever God is about to initiate a new movement of his Spirit, he always begins by mobilising his people to pray. In our time, he seems to be doing so on a breathtaking scale.

> **The greatest answer to prayer is prayer itself. It's easy for God to perform miracles, rare for us to truly humble ourselves and ask.**

From South Korea to South America to South Africa, countless people have begun praying night and day. For instance, just outside Lagos, more than a million people gather to pray all night on the first Friday of every month. This one colossal prayer meeting, led by Pastor E. A. Adeboye, is so big that a bus is required to carry intercessors to the front, if they wish to receive personal ministry. Elsewhere in Africa, the Global Day of Prayer, which began at Cape Town's Newlands Rugby Stadium, expanded at a breathtaking rate to reach every single nation on earth in just eight years. On 31 May 2009, people from 220 nations called upon the name of Jesus "from the rising of the sun even to its setting" (Malachi 1:11, NASB).

The greatest answer to prayer is prayer itself. God can perform miracles easily, but only rarely do we humble ourselves enough to truly ask for them. When the church becomes so hungry for more of God's power and presence that we finally turn to him in persevering prayer, seeking his face day and night, we can be sure that the Lord will not be slow to act. In our time the church of Jesus is certainly arising, seeking God with renewed desire, rediscovering its primary purpose as a *house of prayer* for all nations.

Houses of Prayer

All four Gospels recount the incendiary story of Jesus forcibly driving corrupt traders from the temple courts. It's a decisively important confrontation—especially for those called to build houses of prayer—and it will therefore be explored throughout this book. But while the synoptic Gospels (Matthew, Mark, Luke) place this great showdown near the end of Jesus' ministry as the action that ultimately seals his fate, John's Gospel sets it right at the start. There are two possible explanations for this apparent discrepancy:

- Some people believe that Jesus cleansed the temple twice, once at the beginning of his ministry, and then again at the end. It's as if Jesus was saying, "This is what my ministry is really all about. It's where my message begins and where my mission ends."
- Other people argue that the confrontation in the temple is unlikely to have happened twice. They say that John, with his less chronological, more cinematic approach, must have identified this particular event as the defining moment that could best introduce and contextualise everything else Jesus went on to do. They argue that John repositioned this incident to make it the attention-grabbing opener for the rest of Christ's mission.

It doesn't matter which way you interpret it. If the confrontation in the temple only happened once and John singled out the *house of prayer* story because he deemed it the best possible introduction to Christ's life and work, it gains unique biblical significance. And if it happened twice, bookending his ministry, it assumes double significance. Either way, all four biographers of Jesus clearly want us to feel the force of his "consuming zeal"—that's the way John puts it—for the fulfilment of Isaiah's prophecy about a "house of prayer for all nations."

> **What if the world's great cathedrals were to become houses of prayer again? Not just tourist destinations, but true places of pilgrimage?**

On that fateful day, Jesus stood in the temple courts like a volcano ready to erupt. The grand architecture, the temple's splendid history, the opulence and wild popularity of the place, completely failed to impress him. For all its success as a religious tourist destination, Jesus could see that the temple was failing in its primary task of intercession and hospitality for the nations. This great house of prayer, recently refurbished by Herod, was exploiting the poor and excluding the Gentiles, and this was to be its judgment day.

It is sobering to think that there could be large, impressive, popular churches today which evoke a similar rebuke from the Lord. They may be attracting large crowds and have impressive buildings, strong brands, great wealth, and a remarkable history; but if they have lost the fundamental heart of prayer, they have lost their founding principle. What might happen, for instance, if the great cathedrals of Europe were to truly rediscover their purpose as houses of prayer: places of pilgrimage and not just tourist destinations? It was a senior bishop at a famous cathedral who first posed this question to me.

Blueprint

As the 24-7 movement continued to multiply, we turned to the Bible increasingly for guidance and discovered five vital priorities for contemporary houses of prayer: *presence, prayer, mission, justice,* and *joy.* These five keys help anchor Boiler Rooms,[2] prayer rooms, and churches around the world in a truly biblical blueprint for Christian community. I have therefore used them as the five sections of this book.

1. Presence: "My Father's house . . ." Christ's consuming zeal was not so much for a prayer house as it was for "my Father's house." He was motivated not by the religious activity of prayer but rather by love for his Father's presence. The focus for any true house of prayer should never be prayer itself but rather the Father himself at its heart. Sometimes people come to me in a state of great excitement about the idea of establishing houses of prayer, but when they do so, I am often wary of underlying religious motives. Others come to me talking simply about the Lord: "I'm hungry for more," they say. "I just love spending time in God's presence." This seems to have been Christ's motivation too. His impetus to pray seems to have sprung from a simple desire for interaction with the One he called *Abba.*

2. Prayer: ". . . will be called a house of prayer . . ." Prayer is obviously, by very definition, the primary purpose of a "house of prayer." We respond to the Father's presence with "all kinds of prayers and requests" (Ephesians 6:18)—with adoration and thanksgiving, petition and intercession, spiritual warfare, meditation, and so on. We are called, as God's people, to intercede for the world. Abraham interceded with God to spare the cities of Sodom and Gomorrah (Genesis 18:16-33). Jacob wrestled all night with an angel to secure the Father's blessing (Genesis 32:22-30). Moses begged the Lord not to abandon the Israelites (Deuteronomy 9:25-27). Ezekiel stood in the gap between heaven and earth (Ezekiel 22:30). Daniel knelt three times a day in Babylon to intercede for Jerusalem (Daniel 6:10). Ultimately, Jesus himself "lives to intercede" and calls us to do the same (Hebrews 7:25).

3. Mission: ". . . for all nations . . ." A house of prayer exists to intercede not for itself but "for all nations." Jesus condemned the temple not for its lack of prayer, but rather for its abject failure to love and serve the nations. Prayer rooms and prayer houses are called to be outward looking, actively engaged with the world, missional in their focus, and hospitable in their welcome.

4. *Justice: ". . . but you have made it a den of robbers."* Christ's anger was also provoked by the injustices that were being perpetrated at the temple. Moneylenders were taking advantage of honest pilgrims, and Jesus denounced them forcefully as "a den of robbers." A call to prayer is a call to the poor. That's why we ask all 24-7 communities not just to pray but also to make a measurable difference amongst those who are marginalised and oppressed.

5. *Joy: "I will give them joy in my house of prayer."* A house of prayer is, according to Isaiah's original prophecy, meant to be marked out by joy. He envisages a gathering of "eunuchs . . . foreigners [and] exiles" rejoicing in the temple (Isaiah 56:7). There can sometimes be an unhealthy intensity and earnestness amongst people called to prayer, but this is not a fruit of the Spirit in their lives. If a house of prayer is filled with God's presence, it will be celebratory and joyful, fizzing with gratitude, erupting often with laughter.

Rage against the Beige

Many years ago, long before I understood any of these principles about houses of prayer, before we started our first 24-7 prayer room, before Cape St. Vincent, way back when I was at school, I think that perhaps God had already begun preparing me to be a part of a movement like this.

As a teenager I began gathering my friends to pray. The aim was to find out for ourselves whether Christianity was true. If it was just a list of rules, there were much better things we could all be doing with our teenage years than attending a respectable Anglican church in the suburbs. Surely, we reasoned, you shouldn't be able to squeeze the Creator of tigers into a Volvo? If Christianity was to capture our hearts, it would have to be a big-booted, sharp-toothed, howling thing; a whirl of primary colours, never insipid, never static. There would have to be riots and miracles, wild-eyed adventures, angelic visitations, talking donkeys, pillars of fire, buildings shaking, crazy prophets, signs in the sky, supernatural healings, demons screaming, the gnashing of teeth, money materialising, low-life heroes defying religious bigots, justice for the poor, mercy for the sinner, epiphanies that made you wonder if maybe God was a little crazy, screaming blues, vast Russian male-voice choirs, and even unfortunately a bit of persecution along the way. If faith could be like that, well, God could have us for the rest of our lives.

If the Bible is true, it must surely be a big-booted, sharp-toothed, howling thing; a whirl of primary colours, never insipid, never static.

Feeling this way, and secretly wanting it all to be true because I respected my parents' faith deeply, I gathered my friends in a large shed in my parents' back garden and pro-posed an experiment. We would meet there every Wednesday night to try and make God turn up. If he obliged, if he came, he could have us. That was the deal. But if he stayed away, we all knew that we had some pretty wild parties we could attend instead.

Without realising it, I had just launched my first prayer room.

The Shed

Friends from school and the church youth group began to meet in our shed on Wednesday nights. We sang songs with guitars, out of tune, again and again. We found an old book of earnest Christian poetry by a Catholic priest called Michel Quoist and read these to each other as meaningfully as we could. I think we tried having Communion once or twice. We chatted to God about things and looked for the good bits in the Bible. We really didn't have a clue what to do. None of us knew anything about the Holy Spirit. We just did anything—most of it toe-curlingly embarrassing—to see if we could somehow attract God's attention.

It was truly terrible. Half of it was probably heretical. The local vicar heard about it and told me to stop. And of course that was when I knew we were really onto something.

Then one day, the Holy Spirit turned up and started to do amazing things. Someone received a vision. He saw a sword with the word *envy* written on its blade. I can still remember it, because I had never known anyone to receive a vision before and because it was a personal challenge to me. The living God had just spoken to me directly.

My friend Steve and I prayed for a girl who suddenly started shaking like she was being electrocuted on an invisible bouncy castle. It was the weirdest thing I'd ever seen. A few years later it would happen to me too, on the cliffs of Cape St. Vincent, but this was the first time I'd seen anything like it. Steve and I prayed all our very best prayers, but eventually we couldn't think of anything else to say. The girl, however, just continued shaking like a jelly. Unsure what to do, we went and got choc ices and sat there eating ice cream, watching her shake, unsure what to do. We had clearly found some kind of "on" switch, but we didn't have a clue how to switch her off. Would she now shake like this for the rest of her life?

At last she calmed down, stopped trembling, and whispered, "Wow." Then, with a big grin, she said that God had never before felt quite so real or close.

Word got out. Young people started to come from all over the area. A guy called Mark turned up because he liked a girl called Becky. He wasn't a Christian but probably quite liked the idea of being squashed in a shed with her for the night. We started worshipping as usual, and the Holy Spirit started doing his thing. Suddenly Mark manoeuvred his way out of the shed. He couldn't get out fast enough. I followed him and we sat on the concrete step outside.

"What's up?" I asked.

He was as pale as a sheet. "God's in there!" he whispered.

"Um, yes," I said. "Wherever two or three gather in the name of Jesus—"

Mark cut me off. "Don't quote any of your stupid Bible verses at me," he hissed. "Pete, you don't seem to understand. God—as in Mr. Creator of the Universe—God is in your shed. And the thing is . . ." He paused, and looked at me intently. "The thing is, if I go back in there I'm going to have to sort out some stuff which I really don't want to talk about."

Mark never did set foot back inside my mother's shed. Even Becky couldn't lure him back inside. He had experienced God's holiness in a way that challenged him to change.

Someone kindly gave me a recording of a sermon on the subject of speaking in tongues. The speaker explained in great detail how and why the gift of *glossolalia* no longer exists today. I was completely convinced and became something of an authority on the subject. I would go around our shed group explaining to anyone who would listen how speaking in tongues had died out with the early church, rehashing the arguments I'd garnered from the talk. Everyone was mightily impressed by my knowledge on the subject. Then one day, while I was out walking my dog and trying to chat to God a bit too, I found myself speaking in a language I'd never learned and didn't recognise. I spent several weeks desperately hoping it wasn't tongues, because all thirty of my friends from the shed now knew my views on the subject. To this day I suspect that the Holy Spirit gave me the gift only as a joke.

Eventually those Wednesday night sessions fizzled out. We left school and went our separate ways. But I have rarely, to this day, encountered the presence of God the way we did as teenagers in that shed. I look back now and realise that the Holy Spirit was beginning to teach me, years before the birth of 24-7 Prayer, the life-changing power of passionately seeking the Father's presence in a particular place: "You will seek me and find me when you seek me with all your heart" (Jeremiah 29:13).

The Pursuit

The pursuit of the presence of God has been, without exception or exaggeration, the prevailing passion and common purpose of all the saints in every generation since the time of Christ. Many of these women and men wrote great works, founded churches, fought cruel injustices, or made startling discoveries, but study their lives and you will quickly discover that the universal, all-consuming motivation that fuelled everything else they did was a desire for the presence of God.

In his great work *The Trinity*, Augustine repeatedly cites one particular verse, Psalm 105:4: "Seek his face always." The eminent historian Robert Louis Wilken says of this verse, "More than any other passage in the Bible it captures the spirit of early Christian thinking."[3] In other words, if you want to understand how the early Church Fathers and Mothers successfully constructed a new intellectual and spiritual landscape for their age, the essence of their thinking and motivation was a perpetual search for the presence of God.

"Seek his face always": More than any other verse in the Bible, these four words capture the spirit of early Christian thinking.

You may by now be thinking that such single-minded desire for God sounds worthy but unattainable and a little obsessive. It's precisely what you'd expect of a saint—part of the job description. That's what makes them saints. But people like Augustine never had to deal with screaming kids on the school run. Saints don't generally lose sleep with uncontrollable excitement about the new *Star Wars* movie. A saint would never sneak a game of *Angry Birds* during the sermon.

There are times in all of our ordinary lives when Jesus honestly isn't the most exciting, enthralling reality firing our hearts with desire. He can easily be filed away neatly in the "boring but important" category of life, alongside Leviticus, algebra, and flossing. The modern world effervesces with alluring distractions. How, then, are we, as normal people in such a climate, to prioritise Jesus? Let me tell you two stories about how "seeking God always" can make a difference in real life: during a chronic illness, and in the mess of a broken relationship.

•   •   •

In these days as I write, a dear friend is nearing the end of his current life. By the time you read this he will be with the Lord. He's already halfway there. His body is being ravaged by cancers. Last time I saw Keith he had become a little muddled, and yet, when I suggested reading the Bible together, his entire countenance lit up. He is confused about many things, but at the deepest level of his being, he loves the Lord. And so we sat and read the old familiar words imprinted on his soul even now, especially now. Then we prayed. Simple.

Keith's prognosis is particularly tragic because he has five children. What's more, he had been preparing to retire after a long, hard career. Yet there isn't a trace of bitterness or doubt. I have no idea why the Lord does not answer our prayers for healing. If I were God, I'd do it in a shot. But Keith seems to be trusting for something even bigger than a miracle. There is an unlikely joy around him. Heaven is close. When I spend time with Keith, I come away renewed, aware that I have been in the presence of holiness. How has Keith learned to trust so profoundly?

The Dutch Holocaust survivor Corrie ten Boom pointed out that when a train enters a long, dark tunnel, this is not the moment to disembark! This is the time to sit back and trust the engine driver. He will pull you through to the light. People like Keith have trained themselves over many years to seek the counsel of friends, even when they are tempted to isolate themselves. To trust in the faith of others, even when they doubt their own beliefs. To worship and read God's Word, even when they don't feel like it. Keith has been faithful in the minutiae of marriage, friendship, and holding down a job.

These are the raw materials of a life well lived. Simple choices that shape neural pathways. Habits that nurture virtue through seasons of disorientation and loss. Eventually we approach the longest, darkest tunnel of them all with a hard-won faith in the faithfulness of God. We recall that he has pulled us through a thousand previous tunnels. Every dark Good Friday gave way to a bright Easter Sunday, in the end.

A couple in our church had to learn this lesson the hard way when they decided to separate. We were all deeply concerned. Trial separations rarely move into reverse. Caring souls began streaming to intervene, and pastors sped to their sides with emergency lights flashing, determined to patch up the relationship, but nothing was working. Eventually a man we'll call Matthew, who was one of the least tactful, most brutally insensitive men I have ever known, announced that he was going to "give it a shot" and set off to take the husband out for a drink. By this stage we were all so desperate we figured there was nothing to lose. Matthew told the husband, in no uncertain terms, that he didn't want to talk about the broken marriage because the whole thing was, frankly, getting a bit boring. The husband was surprised because it had been the only topic of conversation for weeks on end. Matthew said that he would prefer to talk about Jesus, maybe once a week. "It's your relationship with the Big Man I'm interested in," he said. "Your relationship with your missus is up to you."

The two men began to meet weekly to pray, read the Bible, and hold each other accountable for their thoughts, words, and deeds. The marriage—or lack of marriage—was strictly off-limits for discussion. And the weird thing is that this tangential approach worked. Matthew's abrasive, tactless, no-messing intervention saved the marriage. The least pastoral, most insensitive man in our church succeeded where all the pastors had failed. At a moment in life when the husband could easily have given up on God, feeling like an abject failure, he managed instead to fix his eyes upon Jesus rather than all the problems at his feet. And as he did so, he was changed, challenged, and comforted. Gradually he and his wife were reconciled, and they have been happily married for many years, ever since.

Satan's not particularly interested in sin. His primary objective has never been to tempt you into violating a particular set of rules. His number-one aim is simply to divert your attention away from Jesus. He'll use sin to do it, for sure. But he's equally able to use busyness, or shame, or pain, or religion, or *Candy Crush Saga*, or an obsessive relationship, or a golf handicap, or a pay rise, or an illness to distract you from the Lord. Satan hates the fact that when we fix our eyes on Jesus, broken relationships get fixed, and when we love him all our lives, as Keith did, then death itself can lose its sting.

The Vision Is Jesus

The point of prayer, the entire impetus behind the 24-7 movement, is not the power that it releases but the person it reveals.

"The vision," I wrote in the first prayer room, "is Jesus. Dangerously, obsessively, undeniably Jesus." I don't pray because I'm into prayer. I pray because I'm into Jesus, so we talk. I don't believe in the power of prayer. I believe in the power of Jesus, so I ask for his help. A lot.

People sometimes ask me how to start a movement. Everyone these days wants to lead a movement. But the only movement that really matters is that of a solitary soul taking a single step toward Jesus. That was all I ever did. If thousands of others choose to join you and there are wonderful consequences you never expected or envisaged—so be it. But if you move toward Jesus alone and no one joins you, that may, in the end, be the most remarkable movement of all.

The point of prayer is not the power that it releases but the person it reveals. The vision is Jesus.

The vision is Jesus. Everything else is secondary—even the mission is less important than the man. Actually I hate evangelism, and so do most of my friends and every non-Christian I've ever met. But because I'm into Jesus, I talk about him a fair bit, in that way you do when you really like someone and you no longer care who knows it, or the way you do when you've seen an incredible movie and you want—you *need*—all your friends to experience it too. "It's incredible," you say. "The cinematography, the plot . . . you've got to see it. It'll blow your mind!" And then, inevitably, you worry that you've overstated it, that they'll be disappointed if the film turns out to be merely quite good, and you feel pretty relieved if they love it too. It's like that with films, with music, with certain foods, and with Jesus. But please don't tag me as some kind of swivel-eyed, radicalised zealot. I'm just not that brave or sure.

My vision is Jesus. Not prayer. Not mission. Not social justice. The Russian novelist Fyodor Dostoevsky argued that without God there is no morality, and if he's right there's no justice without Jesus either. Think about it: If we're all just a bunch of highly evolved animals competing to top the genetic charts in a meaningless universe where our existence is of no consequence, what does it matter if some people get trampled along the way? We're merely cosmic beneficiaries of Tennyson's nature "red in tooth and claw": victors or victims in Darwin's survivalist lottery. It's Sartre's existentialism. It's Nietzsche's super-race emerging. It's tough luck on the losers, but so what? "Attempt to bring justice without Jesus," says author Andy Crouch, "and you may not even get justice. You will certainly not get justice as the Bible understands it—the restoration of all things to their created fruitfulness in relationship with the One who made them. . . . If you follow Jesus, he will use you to bring justice. If you want justice, follow Jesus."[4]

It's Jesus who motivates the church to be the biggest global agency caring for the weak and the marginalised. It's love for Jesus, not justice, that motivates Mother Teresa's Missionaries of Charity to care sacrificially for those who are dying. Day after day those nuns get up and go out to care for nobodies who are probably just weeks or even days away from departing a world that never even knew their name. It's relentlessly pointless unless there is an afterlife and a God. Heroic altruism might perhaps motivate you to spend a few weeks in voluntary poverty engaging in such a thankless task amongst the poorest people on earth, but eventually you would run out of steam if no one ever noticed your work and if it never seemed to make a lasting or systemic difference.

The Missionaries of Charity aren't running out of steam because their compassion for the poor is fuelled continually by passion for Jesus. He notices. He says thank you. His cross reminds them daily that they are not wasting their time at all. For them it's all worship. In fact, their stated aim says nothing at all about fighting injustice or even caring for the poor. Their startling ambition is "to satiate the thirst of Christ on the cross."[5] "We may be doing social work in the eyes of the people," said Mother Teresa when she received her Nobel Peace Prize, "but we are really contemplatives in the heart of the world. For we are touching the

Body of Christ 24 hours. We have 24 hours in his presence."[6] Turns out the Missionaries of Charity are not into justice; they're just into Jesus. So they fight his enemies and befriend his friends, and when they catch sight of him in the faces of the poor, they kneel in worship. Mother Teresa's Nobel medal will mean nothing at all on the day that Jesus looks her in the eyes and says, "I was thirsty and you gave me something to drink" (Matthew 25:35).

Even worship is less important than Jesus. In fact, worship can become an idol in the church. Some Christians probably worship worship more than they worship Jesus. Some worship leaders probably worship worship-leading more than they worship Jesus. It was never meant to be an industry, a genre in Walmart, a karaoke show on Sunday.

Steps to becoming a worship leader:

(1) Practice wonder.

(2) Inspire your friends to wonder.

(3) Learn guitar (optional).

If you really want to lead worship, learn to wonder. Learn to be amazed by the life of Jesus, and your passion will quickly spread. Learning the guitar is entirely optional. Jesus never, to the best of my knowledge, played an instrument—he may have been tone-deaf for all we know—and yet he pursued the presence of his Father with every neuron, every waking choice. He erupted with gratitude. He sought knowledge in his Father's house as a child. He rose early and stayed up all night, just to walk and talk with the Father. I'm not into worship; I'm into Jesus. So when I see him I smile, I bow, and—OK, I admit it—I sing a lot, too.

The vision is Jesus. Not Christianity. Not prayer, mission, and justice. Not worship-leading or church-planting or evangelism. If you love Jesus you'll do that stuff: You'll pray and worship and go to church and preach the gospel. But in doing all those things, don't lose the why, don't get lost in the crowd.

It might be healthier if we all just stopped being Christians for a bit—a week, a month, or even a year. We're just too good at it. It has become habitual. We've been operating out of religious muscle memory for so long we've got spiritual RSI. Urgent voices are calling us to abandon the familiar comforts of Christendom, to strike out into the unknown and rediscover the Nazarene. Let him hack our systems and take us back to the place of willing surrender in which we will simply do anything, go anywhere, say anything he tells us, whenever, wherever, whatever it takes.

We need a theophany, a rediscovery of the terror of his proximity. We are overfamiliar with holy things. We speak in tongues and think it's no big deal. We experience healings. We talk to God and he talks back, for crying out loud. That means we're either clinically insane, suffering from some kind of religious psychosis, or we're experiencing an actual living, conversational, interactive relationship with the Creator of the cosmos. No middle ground. You're insane or you're a saint.

•   •   •

The pursuit of Christ has, I suppose, marked the first half of my life, from that shed in my mother's back garden to the cliffs of Cape St. Vincent and the back-street warehouse where 24-7 began. It's a sort of compulsion. A deficiency in my soul. I find that I watch films subconsciously scanning the storyline for traces of Christ's presence. I throw myself down the flumes at a waterpark, screaming with involuntary praise. In a crisis he's the first person I blame and the one I turn to for help. I am drawn to people, places, songs that somehow remind me of what I think he is probably like. I doubt him still, though not as much as I did. I pursue him because I do not yet feel that I have found him. And yet he has, I think, found me. Whenever I glimpse him, or sense him, or think I understand him, the moment is elusive and tantalising. Like a powerful drug, he continually makes me hungrier for more.

"Let us then," as Augustine writes, "seek as those who are going to find, and find as those who are going to go on seeking."[7] The joy, he says, is in the journey.

The road is different for all of us. Mine began unglamorously in a shed, led into pastoral ministry, and then, just a year before the birth of the 24-7 movement, took a very suprising turn indeed, carrying me unexpectedly to a remote Scottish island where I was about to learn one of the most important lessons of my life.

SELAH

Thou hast put salt on our lips, that we may thirst for Thee.
ST AUGUSTINE

Lord, where I am thirsty for your presence, fill my cup and let me drink.
And where I am not thirsty at all, rub salt on my lips that I may desire you deeply and seek you first.
One thing I ask from the LORD,
this only do I seek:
that I may dwell in the house of the LORD
all the days of my life,
to gaze on the beauty of the Lord
and to seek him in his temple.
PSALM 27:4

You love me unconditionally; you like me and long for my presence more than I will ever long for yours. Please grow that longing for home within me. May we walk together and talk together intimately through the pages of this book. Amen.

4

THE PRESENCE PARADIGM

SCOTLAND · ENGLAND · ISRAEL

The road and the hillside become sacred spots to many when the
winds of God blow. Revival is a going of God among his people, and
an awareness of God laying hold of the community.
DUNCAN CAMPBELL

Frenzied ghosts hissed and groaned, spitting rain horizontally across the island from the North Atlantic Ocean. Weary from two days on the road, I dialled home merely to hear the sound of a friendly voice. "Honey, this is crazy. I don't know what I'm doing here. I wish I was there with you."

The Outer Hebrides constitute some of the wildest and remotest of all the British Isles. More than sixty granite islands lie scattered like a necklace in the jade-blue seas to the west of the Scottish mainland. Fringed in white sand, they rise to jagged heights beneath glowering skies like the teeth of a smoke-breathing dragon. A thousand years before Abraham and three thousand miles north of his birthplace, Neolithic tribes were already eking a life out of these shores, pulling fish from the sea and erecting stone circles that huddle mysteriously around the land to this day.

When Columba first brought the gospel here in the sixth century, it took root readily and spread vigorously, displacing paganism as a constellation of monasteries and simple prayer cells coruscated out across the Hebrides from the abbey at Iona. Eventually this unlikely region of the world became the greatest centre of Christianity outside the Mediterranean basin. The Hebridean islands continued to thrive as an epicentre of apostolic faith for almost 300 years, until marauding Vikings (with colourful names such as Harald Fairhair, Ketill Flatnose, and Bjorn Cripplehand) sacked the archipelago, desecrating its many monasteries and killing its priests.

Most of the Hebridean islands today are uninhabited, and I was starting to understand why. My jeans were wet, it was dark, I was almost a thousand miles from home, and I couldn't get a signal on my mobile phone. I dashed from my car to an old-fashioned red phone box. Rain was crackling like shingle against the glass. The wind was howling under the door. But Sammy's voice was warm as caramel, reassuring me that God had sent me to this place for a reason. She was right. I was here on a pilgrimage of sorts, visiting the scene of the last Great Awakening and investigating a peculiar set of clues I'd recently unearthed in my late grandfather's archive.

●　●　●

Something had happened here in those postwar years in the Outer Hebrides, and particularly on the Isle of Lewis, that cannot be fully explained to this day. Between 1949 and 1953, the majority of the population surrendered their lives to Christ, empty churches were repopulated with young people, there were miraculous signs and wonders, and the entire fabric of Hebridean society was transformed by the gospel. All in just four years. Those who lived through those years insist that their experiences can only be attributed to a sovereign act of God in answer to their earnest prayers. They describe the Holy Spirit sometimes seeming to hover over specific geographical areas so that anyone who stepped into those particular zones could feel his presence tangibly and undeniably. On one occasion, at a prayer meeting in the village of Arnol, the room physically shook as they cried out to God.

God's presence sometimes became so palpable in parts of the Isle of Lewis that 75 per cent of those who gave their lives to Christ, on one particular night, did so before they even reached a meeting. Workmen knelt in the mud by the roadside, repenting of their sins. Housewives woke in their beds feeling so deeply disturbed by the state of their souls that they dared not wait until morning to get right with God. A group of young people left a party and travelled together by bus to surrender their lives to Jesus at the church. Some historians argue that there hasn't been an equivalent movement of transformational revival anywhere else in the Western world since then. Certainly anyone who prays and longs for the renewal of the church and the transformation of nations has good reason to explore the remarkable events that shook these islands in the postwar years.

> **God's presence was palpable. Seventy-five per cent of those who gave their lives to Christ did so before they even reached a meeting.**

Huddled in the phone box that night, I reminded myself that this was holy ground. People in this place had, within living memory, experienced the sort of phenomena we read about in the Bible, where it is said of the early church: "After they prayed, the place where they were meeting was shaken. And they were all filled with the Holy Spirit and spoke the word of God boldly" (Acts 4:31).

• • •

The Hebridean revival began in the tiny village of Barvas on the Isle of Lewis, where two elderly sisters, Christine and Peggy Smith, were sitting by their peat fire lost in prayer. One of them was eighty-two, bent double with arthritis, and the other was eighty-four and blind. They couldn't do much, but they could certainly still pray, and on this particular night their souls were burdened deeply by the complete absence of young people from the church across the fields. Outside, the moon hung high in the sky and the wind swept in from the sea, but inside the fire sighed and crackled, casting gentle shadows across the room as the Smith sisters poured out their hearts to heaven in their native Gaelic tongue.

Suddenly one of the women received a vision of young people filling the church. It was as simple as that—the sort of thing we might gloss over in many of our meetings today. But these two old prayer warriors were not so flippant. They summoned the minister to their house the following morning and informed him quite unequivocally that he would be needing to get ready. "Revival is coming."

"What do you suggest I do?" he asked a little helplessly.

"What should you do?" they gasped. "You should *pray*, man!" And then these two octogenarian saints proposed a deal. "If you will gather your elders and pray in the barn at the other end of the village at least two nights per week," they said, "we will do the same here from ten at night 'til three in the morning."

And so a remarkable series of late-night prayer meetings began in the village of Barvas on the Isle of Lewis in the year 1949. They persevered like this, praying for five hours a night, twice a week, because they were convinced that God had spoken—and that when he gives a promise it's our job to pray it into being.

There were no instant answers, no further visions, and certainly no teenagers miraculously turning up at church. But they refused to relent. The Smith sisters kept praying in their cottage, and the church elders kept praying in their barn for many weeks, until a particular night when one of the elders stood to read Psalm 24:

Who may ascend the mountain of the LORD?
    Who may stand in his holy place?
The one who has clean hands and a pure heart,
    Who does not trust in an idol
    or swear by a false God.
They will receive blessing from the LORD
    and vindication from God their Saviour.

"Brethren," he said, "it is just so much humbug to be waiting thus, night after night, month after month, if we ourselves are not right with God." They nodded and he continued, "I must ask myself, 'Is *my* heart pure? Are *my* hands clean?'" He lifted his head and emitted a strange cry; then he fell to his knees and crumpled to the floor.

The barn was suddenly filled with the presence of God. It was a moment that would later be identified as "the catalyst that let loose a power that shook the Hebrides."[1]

The following morning the minister sent word to an organisation called The Faith Mission in Edinburgh, requesting a Gaelic-speaking evangelist to be sent to the island without delay. A preacher by the name of Duncan Campbell was duly dispatched and made his way north. By the time he reached the village of Barvas, Duncan Campbell found the church building packed with inquisitive locals who wanted to make sure that they didn't miss out on whatever peculiarities might happen next.

What happened next is a holy thing, and I write about it even now with a sense of awe. It was as though the Holy Spirit began moving in the building. Many in the congregation actually cried out as if they were in physical pain. Some people arrived at the church after midnight, having been woken at home with an irresistible urge to come. That first meeting continued until four in the morning. Duncan Campbell himself had intended to stay in the Hebrides for just ten days but remained for more than two years, travelling from place to place, praying and preaching everywhere he went, leading countless people to Christ.

• • •

Standing in the phone box that night, with the rain beating against the glass, I didn't want to stay in the Hebrides for another two minutes, let alone ten days or two years. But Sammy's voice was reassuring, reminding me patiently of the ways the Lord had led me here. The journey had begun several weeks earlier as I flicked through some old papers belonging to my grandfather who had recently died. Buried amongst endless cuttings from newspapers, yellowed with age, I'd made a discovery so startling that it had compelled me to come.

I'd found out that The Faith Mission had been started by a man called John Govan with help from his brother, my great-grandfather James Govan. As a member of The Faith Mission and a contemporary of the Govan brothers, Duncan Campbell would have been trained, commissioned, and sent to the Isle of Lewis by members of my own family. I'd always loved the stories of the Hebridean revival, but suddenly, unexpectedly, I felt the excitement of a personal connection.

The Faith Mission had begun, I learned, with a season of intense prayer at The Water Street Hall in Edinburgh led by John Govan. For ten days, people had gathered to seek God each evening after work, sometimes continuing all night until dawn. "A day came," my great-grandfather wrote, "when the very room was shaken, as in the days of the early church and we were filled with the Holy Spirit, with 'joy unspeakable and full of glory.'"

It was hard to imagine those stern-looking brothers with their starched collars and bushy moustaches ever smiling, let alone experiencing "joy unspeakable" during an all-night prayer session, at which the building physically shook. Stirred in ways I couldn't quite articulate, I poured out my heart to a trusted older friend and immediately regretted it. Interest in ancestry and family trees is a sure sign of ageing. But she listened carefully. "I think you need to go to the Hebrides," she said eventually. "The Lord has something there for you, something in your history that he wants to release into your destiny."

God sometimes identifies something in your history that he wants to release into your destiny.

This sounded fun, and I immediately began envisaging the group of friends I would cajole into coming along for the ride. We could climb a couple of mountains, take in a distillery along the way. But then she fixed me with a beady stare. "Pete, I think you should go alone."

• • •

I flew to Scotland, drove up through the majestic mountains of Glencoe, crossed the bridge to the Isle of Skye, and drove its length in the shadow of the Cuillin mountains. I boarded a Caledonian MacBrayne ferry to sail forty miles northwest across the Minch to the Outer Hebrides. When we landed at Tarbert, I drove another fifty miles north, along narrow roads across deserted moorland, as the night and the rain settled in. Finally I arrived in the tiny, unlit village of Barvas where I was now standing, dog-tired in soggy jeans, wondering if this whole expedition had been a terrible mistake.

I left the phone box, dashed back to the car, and began driving down unlit roads to find the lodgings my mother had kindly arranged through one of her Scottish friends. I wasn't quite sure what to expect. My mum's friend had apparently called another friend, who had called someone else, who had said that they knew someone in the Barvas area. This woman's house had been full, but she had suggested that perhaps her neighbour might be willing to accommodate a complete stranger. It was a tenuous invitation, to say the very least. My hosts probably weren't even Christians. How on earth, I wondered, was I going to explain the reason for my visit, when I barely even knew the reason myself?

I was greeted at the door by an elderly lady with a warm smile and white hair coiled lazily into a bun. "Come away in," said Morag McPhail, as if I was an old friend. "You look half-drowned!" She took my coat and ushered me into the kitchen where her husband, Donald, was sitting by the range—a tall, lean man, with white hair and the most penetrating blue eyes I'd ever seen. *Some Viking blood in there for sure*, I thought.

Morag busied herself making tea while Donald plied me politely with questions. At first he asked about my family and my connection to his neighbour. Then he asked about the reason for my visit.

A little hesitantly, I explained that, in case they weren't aware, there had been an extraordinary revival of Christianity here way back in the 1950s.

My elderly hosts nodded politely, indicating that, yes, they were perhaps somewhat aware of the revival.

A little more confidently, I explained that I was a Christian and that I had come to the Hebrides on a sort of pilgrimage.

Again they nodded as if perhaps they understood that, too.

Then I explained about my great-grandfather and The Faith Mission and the link to a preacher called Duncan Campbell.

At this point my hosts erupted with laughter, as if they'd been holding it in. They started talking, both at the same time.

"Aye, we knew Duncan Campbell," laughed Donald.

"So you're related to The Faith Mission?" enquired Morag.

"He led me to Jesus!" continued Donald.

"Me too," said Morag, beaming.

"Mr Campbell was our son's godfather," Donald chipped in.

"Aye, he was a dear friend."

"But you said you're related to John George Govan?"

The population of the Outer Hebrides today is little more than 27,000 inhabitants stretched across more than sixty islands and a thousand square miles. Very few of its contemporary residents were even alive in the days when revival shook the land. But my hosts had experienced the awakening firsthand. In fact, they had become Christians through it and had even known the late great Duncan Campbell personally.

But it was even more remarkable than that. Donald McPhail was too humble to tell me about the important role he had played in the revival, but subsequent research left me in no doubt that God had set me down in the home of the man who had been the main intercessor of the awakening, aged just sixteen.

There were times during the revival when Duncan Campbell's preaching was surprisingly ineffective and he would turn to Donald McPhail for prayer support. On one occasion he was preaching to a group gathered in a police station, but his words were falling flat. Donald rose to his feet and prayed a single word with deep emotion: "Father," he said. That was all. Just two syllables and the Holy Spirit came in power, like a rushing wind. People began to cry out for salvation without another word being preached.

On another occasion, the teenage prayer warrior took a naval officer to catch a bus. "When Donald shook my hand," the sailor later recalled, "it was as if God himself touched me." As the bus drove away, that man gave his life to Jesus.

Donald was now an old man, but he kindly took me to different locations on the island, recounting the astonishing stories of God's work in each place, without ever mentioning the ways in which he himself had been deployed.

There is a telling story about a visit Donald received one day from Duncan Campbell at his family home. Donald's mother rushed out to the barn to let her son know the exciting news that the most famous man in the land had come to call. She found him kneeling with his Bible, deep in prayer. "Please tell Mr. Campbell," said Donald firmly, "that he shall have to wait because I am having an audience with the King."

At the end of my stay, Donald stood in the kitchen, laid his hands on my head, and gave his benediction. The teenage intercessor was now old and grey, but the glory of those years was still undeniably etched in his features, and I felt the fire.

•　•　•

The book of Hebrews describes a great cloud of heavenly beings and heroes of the faith cheering us on as we seek to live for Jesus. Whenever I'm flagging in my faith, I find it helpful to remember that these saints, whose lives have inspired mine, are watching my choices, applauding my efforts and crying out, "Come on!" I can imagine Christine and Peggy Smith, the two elderly sisters who prayed until the Hebridean awakening began, standing in that great cloud of witnesses, applauding the young intercessors praying night after night in 24-7 prayer rooms, as they once did in their little cottage.

Next to the Smith sisters I can picture that dignified elder from the barn. He's solemnly waving his Bible and exhorting us to holiness, urging us to ensure that we have "clean hands and a pure heart."

Beside the elder stands Duncan Campbell, the great Gaelic preacher, calling out in that booming voice, challenging us not just to pray but to preach the gospel courageously. Behind Duncan Campbell I see his mentor, my ancestor, John Govan, urging us not just to pray and not just to preach, but also to train and release the next generation of revivalists, as he once did.

Finally, I see a tall, impressive man with white hair and the most piercing blue eyes you've ever seen. It was 6 September 2004 when Donald McPhail went to join that great cloud of witnesses. In his left hand I imagine him holding one of Morag's cups of tea, and with the other he's punching the air cheering on all the teenagers, reminding them that it all begins and ends in "an audience with the King."

Then suddenly everything becomes silent and still. Every eye has turned to Donald as if they know what will happen next. Slowly a smile spreads across his face. He raises his hands (spilling a little tea), throws back his head, and issues a cry of delight: "Father!"

And at the sound of his voice all heaven roars.

* * *

Donald McPhail's remarkable spiritual authority flowed directly from his intimacy with the Father in prayer. As the apostle Paul says:

> This resurrection life you received from God is not a timid, grave-tending life. It's adventurously expectant, greeting God with a childlike "What's next, Papa?" God's Spirit touches our spirits and confirms who we really are. We know who he is, and we know who we are: Father and children.
>
> ROMANS 8:15, MSG

The public authority of Jesus also flowed from his intimacy with the Father. Jesus was the same. His public authority flowed from his personal intimacy with the Father in prayer:

For the Father loves the Son and shows him all he does. Yes, and he will show him even greater works than these, so that you will be amazed. For just as the Father raises the dead and gives them life, even so the Son gives life to whom he is pleased to give it.

JOHN 5:20-21

The most important discovery you will ever make is the love the Father has for you. Your power in prayer will flow from the certainty that the One who made you likes you, he is not scowling at you, he is on your side. All the other messages of this book lose their meaning without the infilling presence of God the Father. That was the significance of the temple for Christ: It was "my Father's house." It was home. Unless our mission and our acts of mercy, our intercession, petition, confession, and spiritual warfare begin and end in the knowledge of the Father's love, we will act and pray out of desperation, determination, and duty instead of revelation, expectation, and joy.

> **Your power in prayer flows from an inner certainty that the One who made you likes you. He is not scowling at you. He is on your side.**

Our Father

As a natural activist, I don't find this easy. I tend to want the authority without the intimacy, the power without the hidden hours enjoying the Father's presence. I am ashamed to admit that my tendency in prayer is to rush through the preliminaries ("Our Father") to get down to the "real" business ("Thy kingdom come" and "give us this day"). I tend to justify prayer by its results, and want to prove to the world (perhaps even in this book) that it is productive, that it works, that it is not a total waste of time.

But as the 24-7 movement unfolded around the world, Sammy's illness meant that I was unable to travel much. At a time when I might otherwise have been visiting exotic prayer rooms, clocking up air miles, and speaking at conferences, I was in fact at home changing nappies. And it was through the frustrations of this apparent restriction that God began to teach me a great deal about waiting and worshipping in the hidden places, dwelling quietly in the Father's house, sitting at the feet of Jesus like Mary of Bethany instead of rushing around serving him like Martha, *being* rather than *doing*. The Father began coaching me, speaking to me powerfully through the mundane circumstances of my new domestic realities.

On one particular occasion, when I had just finished writing a book, I gathered Sammy and the boys in front of my computer. I'd been working so hard for so long, the children were fractious and I was exhausted. We committed the book to the Lord, said "Amen," and dispatched the manuscript to the publisher. It was a moment I'd been anticipating eagerly, and I knew exactly what we should do next.

We drove to a pub with a large leather couch for me and a playground for the kids. Collapsing into the soft embrace of the sofa, I pointed the boys towards the swings and slides: "Go and have fun!" I grinned, a little too enthusiastically. "Play as long as you want."

They whooped with excitement and bounded towards the door. One of them ran right on outside to the playground, but our other son paused, watched his brother running to the swings, and then looked back at me quizzically. Slowly he turned round and walked back into the room as if he'd forgotten something or had something to ask. But instead he just climbed into my lap, threw his arms around my neck, and said four words that sucked the air from the room: "Daddy," he whispered, looking into my eyes and nodding his head with each syllable to emphasis the point, "Daddy, I missed you." While our other son laughed on the slides and swings outside, I sat quietly inside, breathing in time with the little man in my arms.

He didn't become any more my son at that moment just because he'd preferred me to the playground. I didn't start loving him more than our other boy outside on the swings. But his act of unnecessary affection ministered to my tired father's heart at depths he could never have known. And the Bible says that this is precisely the opportunity we have in Christian prayer: to minister to the Father's heart, with unnecessary acts of deep affection. When we choose God's presence at 3 a.m., he won't love us any more than all the sensible

> **We can minister deeply to the Father's heart with unnecessary acts of deep affection.**

people asleep at home, but our desire to be with him in those moments is the sweetest song we will ever sing.

God's Oscar Speech

When Jesus was baptised, the Spirit descended and the Father announced to the world how very proud he was of his boy: "You are my Son, whom I love; with you I am well pleased" (Luke 3:22). At this point in his life, Jesus hadn't done anything publicly to merit such approval. He was thirty years old at a time when people rarely lived beyond forty-five, and his ministry had still not begun, yet the Father was already pleased with him. God's pleasure in us is never dependent upon our achievements. He doesn't grade our performance like a wannabe celebrity in a reality show. He loves us because he likes us because we are his kids.

There are just two other occasions on which the Gospels report the actual words of the Father speaking audibly to Jesus, and since it has only been recorded three times in the totality of world history, all three moments surely deserve our particular attention. This first instance occurred at Jesus' baptism in the River Jordan at the start of his ministry. The second occurred during his transfiguration on a mountain in the middle of his ministry (Luke 9:35). The third occurred in the temple at the end of his ministry during Jesus' final week (John 12:28). The weird thing is that, on all three occasions—in the river at the start, up the mountain in the middle, and at the temple near the end—the Father says pretty much the same thing. At Jesus' transfiguration the Father says, "This is my Son, whom I love; with him I am well pleased" (Matthew 17:5). Almost identical to his words at Jesus' baptism. And the third time he simply affirms Jesus, assuring him that his life has already brought glory.

God's Oscar speech, the words he wants to write in the sky on your birthday, are these: "I love you. I'm proud of you."

These three exchanges which punctuate the three years of Jesus' ministry must surely rank as some of the most important verses in the whole of Scripture, and yet they say so little. The Father could have denounced the Romans, rebuked his Son's detractors, told people to repent, or revealed the meaning of life. This, after all, is God speaking audibly to his Son for all to hear. But instead, on each occasion, all he says is "I love you" twice and "I'm proud of you" three times. And it seems to me that, in the absence of any other evidence, these three exchanges alone tell us all we need to know about the unconditional affection and affirmation within the heart of the Trinity, and consequently the relentless love of the Father towards all of us as his children: His priority is relationship, and his default is kindness. The Father's Oscar speech, his one phone call, the words he wants to write in the sky on your birthday, are these: "I love you. I'm proud of you."

Of course, this can be frustrating. Most of us would prefer God to speak in specifics: to tell us what to do, when to do it, and how. But he generally refuses to micromanage our lives. When I say, "Where should I go?" he says, "I love you." I ask, "What should I do?" and he says, "I'm proud of you." I say, "How should I handle this situation?" and he says, "Let's hang out." Time and time again God ignores my most pressing questions in order to answer the deepest longing of my heart.

A prayer room may sometimes become a sort of classroom in which we learn from God, or it may occasionally become a boardroom for doing business with him, or a war room in which we fight for the extension of his kingdom. But first and foremost a prayer room is not a classroom, a boardroom or a war room; it's a living room for intimate interaction with the Father. Carol Arnott, who with her husband, John, has spent more than twenty years helping Christians to wait and to "soak" in God's presence at their church in Toronto, puts it like this:

> There must be time for Him, just to love Him and have Him love us, no other agendas, no shopping lists of prayer requests. These may come later, but we need to put loving Him first, because only as we are filled with His love, do we have love to give away. So many Christians cannot rest in His presence but must constantly "be on duty." . . . I do not want to hear the words, "Depart from me; I never knew you." I want the love affair to begin now.[2]

Couch Time

Resting in God's presence is one of the most important and one of the most difficult things we will ever learn to do. I went on retreat to an old monastery with my friend James, an Anglican priest. It was only a two-day retreat, but I arrived with long lists of all the problems I needed to pray about, questions I needed God to solve, and three big books I was determined to read. All in forty-eight hours. Noticing how unrealistic and driven I was, even in my prayer times, James told me a simple, beautiful story that helped slow me down.

James's son Connor was in his final year at school, and most days, when he got home he would come and find his dad in the study, remove his tie, and flop down onto the sofa. He would remain there for a while as James continued to work—silently sprawled out on the cushions, staring at the ceiling, idly thumbing his phone, never particularly wanting to talk. Connor didn't

God doesn't micromanage. His guidance speaks to identity more than activity: the who, how, and why more than the where, when, and what.

have any agenda other than to unwind for a bit in the presence of his dad. Later in the evening he would chat about his day and ask to borrow the car. But when he first got home all he wanted to do was to be with his father without doing or saying anything. "You have no idea," said James, eyeing the ambitious pile of books I'd brought on retreat, "how deeply I treasure those wasted moments, simply doing nothing together every day."

Our Father in heaven longs for us to seek out his presence in the Holy of Holies without an agenda. Not out of duty. Not because we have favours to ask or things to get off our chests. He wants us to seek him out simply because we are happier in his presence than anywhere else. "One thing I ask from the Lord," says the psalmist:

> this only do I seek:
> that I may dwell in the house of the LORD
> all the days of my life,
> to gaze on the beauty of the LORD
> and to seek him in his temple.
>
> PSALM 27:4

Of course there are times to be intentional in prayer: to petition the Father for provision, to cry out for help, to ask for advice, to borrow the car keys. But if we only ever make demands of God, we will gradually reduce our relationship with him to a self-interested wishlist of transactional requests. Instead, in the words of Pope Francis:

> Prayer should be an experience of giving way, of surrendering, where our entire being enters into the presence of God. This is where dialogue, listening and transformation occur. Looking at God, *but above all sensing that we are being watched by him.*

The Pope even admits: "Sometimes I allow myself to fall asleep while sitting there and just let Him look at me. I have the sense of being in someone else's hands."[3]

Learning to dwell (and even to sleep) in the love of the Father in this way is offensive to the strategic part of our brains—a violation of the ego, a sort of dying. It can seem irresponsible, like David dancing in his underpants when he should have been thinking about his reputation as a national leader (2 Samuel 6:12-16). It can appear profligate and super-spiritual, like the psalmist "yearning," "fainting," and even "crying out" simply to be in God's dwelling place (Psalm 84). It can seem naïve and scandalous, like Mary of Bethany splashing bottles of Chanel on Jesus' feet, when the money could have been used to feed the hungry (Mark 14:3-4). It can be inefficient, like Jesus staying up all night in prayer when he really needed to be sharp the next day (e.g., Luke 6:12). It can appear selfish, like Mary abandoning her sister peeling potatoes in the kitchen so that she could recline at the feet of Jesus (Luke 10:38-42). It can seem rude, like Donald McPhail ignoring his important guest to continue his "audience with the King." It can seem unstrategic, like me swapping church-planting for mere prayer. "To be a witness," says the writer Madeleine L'Engle, "is to be a living mystery. It means to live in such a way that one's life would not make sense if God did not exist."[4]

> "To be a witness is to be a living mystery. It means to live in such a way that one's life would not make sense if God did not exist."
> —CARDINAL EMMANUEL SUHARD

23-7 Prayer

Near the start of the 24-7 movement I shared a pizza with Brennan Manning, the much-loved priest and author of *The Ragamuffin Gospel*. "How do you know when you've prayed enough?" he asked me with a twinkle in his eye.

"I guess I don't," I admitted eventually.

"So you feel guilty most of the time?" he continued.

"Well, I try not to . . ."

"Let me tell you," he continued, waving a piece of Hawaiian pizza in my direction, "how we see prayer in the contemplative tradition. For us," he said mischievously, "the hour you might spend in a prayer room each day would be the one hour in the day when you *don't* pray."

He paused, but I just stared at him blankly.

"It's like this," he continued. "The hour you spend in the prayer room is when you refocus, re-centre on Jesus, becoming fully aware of his presence once again. When this happens, you can carry God's presence with you into the other twenty-three hours of the day, knowing all the time that he is with you, he is for you, he likes you, and he hears your thoughts. You'll see people and situations the way he sees them. When problems arise you'll pray in real time, right then and there, instead of compiling prayer lists for a later holier moment. In fact, your life will become that moment: a continual conversation with God."

I nodded. This was a strange concept to someone who had grown up in a tradition that anchored prayer securely in an all-important daily devotional time, or at an optional weekly prayer meeting, or at church on Sunday morning. It seemed strange, and yet it also made a lot of sense in the light of the things we were learning about the presence paradigm. Here was a way to move from just saying our prayers to *being* our prayers, from asking for God's kingdom to come once or twice a day to carrying his presence with us continually. It meant that the real purpose of a 24-7 prayer room is to multiply itself into the lives of those who use it, sending them out from the presence of God as walking, talking prayer rooms, carriers of his presence—living temples of the Holy Spirit.

Nice Tree

God spoke to me about this very clearly one day, as I walked down a road near my house. It wasn't an audible voice, but it was so unmistakably and unexpectedly him that I stopped immediately, mid-pace, right there in the crowded street. God said, "Look at that tree."

I froze and stared at it with my heart racing. Something momentous was obviously about to happen. Perhaps this was to be my burning-bush moment? Or perhaps the tree was about to fall, and I was to heroically save someone? Or maybe the Lord was about to give me a powerful prophetic revelation or even an angelic visitation.

I stood there transfixed, staring into the branches of a fairly average hawthorn (if my memory serves me correctly), hardly daring to breathe. And gradually . . . absolutely nothing happened. I waited undeterred, rooted to the spot, eyes aloft, muscles tensed, while fellow pedestrians gave me sideways glances, probably concerned that I'd lost my cat, or cricked my neck, or was having some kind of awkward "episode."

"OK, I'm looking at the tree," I hissed eventually, just in case God hadn't noticed or had got distracted with events in the Middle East. "What happens now?"

But God didn't seem to be in any great hurry to reply. Eventually, a little reluctantly, he said, "I just thought it was a pretty good tree, Pete," before adding, "Why do you always have to get so intense about everything?"

I found myself muttering, "Nice tree, Lord. Good job on the tree." Then I wandered off down the road a little dejectedly, having experienced the most underwhelming epiphany of all time.

Your relationship with God is at its best when you talk to him about trivia: trees and trains and parking spaces. I'd hate it if my children only ever talked to me about Grave Matters of Serious Concern. What's more, if you only pray about big, important, weighty matters, you will only occasionally be grateful. But if you learn to pray about things like nice-looking trees or your daily bread when the supermarket is full of the stuff, then you will live in a state of continual gratitude for miracles so common that most people take them for granted.

I often wonder what Adam and Eve talked to God about when they walked with him in the cool of the evening before there was any sin or sickness or suffering in the world, before there were any problems at all in the world, before there was any need for intercession or spiritual warfare. I presume that they merely said "Thank you" and "Wow" a lot. Perhaps they pointed out things they had discovered in Eden that day and asked a lot of questions. Maybe they explained the weirder names they had chosen for the animals. They must surely have said a lot of things like "Nice tree, Lord."

One day we will be with the Lord for ever. But what will we talk to him about once there are no more sicknesses to be healed, sinners to be saved, churches to be planted, and injustices that need to be fought? Too often we only pray about problems: conflict at work, friends who need healing, prodigals far from God. One day, when the Lord invites us to walk with him in the cool of the evening, and there are no more problems we can possibly address in prayer, will we have learned simply to enjoy his presence, hallowing his name without asking for anything in return?

> **Your relationship with God is at its best when you talk to him about trivia. An attitude of gratitude grows from a daily conversation with him.**

*   *   *

A friend of mine attended an intensive residential interview for a particular role in senior church leadership within a major denomination. They gave him psychometric testing, asked him to facilitate group discussions, quizzed him about his theology, and set him essays on complex ethical dilemmas. These were probably all good things to do, but at no point in the whole two-day process did anyone simply sit him down, look into his eyes, and ask the most important questions of all: "Do you love Jesus? How did you meet him first? Was it him who sent you here? Did you carry the presence of God with you when you stepped through the door today?"

This is peculiar, because there isn't a single biblical character used significantly by God who did not have a life-changing encounter with his presence. Not one. Ezekiel would probably have failed a psychological test. The apostle Peter would have flunked a group-facilitation exercise for sure. James and John had unhealthy ambition. Thomas was plagued by doubt. Paul had been a Machiavellian aggressor against Christians. But none of this really mattered because they had all encountered Christ and become carriers of his presence.

Jesus called the twelve disciples to himself primarily so "that they might be with him" and only secondarily "that he might send them out to preach" (Mark 3:14). Before we do great things for Jesus, we are called very simply to become his friends. Henri Nouwen, who swapped a successful career as a university pro-fessor for life amongst the physically and mentally disabled, said that the most important question for any min-ister of the gospel is not "How many people take you seriously? How much are you going to accomplish? Can you show some results?" but "Are you in love with Jesus?"[5] This means that we are qualified for Christian service by our praying and not our preaching, by our desire to worship him and not our workload on his behalf, by knowing Jesus personally and not just by knowing a lot of interesting things about him. If you lose God's presence you lose everything, but if you know his presence you already have everything you will ever need.

> **We are qualified for Christian service by our praying not our preaching, by our worship not our workload, by knowing Jesus personally.**

The Secret of Obed-Edom

I have always had a particular soft spot for a very minor biblical char-acter called Obed-Edom, whose life epitomises the sheer joy available to us all in the presence paradigm. But blink and you'll miss him. He photobombs the story of David a couple of times, and then he's gone. And yet Obed-Edom knew all about hosting the presence of God because he had once accommodated the Ark of the Covenant in his own home. Indiana Jones, eat your heart out.

You may recall that the Ark had been on its way into Jerusalem, carried clumsily on the back of a cart, when an unfortunate ox-driver called Uzzah reached out and touched it. He was only trying to stop the holiest object in the world tumbling to the ground. It should never have been carried so casually in the first place, but poor old Uzzah dropped dead on the spot. Everyone was suddenly terrified—so much so that King David gave orders to abort the procession and approached the nearest landowner with one of the most extraordinary requests in world history: "Would you mind housing the Ark of the Covenant for a while?" David needed time to work out what to do.

I assume that Obed-Edom had a large house, and that he had children. Imagine how worried he must have been when he commanded them not, under any circumstances, to touch the big box with the angel wings in the spare room. Obed-Edom had no guarantee at all that housing the symbol of God's presence was not going to cost him his life or the life of at least one of his children. Caught somewhere between wonder and fear, he must have thanked God for the unspeakable honour of his presence with one breath and begged God to spare his life with the other. More than a thousand years before the cross of Christ, Obed-Edom was forced to gamble his life upon grace.

The glory of God's presence must have been heavy throughout Obed-Edom's home for the three months in which he housed the Ark. I imagine worship and prayer erupting continually; revelation flowing freely; his marriage happier and more fulfilled than it had ever been; the children laughing, thriving, and healthy; neighbours coming round just to enjoy the atmosphere of peace and joy; arguments getting resolved quickly; and consciences sensitised to holiness. We're told that, during this season, Obed-Edom's business prospered so much that eventually King David was provoked to envy. You have to be significantly successful in business to leave a king feeling like he's missing out. Wanting the blessing of God's presence for his own family and city, David eventually determined to retrieve the Ark and resumed the procession, but this time he did so with appropriate reverence and lavish attention to every detail. It became such a joyful carnival, so full of the presence of God, that David himself was eventually overwhelmed with worship, dancing in complete abandonment in his underwear.

The story moves on. Obed-Edom's fifteen minutes of fame have passed. But then, when we are just about to forget him altogether, the name of Obed-Edom begins to pop up again and again. First as a temple porter, then as one of the "singers with instruments" appointed by the Levites, and finally as a treasurer in the temple (1 Chronicles 15:18, 21; 2 Chronicles 25:24). If this is the same fellow, we may well wonder why such a successful businessman would take a relatively humble job as a porter, and then as a musician in the worship band, and finally as the temple treasurer. We can't know for sure, but it is a reasonable guess that Obed-Edom had fallen in love with the presence of God. The one commonality between these three roles is that they all orbited the Ark of the Covenant, now housed in the temple. Having experienced the blessing of proximity to the Lord, Obed-Edom knew that nothing else and nowhere else could be as satisfying. He simply didn't care whether he was a treasurer, a porter, or a musician. He would do anything to get as close as he could to the Ark once again. Obed-Edom's overwhelming passion for the presence of God is captured in Psalm 84. The psalm itself is anonymous—no one knows for sure who wrote it—but I have a theory that Obed-Edom was its author. I should say at this point that there is absolutely no academic evidence whatsoever to support my theory. But even if he didn't write Psalm 84, it's certainly easy to imagine Obed-Edom happily reciting it as he went about his duties at the temple:

How lovely is your dwelling-place, LORD Almighty!
My soul yearns, even faints, for the courts of the LORD;
my heart and my flesh cry out for the living God. . . .
Blessed are those who dwell in your house; they are ever praising
    you. . . .
Better is one day in your courts than a thousand elsewhere;
I would rather be a doorkeeper in the house of my God
than dwell in the tents of the wicked.

When we host God's presence in our homes, schools, businesses, and churches, we unlock Obed-Edom's secret. The joy of the Father's house ruins us for the suburbs of religious mediocrity. Augustine knew this secret too: "You arouse us so that praising you may bring us joy, because you have made us and drawn us to yourself, and our heart is unquiet until it rests in you."[6] That is often my experience when I step into a prayer room. The door shuts, and I sigh with the sense of homecoming. All the voices that have been conspiring to distract me from the presence of God are exposed in that moment as convincing lies. I remember again that my main purpose in life, my highest calling, the primary reason for my existence, is simply, wonderfully, in the famous words of the Westminster Shorter Catechism, "to glorify God and to enjoy him for ever."[7]

• • •

As the 24-7 movement continued to expand, we were certainly experiencing the joy of God's presence and sometimes even felt a bit like Obed-Edom, almost addicted to the Father's house. The stories I'd heard from Donald in the Hebrides still lay far beyond anything we'd so far witnessed, but there were certainly many encouragements. And so we had gathered the 24-7 tribes in Amsterdam to seek God in the wake of 9/11. We were focused on Europe and the Middle East, and when *Rolling Stone* unexpectedly crashed the party and the movement began to take off in America, we started to wonder whether maybe the Holy Spirit was calling us to look west as well. The answer was coming, but we were going to face one of the most supernatural and terrifying encounters of our lives to find it.

Many centuries before Europeans arrived in America, around the time of Abraham, the ancient Celts stood on the beaches of places like the Outer Hebrides, gazing west as the setting sun sank flaming into the sea. They would wonder what lay beyond that distant horizon, and would sit around fires at night weaving magical stories about a place they called *Tir na Nóg*, "Land of the Young." The citizens of this land were, they believed, always happy and eternally young. Paradise awaited them somewhere beyond the sea.

It's fascinating to me that the modern mythology of America as a land of dreams, of plenty, of eternal youth may well be as old as these stories of *Tir na Nóg*, nurtured over many centuries in the imaginations of the very Celtic peoples who first left Ireland, Scotland, Wales, and England, lured so easily by the promise of a New World located, as it always had been in their oldest thoughts, beyond the western horizon where the sun slips into the sea.

Tir na Nóg sounded pretty good to Sammy and me. We were learning to find the presence of God in the midst of our trials, but with terrorist attacks filling the headlines in Europe and regular seizures still afflicting our lives at home, a bright new land of happiness and eternal youth sounded great. Exchanging the English rain for *Tir na Nóg* was a beguiling dream, but it was to be an unexpected nightmare that would propel us, soon enough, to its shores.

SELAH

Be still, and know that I am God.
PSALM 46:10

I pause now to become more aware of your presence in the stillness of this moment. Grant me epiphanies of the ordinary today—glimpses of your presence in the places I go, the people I meet, the routine things I do. Teach me to perceive and receive your presence in all things. Amen.

It is not necessary for being with God to be always at church; we may make an oratory of our heart wherein to retire from time to time, to converse with him . . . Everyone is capable of such familiar conversation with God.
BROTHER LAWRENCE, *THE PRACTICE OF THE PRESENCE OF GOD*

PRAYER

GOD'S PRESENCE IN POWER

. . . will be called a house of prayer . . .

ISAIAH 56:7

*When I shut up the heavens so that there is no rain, or command
locusts to devour the land or send a plague among my people, if my
people, who are called by my name, will humble themselves and pray
and seek my face and turn from their wicked ways, then I will hear
from heaven, and I will forgive their sin and will heal their land.*

2 CHRONICLES 7:13-14

5

ALL HELL

ENGLAND · SWITZERLAND · AMERICA

We are up against the unseen power that controls this dark world,
and spiritual agents from the very headquarters of evil.

EPHESIANS 6:12, *PHILLIPS*

The sound of the siren seemed to emanate from another place entirely. Another ambulance. Another family. Not us. Somewhere else. Surely, not us again.

Hudson, who was now four years old, lay in my arms, clutching his favourite cuddly toy, Lala, with one hand and gripping three of my fingers with the other. "Daddy?" he said, so quietly that I had to bow my head. "Daddy, my legs feel funny."

We were slaloming down country lanes, scribbled across the English landscape years before cars and trucks and speeds like these. I counted numbers in my head, and tried to ignore the ominous, involuntary twitching in my son's legs.

"It's going to be OK, Huddy," I whispered, brushing his hair softly and banishing the helium from my lungs. "We'll be at the hospital soon and they will make you better. Try to stay awake."

The National Poisons Clinic had warned us that it was probably too late to remove the powerful drugs from his tiny body.

I glanced nervously across at Sammy, searching for reassurances of my own. Strapped into a fold-down chair by the ambulance door, she was beautiful in her evening clothes, a touch of mascara around those big blue eyes, ready to party. It had been several months since the encounter with *Rolling Stone* in Amsterdam, even longer since that fateful return to Cape St. Vincent, and she was slowly getting better. Her hair was tied back to hide the scar, but a few strands were playing across her face as she stared down at her phone, frenetically texting friends, begging them to wake and pray for our little boy.

Instruments rattled in their allocated drawers. Lights strobed out across the fields. The swirling of the van and the smell of diesel. I closed my eyes, caught in a nightmare, hardly believing that we were back here again.

• • •

Two years had passed since Sammy's surgery, eighteen months since our return to Cape St. Vincent. Things had been going well. Maybe too well. Much of the day had been spent with one of my heroes: an old American missions statesman called Floyd McClung. Having heard the near-mythical tales about Floyd's pioneering work in Afghanistan on the hippie trail in the 1970s, and later in Amsterdam's infamous red-light district, and having been profoundly impacted as a teenager by his book *The Father Heart of God*, I had been thrilled finally to meet this smiling giant. His seven-foot frame, wide smile, and white socks worn with Crocs combined to remind me of Roald Dahl's Big Friendly Giant.

Floyd was visiting England to speak at a large conference with four impressive young men. We didn't know it at the time, sitting in that ambulance, but these people were about to become firm friends, key players in the unfolding story of 24-7 Prayer. In fact, the terror of that night would catapult us into their world in a remarkable way, almost against our wills.

One of the young men, Adam Cox, seemed to burn with quiet intensity. But where Adam was intense, his friend Nate Chud—a handsome Alaskan with a toothpick perpetually lodged in his perfect dentistry—was so laid back he almost seemed stoned. And then there was Travis, with a long blond ponytail and a remarkable call to the Native American reservations. Beside Travis was David Blackwell from Chicago, a man without an ounce of fat anywhere on his body, who could talk more enthusiastically about food than anyone I'd ever met. David once spoke for almost half an hour about a single Chicago hot dog. I timed him.

I had asked them about the impact of the recent terror attacks on their nation, and about Afghanistan, where Floyd once lived. The gentle giant sighed. "Pete," he said eventually, "there's an urgent need in America, in Afghanistan, in the Middle East right now for . . . *Jesus*!" He laughed at the naïvety of his statement, raising his hands above his head in mock surrender. "That's why we need to pray!" He turned his attention to Sammy, staring at her over the top of his grandpa spectacles, and then looked back at me. "The 24-7 movement isn't a coincidence. You have been raised up—by God—precisely for such a time as this."

Emboldened and sobered, I embarked upon our story, starting with the vision at Cape St. Vincent, and our return on 9/11. I described the red moon that had risen above us the night we launched 24-7 in Guildford, about *Rolling Stone* in Amsterdam, about the unexpected explosion of prayer rooms and the way the movement seemed now to be morphing into mission.

Floyd just laughed and nodded like he was remembering the whole thing. And then, leaning back in that tiny chair and crossing his legs so that one giant Croc was almost as high as my head, he sighed. "OK, count me in. How do I join?"

"What we really need," I said, "is a few older people, mothers and fathers who've been around the block a few times, who'll believe in us enough to want to help us without trying to take control."

Floyd said he'd love to be one of those people, and casually suggested that we think about opening an office for 24-7USA at the new mission college he was establishing in Kansas City. It sounded exciting, and we agreed to talk together more the following day.

But maybe someone somewhere didn't want us to talk more the next day, the day after that, or ever. Within twenty-four hours of that first meeting, all hell had been let loose in both Floyd's family and ours.

Blasphemous Prayers

Worshipping in such a large congregation later that night, I surveyed the sea of shining faces and smiled at Sammy. Over the previous three years we had countless seizures, a brain tumour, the birth of a child, and the beginnings of a global movement. The encouragement from Floyd that day, and the atmosphere of celebration in the venue, felt like a milestone on Sammy's incremental road to recovery. Life was, at last, starting to feel less scary, more fun.

After the meeting, Sammy and I popped back to our accommodation to check on the boys before heading out to a reception for fellow speakers. The babysitter had put Hudson to sleep in our bedroom so that he wouldn't disturb his younger brother. Poking our heads around the door, we could see that he had wriggled down under the covers so that only his mop of blond hair was visible above the blankets. We whispered his name, but he didn't move. Sammy tiptoed into the room and risked turning on a light to refresh her make-up. He didn't stir. Didn't move a muscle.

Then God spoke.

Not audibly. Not undeniably. But now in the ambulance, with the benefit of hindsight, it did seem that something supernatural must have taken place—and the thought granted me a faint glimmer of hope. You can call it female intuition, call it a hunch, call it luck if you really have that much faith in fate, but something caused Sammy to put down her hairbrush and go to a special container, tucked away in one of the drawers where she had been hiding her medication from the kids.

Bemused and frustrated, I watched her empty a pile of those

powerful brain-drugs onto the bed in which Hudson was sleeping and laboriously count them out. A blue pill. A yellow pill. A white one. A pink one. Another white one. And so on. We were already late for the party. I was checking the time. Pacing the hallway. The moment she finished counting, I said, "Come on, let's go," and stepped towards the door. But Sammy just ignored my impatience and began the whole pointless exercise all over again, counting faster.

"Twenty," she said at last. Then she looked up, fear in her eyes. "Pete, twenty of my pills are missing."

For a split second I paused. Had she miscounted? Left some pills at home? But then, with a single thought, we both lurched towards Hudson, flung back the covers and froze with horror.

Hudson was lying on his side, curled up in his tartan pyjamas. A single yellow pill lay half-sucked on the ice-white pillow. A pretty pink one was trickling even now from his baby lips. How many anti-convulsant drugs had he swallowed, searching for one that would taste as nice as they'd always looked?

"Huddy!" I commanded, shaking him to wake him. But he barely stirred. Sammy was talking hysterically. The babysitter rushed in. There were those two wet pills on the pillow, but no trace of the other eighteen.

Scooping Hudson into my arms, I bounded out of the building in three or four strides, yelling instructions over my shoulder, running with his listless body towards the site office.

"Call an ambulance!" I shouted, barely recognising my own voice. My lungs were empty and the world was moving way too slow. The hospital, they said, was twenty-six miles away. Twenty-six miles at night on narrow country roads designed for horses. Lanes scarcely wider than the van in which we were travelling.

Many years ago, God spoke through the prophet Jeremiah to a terrified people: "I know the plans I have for you," he promised, "plans to prosper you and not to harm you, plans to give you hope and a future" (Jeremiah 29:11). Sitting there in the site office a little earlier, holding our semiconscious four-year-old, awaiting the ambulance, I'd felt all such hope draining from my body. Could the very drugs that saved my wife now damage or destroy our firstborn son? My own triumphant sermon, preached with such conviction barely an hour before, now seemed hollow.

The National Poisons Clinic had fired questions down the phone. I heard myself confirming that, yes, a four-year-old boy had indeed ingested up to eighteen epilepsy pills and sucked on two more. I had recited the names and the strengths of my wife's medication. Some of the strongest anti-convulsant drugs on the market. At least ninety minutes previously.

"Nineteen?"

"No. Nine-oh," I replied flatly.

A slight pause.

I had tried to describe the way that his legs were occasionally spasming. They said it was probably too late to get the drugs out of his system. Someone muttered something darkly about his liver and other organs. I shut it out. The thought of those powerful drugs irretrievably damaging our child was simply too terrible to accommodate.

Sitting in the ambulance now, I held my son, closed my eyes, and prayed desperately in sighs and mumbled blasphemies.

• • •

We arrived eventually at the hospital where night staff hurried us, blinking, through bright lights to an observation room. Sammy's frenetic texting seemed to have mobilised a small army of intercessors, and yet it felt foolish to admit such things amidst the cold, clinical tools of medical science.

A doctor arrived to conduct some initial observations. He instructed a nurse to take a blood sample and hurried away. Sammy and I sat talking as calmly as we could, holding hands, exchanging worried glances. We noticed that Hudson's spasms had stopped. What did it mean? He began to stir. And then he suddenly sat up and asked where he was. We stared at him in amazement, hardly knowing what to say.

The nurse returned to take Hudson's blood. She ran a few checks and took his sample away for analysis.

Eventually, the doctor returned with the results. "Hudson Greig," he said slowly, checking his clipboard, looking at us and then at the blinking boy in the tartan pyjamas staring up at him. Were we certain, he asked, still staring at Huddy, that our child had ingested so many pills? Because there was no sign of any poison whatsoever in his system. All Hudson's vital signs were fine, he said, his eyebrows arching with doubt. And then, with a weary shrug, he said we were free to go.

We arranged a new prescription for all Sammy's missing drugs and climbed into a taxi, hugging Hudson especially tight. Had we really just experienced a miracle? How could a child who had been convulsing and half-conscious when we carried him into the ambulance a few hours earlier now be heading home completely fine without any clinical intervention? We would later interrogate the babysitter, check and double-check the apartment for any sign of the missing pills, and search in vain for a way to explain Sammy's mysterious compulsion to count her drugs. In the end, however, we never did find a better explanation than the simplest one of all: God really had spoken to Sammy and answered our prayers. He had intervened miraculously to spare the life of our little boy.

You don't kiss your brains goodbye when you become a Christian. God doesn't get insecure if we ask a few sensible questions.

Of course, people question miracle stories like these, and so they should. In a world full of charlatans and sweet, gullible suckers, it's only rational to wonder about the number of serious, verifiable illnesses which remain uncured while Jesus appears in a tortilla, sends gold dust around Christmas time, or makes a leg grow by half an inch. We were never meant to anchor our faith in tortillas and Pentecostal osteopathy. We didn't kiss our brains goodbye when we gave our lives to Jesus. And he doesn't get insecure if we ask a few sensible questions.

However, although miracles can be misreported, and they certainly don't happen as frequently as we might like, this does not mean that they don't happen at all. Jesus performed many miracles and told us to expect the same (John 14:12). It was Einstein who said that there are really only two ways to live: as if nothing's a miracle or as if everything is. The very intellectual capacity we possess with which to question miracles is in itself a kind of miracle beyond explanation. We might as well deny our own ability to think and blink and read a book. Waking up as we do in a cosmos where a billion planets have apparently been perfectly choreographed to orbit a million stars, it's absurd to question the possibility that sometimes a car might swerve unexpectedly to spare the life of a child. Finding ourselves to be intricately designed, sentient beings, it seems ridiculous to doubt the occasional wonder of an eye opening, or a virus dying, or a depression lifting, or a cancer that had been inexplicably growing one day inexplicably shrinking the next, or a collection of anti-convulsant drugs disappearing from a child's bloodstream at the command of the One who constructed his cardiovascular system in the first place.

•   •   •

We paid the taxi driver a small fortune and trudged wearily back towards our apartment, muttering something about docking Hudson's pocket money for the next twenty years. But there was still one more shock in store, as we discovered from a steward on night duty.

"Quite a night," he muttered.

"Quite a night," we agreed.

"First this little monkey scares us all witless," he said, winking at Hudson, "and then this terrible business with Floyd McClung's daughter."

"Why?" we both exclaimed. "What's happened?"

"I guess it was while you were gone. Misha—that's her name. She was pregnant and went into labour, but something went wrong. She's in a coma. Fighting for her life, and the baby too. Not looking good, I'm afraid. Need to pray."

At the door of our apartment, Sammy paused to gaze at Hudson asleep in my arms, his head resting on Lala sandwiched against my chest. "Thank you, Lord," she whispered softly, stroking his blond hair. "I don't know what's going on round here," she continued, staring now at the long row of identical doors. "But please, Lord, would you do for Floyd and his daughter what you just did for us?"

We opened the door and went in to bed.

• • •

I spent much of the next day online and on the phone, furiously mobilising prayer for Floyd's daughter, doing what little we could to support them. There was no time to process our own trauma from the night before—the news coming through from America was terrifying. Misha had suffered an amniotic embolism and was being kept in a coma. Some of the fluid from her womb had leaked into her heart, and this had caused cardiorespiratory collapse. She had gone eight minutes without breathing. The medical prognosis for both mother and baby was utterly bleak. Misha, it seemed, was suffering from one of the most dangerous and untreatable conditions in obstetrics, a set of complications associated with an 86 per cent mortality rate.[1] Even if she survived, Floyd had been cautioned to prepare himself for the probability that his daughter would suffer long-term neurological damage. As for his new grandchild, it was a boy called Luke born by emergency C-section, but he had probably been starved of oxygen for as many as fourteen minutes.

The prognoses for both Misha and baby Luke were terrifying, and yet we prayed for them with a new level of faith fuelled by the miraculous events of the night before. Hadn't God just delivered our own son supernaturally? Couldn't he do it again? We prayed because it was all we could do, but also because it was the most powerful thing we could do, and we mobilised the 24-7 networks around the world to join us.

The following night Floyd was scheduled to preach to the big crowd in the circus tent, but with his daughter lying in a coma on the other side of the world, we assumed he wouldn't do it. Some said he *shouldn't* do it.

He was white as a sheet, clearly traumatised, but he was also determined to preach. "I've come here to deliver a message and Satan's not going to stop me," he said quietly. "I can't make any difference back home, right now, and I'm not going anywhere until I've done the thing God brought me here to do." And so, armed with just a pocket Bible and without notes, this broken-hearted father took to the platform and conveyed the Father heart of God to a spellbound congregation. I had never heard such a defiant sermon; the passion and the pain were written across his face on the large screens. Many people responded to the message and streamed to the front of the tent to ask for prayer. Floyd stepped out of the spotlight and down into the twilight at the side of the stage. Quietly switching on the mobile phone I had lent him, he dialled home.

The phone glowed blue, highlighting Floyd's features as he lifted it to his ear. I watched him smile wearily at the sound of his wife's voice, but then his features froze. He ended the call looking shocked. "It's Misha," he said, half-whispering. "She's, um, awake, and she's . . . she seems fine. No sign of brain damage. And we have a new little grandson, Luke. They think he's gonna be OK too." At last Floyd's features broke into a smile of pure joy.

We would later discover that medical staff at Misha's hospital had been so stunned by this dual miracle that they set about calculating the statistical probability of what had taken place. The likelihood of both Misha and Luke surviving an amniotic embolism without lasting neurological damage was 1 in 1.2 million. Virtually impossible.

What were we to make of it all? It had been a day unlike any we'd ever known. Within hours of meeting Floyd and discussing the possibilities for 24-7 Prayer in America, we had both nearly lost our firstborn children, and had both received miracles of deliverance.[2]

* * *

It's easy to overplay our own significance in the greater schemes of life, but we must also avoid the opposite pitfall of underestimating the authority we have as children of God, especially when we pray (Ephesians 6:18). The great Swiss theologian Karl Barth insists that "prayer exerts an influence upon God's action, even upon his existence."[3] Jesus promises unambiguously to do "whatever you ask in my name" (John 14:13). A little later he sends his disciples out with "all authority in heaven and on earth" (Matthew 28:18-19). That's a lot of authority. Our prayers can often be more powerful than we dare imagine. Hudson, Misha, and baby Luke could easily have died or been brain-damaged on the same day, but instead we prayed and they were saved.

Put Your Fists Together and Pray

The Bible is clear that we are engaged in a vicious spiritual battle, in which God's purposes are contested constantly. Prayer (in which we harness our wills with God's will to resist Satan's will) is our greatest weapon of defence as well as attack. People sometimes ask why God requires us to pray, as if it were merely a form of relentless begging: "please, please, please" in the tone of a child beseeching his father for a treat, or a football fan wishing like mad for a goal in the final minute. But to pray is not to plead from the sidelines; it is to invade the field of play. In prayer we join the team, actively shaping the outcome of the match, challenging and occasionally outplaying an aggressive opponent (Revelation 12:10-12). Martin Luther went so far as to describe prayer as "a constant violent action of the spirit as it is lifted up to God, as a ship is driven upward against the power of the storm." He continues:

> Thus we must all practice violence and remember that he
> who prays is fighting against the devil and the flesh. Satan is
> opposed to the church . . . the best thing we can do, therefore,
> is to put our fists together and pray.[4]

It can be troubling to recognise the militancy of prayer and the level of authority we may wield to affect the outcome of spiritual battles. But the truth is this: There are terrible evils that will only be restrained, and wonderful blessings that will only be unlocked, by our prayers. "You do not have," says the apostle James very simply, "because you do not ask God" (James 4:2). The Lord's purposes are contingent upon our prayers because he has chosen to work in partnership with our free wills. He has not made us automatons preprogrammed to do his bidding. He is love, and love liberates, love trusts, love risks, love collaborates. It does not dominate, control, coerce, or enslave.

> "He who prays is fighting against the devil . . . The best thing we can do, therefore, is to put our fists together and pray."
> —MARTIN LUTHER

The Creator is still creating. He invites those made in his image to join him in imagining and forming the future—new songs and movies, new scientific theories, innovative businesses, revolutionary social policies, brilliant computer games, medical breakthroughs, recipes for soup. In the words of the great French philosopher Blaise Pascal, God has "instituted prayer . . . to impart to his creatures the dignity of causality."[5]

Fool's Gold

One of the most confounding miracles we've experienced in more than fifteen years of continual prayer involved a much-loved Swiss prayer warrior called Susanna Rychiger. She relinquished the prospect of a senior post in her successful family business to pioneer a 24-7 community in the beautiful Alpine town of Thun. One day the Lord spoke to Susanna, directing her to move into a particular, strategically located apartment in the centre of town where she would be able to reach out to many of the neediest people. The rent on this new apartment, however, was way beyond Susanna's modest budget, so she cut back on all luxuries and began to pray for provision daily, claiming the promise of Psalm 55:22: "Cast your cares on the LORD and he will sustain you; he will never let the righteous be shaken."

If I had known about Susanna's financial challenges at that time, I probably wouldn't have asked her to consider flying to South Africa, at her own expense, to represent 24-7 at one of the first meetings of the Global Day of Prayer. I certainly wouldn't have promised her so casually that God would provide the money for her flight if he wanted her to go. But Susanna, being a godly woman, just smiled and promised to pray about it. Almost immediately someone did indeed offer to fund her trip.

The meetings in Cape Town furthered an important friendship with the organisers of the Global Day of Prayer, so it's easy to see why God had so speedily provided the funds for Susanna to attend. But of course, while she was in Cape Town, she continued to pray for the money to pay her rent back home.

A friend called Rebecca was house-sitting Susanna's apartment while she was away. Deciding to clean the place before Susanna returned, Rebecca went to the cleaning cupboard, opened the door, and gasped. Thousands of Swiss francs lay scattered around the boiler and over the floor. Why was Susanna hiding so much money while pleading poverty? Why had she left it like this, strewn across the floor? Why hadn't she put it in a bank like everyone else?

Understandably perplexed, Rebecca piled the bank notes neatly in the corner of the cupboard, scribbled a note asking Susanna to call, and went home to her parents wondering what to do.

"Did you find the money?" asked Rebecca, without any introduction, when Susanna finally called.

"Money?"

"The pile of money. The pile of money in your cleaning cupboard, Susanna."

Unsure what to think, Susanna initially opened the door of the wrong cupboard. The voice on the phone redirected her, and she gasped at the sight of the cash. With her mind reeling and her hands trembling, she knelt to count 14,000 Swiss francs—half a year's wages. Could Rebecca be playing some kind of game? But Susanna knew for sure that she didn't have that kind of money. And even if she did, why would she leave it like this or decide to give it in such a convoluted way? Rebecca was clearly freaking out too.

Maybe a generous friend had secreted the bank notes in her cupboard while she had been away? It was a lovely thought, but since Rebecca was the only person with a key, this would have involved breaking into the apartment. And why would anyone go to such lengths when they could easily just post it through the door, or make an anonymous payment into her account? No one would scatter money in a weird little cupboard, especially while someone else was staying in the house. It didn't make sense.

Perhaps the previous tenants had left the money there? Quite apart from the fact that people tend not to forget that much cash, Susanna had been living in the apartment for several months, had obviously often used the cleaning cupboard, and knew that the money certainly hadn't been there previously.

> "Each miracle writes for us in small letters something that God has already written . . . in letters almost too large to be noticed, across the whole canvas of Nature."
> —C. S. LEWIS

Susanna carefully searched every nook of the tiny cupboard in case the cash could somehow have been hidden for some time, but there was no way it could possibly have been missed.

The bank told Susanna that no one had reported the money lost. The police said that it hadn't been stolen. Nobody could explain how it had appeared in her house. In the end there were only two possible explanations: "Either the world's most confused burglar had broken into my apartment and deposited thousands of francs in my cupboard before leaving without a trace, or God really had heard my cries for provision and made the money materialise in my cupboard."

Susanna took the money upstairs, laid it out in front of her, and prayed. She thanked God, repented for doubting his power to provide, and told him it was his money, not hers.

Susanna was surprised by how many people—even senior Christian leaders—struggled to accommodate the notion that God could, or would, do this kind of miracle. "I discovered that a lot of people believe God can make trees but not paper! They believe that story where Jesus uses a fish as an ATM, because it's in the Bible [Matthew 17:27], but doubt that God would ever choose to do anything remotely similar today. I think it's because money is such a stronghold in our material-istic mindsets," she says. "We worship money, we put our faith in it. If God can make money so easily, our currency gets devalued, our value system is undermined; our idol comes tumbling down."

We may accept the vast credal miracles of creation, resurrection, and salvation whilst doubting the smaller miracles of healing, guidance, protection, and provision. We trust God for our eternal salvation yet struggle to believe that he will sometimes still intervene in ways we can't explain when we cry to him for help.

Three days after discovering the cash, a friend asked Susanna to show her the cupboard. Susanna opened the door laughing, but then she froze. Another 200 Swiss francs had appeared out of nowhere on top of the boiler. "I freaked! There was no way that we could have missed any remaining money the first time. We had checked every millimetre of that cupboard, you can bet on it!" It was as though God was just adding a little extra, playfully blessing his daughter and enjoying her surprise.

The next morning Susanna got up early, opened the cupboard again, and found another 200-franc bill. Susanna just handed the money to her friend. "This is for you—I don't need any more!" At that moment she made a solemn decision to give away whatever else God provided through the cashpoint he'd installed in her kitchen. And of course, inevitably, whenever friends came to visit they would all ask to see the cleaning cupboard as if it was some kind of holy shrine.

Eleven days later, Susanna hosted a meeting to plan a youth confer-ence with her friend Michael. When he arrived he went straight to check the cupboard like everyone else. There was nothing in there, so Susanna laughed, he closed the door, and she made tea. Minutes later they were standing in the kitchen, drinking the tea, and discussing the conference, when a gentle shuffling sound suddenly came from the cupboard. They froze for a second, looked at each other, and lurched for the door.

Michael opened it and gasped. Another 13,600 Swiss francs lay scattered on the floor of the closet which they had checked just minutes earlier. "Michael and I never did manage to prepare our conference that day," recalls Susanna. "We were on our knees laughing, crying, and thanking God."

That was the last cash to appear in Susanna's cleaning cupboard, but overall, in less than a month, a total of 28,000 Swiss francs—a year's wages—had materialised, on four different occasions, witnessed variously by Susanna and three of her friends.

> **28,000 Swiss francs had materialised on four different occasions in less than a month, witnessed by Susanna and three of her friends.**

Susanna paid her rent and taxes, then gave the rest of the money away. As she did so, many of her friends and family who didn't know Jesus came to believe in God's power to provide supernaturally more readily than some of her Christian friends. One pastor actually admitted that he didn't want it to be true because it would destroy his theology. Susanna just replied, "Hallelujah!"

The Power of Normal

Susanna told me these stories, and I confess that I checked my own cleaning cupboard on more than one occasion! The 24-7 movement had significant financial challenges at that time. I couldn't understand why God didn't just make the money materialise for us, the way he'd made it for Susanna. But as I thought about this, he taught me one of the most important lessons I have ever learned about money.

The fact that God can create banknotes supernaturally at will means that when he chooses not to do so (which, let's face it, is pretty much always), it is because he wants to provide for us in another way. Generally, God prefers to bless us through relationships, allowing money to flow from person to person through generosity and merit. In fact, the word *currency*, which we use to describe money, derives from the Latin *correre*, meaning "to run." It has given us our modern term for the current in a river, or an electrical current, or a "common currency" of ideas.

Money is designed to move around, to flow dynamically between people, whether through a monthly wage or a commercial exchange or in the form of a gift. Money loses its purpose as a catalyst for creative exchange when it is allowed to stagnate, merely accruing interest in a bank or becoming a number on a screen. Nine times out of ten, therefore, God chooses to provide for our needs—whether financial, medical, or emotional—naturally through people, not supernaturally through angelic visitation, manna from heaven, or cash materialising in cupboards. This may be less mysterious, but it is actually ultimately far more creative and relational. As one theologian says, God tends not to work by "violently ripping into the fabric of history or arbitrarily upsetting the momentum of its powers," but rather "within and through the closely textured and natural historical processes of our modern experience."[6]

The supernatural may well be "super," but it is also natural. It may be surprising and unusual, but it is never unnatural when it's from God.

Susanna prayed for rent, and God provided for her needs. Floyd and I prayed for our kids, and their lives were miraculously spared. The Smith sisters prayed for young people in the Outer Hebrides, and revival came to their land. We prayed for God's help in marketing a book in America, and he lined up an interview with *Rolling Stone*. Miracles happen. But between such mountaintop moments, we must all traverse the long, predictable valleys of the mundane.

If our days were continually punctuated with the kind of supernatural interruptions described in this chapter—if our prayers were all immediately granted—we would be like spoiled children with weak bodies and rotting teeth. We are strengthened and matured by seasons of boredom and even pain that demands perseverance. In fact, it is often during these unglamorous, in-between times that we mature; our faith fills up into faithfulness, we learn to push into community and into God's presence, which is, after all, the greatest miracle of all.

Mr. Tumnus and Us

As the 24-7 movement began to expand internationally, I asked the Lord for someone to share the load by coordinating the work at home in the UK. I needed a friend I could trust, someone passionate about prayer, highly relational—and able to work without a salary! The obvious choice was my old friend Phil Togwell, who was working at that time with homeless young people in central London. In his spare time he was running a youth church in Romford which had been going crazy with 24-7 prayer. Nervously I asked Phil to consider quitting his job to work with us, adding as casually as I could that we wouldn't be able to pay him anything. It was obviously an outrageous suggestion.

Phil's long, wiry goatee and twinkly eyes always reminded me of Mr. Tumnus, Narnia's half-human faun. When I asked him about quitting his job and working for us for free, his eyes twinkled and his beard quivered even more than usual. He pointed out very gently that he loved his current job, and then he asked (not unreasonably) how he would feed his wife and daughters. But there was also an excitement in his eyes. He admitted that he was longing for a deeper sense of community and a greater adventure from life, so he agreed at least to pray about it.

It was a decision that would change Phil's life, and the lives of thousands more to this day.

The Holy Spirit began by whispering to Phil through a line in *The Lord of the Rings*:

"And now," said the wizard, turning back to Frodo, "the decision lies with you. But I will always help you." He laid his hand on Frodo's shoulder. "I will help you bear this burden, as long as it is yours to bear. But we must do something, soon. The Enemy is moving."[7]

Sensing that the Holy Spirit was giving him the choice, asking him to decide, Phil sat down to take a long hard look at their family finances. How much money would they actually need to survive? They could use all their savings—it didn't seem right to ask others for support, if they themselves were sitting on a nest-egg—but God would still have to provide an additional £1,000 per month just to pay the bills and put food on the table. Phil and Emma quietly shared their need with a few friends who offered to support them with small monthly gifts. In this way they raised a total monthly pledge of £310—way short of their target.

On 9 January, Phil and Emma did a secret deal with God. They'd been trying to raise money for several months, with meagre success. To add to the pressure, Sammy and I were due to come and stay with them three days later, on 12 January. "Give us just half the money we need in the next three days," they prayed, "and we'll trust you for the rest. But if you don't, we'll just have to tell Pete and Sammy we can't afford to do the job."

By the day of our visit, the Togwells were still £190 per month short of that all-important halfway mark. With heavy hearts they greeted us at the door, knowing that we would be almost as disappointed as they were.

At the first opportunity to be alone, Phil told me he had something important to tell me. This reminded me that I also had some news to share.

"OK, you go first," he said, trying to delay the inevitable.

"Well, three days ago, I bumped into an old friend in Portsmouth and he's just got a new job, but, um, he's not in a great place with God right now. He certainly isn't going to church, but he was asking me all about 24-7."

"OK," said Phil, a little wearily.

"Look, the point is," I continued, completely failing to read Phil's bleak mood, "I told him about you guys and how you're total rock stars and you're wanting to start working with us but you need a bunch of money and, well, he said he'd like to support you."

Phil knew that unless this new donation amounted to at least £190 per month—by far their biggest gift so far—it wasn't going to make any difference. "How much?" he asked, testily.

"Two hundred pounds per month," I replied.

"No way!" Phil began laughing. Then he yelled, "Hallelujah!"

Our wives heard the commotion and rushed into the room. Still grinning wildly, Phil told Sammy and me about their deal with God and the secret deadline they had set three days before.

"Three days ago?" I said, counting back through the week. "That was the day my friend made his pledge."

"Perfect timing then," laughed Phil. "God really does hear our prayers, huh?"

"Glad you think so, Phil," I grinned, "since you just became the UK coordinator of a prayer movement."

"And God's given us an extra tenner a month too," said Phil.

"That's obviously my commission," I joked, already looking forward to recounting the story to the donor and blowing a couple of his non-churchgoing fuses.

That night Phil and Emma Togwell agreed to coordinate 24-7 Prayer in the UK. They were only halfway towards their target, but God was on their side. "I feel like Moses refusing to heed the call at the burning bush and asking God to send someone else," wrote Phil in his journal. "And yet this is my call."

Early the next morning, Phil received another financial pledge. It was anonymous, via a Gmail account. To this day neither of us knows where it came from. It covered the exact amount they needed to achieve their £1,000 monthly target. Overwhelmed, he woke Emma to show her the email, phoned me, and turned to his journal again. "God forgive me my lack of faith! Forgive my double-mindedness! Forgive my needing-to-know-it's-you every few seconds! You have swept away my feeble wonderings!"

Phil Togwell stepped into his role with 24-7 knowing for sure that it wasn't just a job. This was a call from God himself, and the people who'd pledged to support them financially were also going to do so in prayer. He and Emma decided to risk all their security, to use up all their savings, and to live very simply indeed in order to serve the purposes of God. It was to be the beginning of a faith adventure which continues to this day, touching countless lives. And we were just about to discover that it had come in the nick of time for something new that God was planning.

• • •

The spiritual warfare around our encounter with Floyd had been so dramatic and traumatic that on my next visit to America I made a beeline to see him in Kansas City. I was determined to continue the conversation that the enemy had so violently sought to abort.

Floyd greeted me warmly, still wearing his Crocs with socks, and took me to a microbrewery for fish and chips.

"So I feel like we went way too far on our first date," I ventured, squirting ketchup on my fries. Floyd threw back his head and roared with laughter.

I could tell you that I had no idea, as we talked that night in Kansas City, that another amazing chapter of the 24-7 story was about to begin, but I'd be lying. The truth is that I knew with every fibre of my being that God was on the move, turning the page, initiating something immeasurably beyond my imagination. The sense of destiny was palpable, and I returned to England convinced of two things: First, Satan hated the idea of us establishing any kind of bridgehead for 24-7 in America; second, we should do the very thing he so feared.

SELAH

Our struggle is not against flesh and blood, but against . . .
the powers of this dark world.
EPHESIANS 6:12

*Holy Spirit, please open my eyes to see the reality of the
spiritual battle today. Deliver me from evil. Soften my heart to
discern spirits, sharpen my senses to detect the Enemy's lies.
Teach me to rule and reign with the authority you have given
me in and through Jesus. Amen.*

There is no neutral ground in the universe: every square inch,
every split second, is claimed by God and counter claimed by
Satan.
C. S. LEWIS, *CHRISTIAN REFLECTIONS*

6

SUPER BOWL

ENGLAND · USA · SCOTLAND · INDONESIA

Miracle is just a word we use for things The Powers have
deluded us into thinking that God is unable to do.

WALTER WINK, *ENGAGING THE POWERS*

I found Sammy in tears after church. "I'm sick of being sick," she sobbed. The only thing anyone had asked her about that morning had been her illness. "I know they all mean well, but I hate being seen as a victim, a problem, someone to feel sorry for."

Word was out about Sammy's recent, unexpected return to hospital. She had developed a dangerous condition called *status epilepticus* in which every seizure triggers another one. Without medical intervention, she would get locked into a terrifying cycle of fits. This had been a devastating setback, but there was something deeper going on too. "I feel like I'm losing my identity to this ugly, vicious, horrible thing. It's just so . . . *boring!*" She almost bellowed the word. "I used to be Sammy the singer, Sammy the leader, Sammy the mother, happy Sammy, scatty Sammy. Now it's just 'poor Sammy.'" She deflated into my arms with a sigh. "Pete, this is not who I am."

Recent MRI scans had confirmed that Sammy's greatest enemy, the brain tumour, was not growing back, and 24-7 continued to be wildly exciting. But behind closed doors we were becoming quietly desperate, wrestling with the emotional, relational, and spiritual fallout that can accompany any long-term illness. "Lord," I whispered, "we've had enough. We're trying our best here, but, well, where are you? We've run out of energy. We've run out of hope. Please, tell us what to do. Please, help us."

It was a desperate prayer from a vulnerable place, and with it came the unruliest of thoughts. We should run away! Why did we have to send someone else to take Floyd up on his invitation? Why couldn't we be the ones to go to America? Sammy could maybe recover her identity in another country. And we could all do with a break.

I rebuked the idea immediately. It would be impossible, impractical, disobedient, and unwise. This wasn't a time to be jetting off to the other side of the world, when Sammy so clearly still needed her medical team on hand. Hudson had also just started at school; it would surely be irresponsible to unsettle him. On top of all this, the ministry in England was all-consuming. We could hardly just abandon our small, loyal team to cope alone while we swanned off to *Tir na Nóg*. We knew that our call was to Europe—arguably the toughest mission field on earth—not to the highly churched American Midwest.

In addition to all these significant objections around Sammy's health and Hudson's schooling and the demands of 24-7 and our own call to Europe, there was also the small matter of money. We were receiving a small stipend from the church, and one or two friends were supporting us each month, but in the United States we would presumably have to start again from scratch.

With a sigh I accepted that the American idea was a really bad one. I didn't mention it to Sammy. It would be escapism at best and might even be a distraction from the front lines of our call. And yet a few weeks later, in an unguarded moment when I was preparing for a scheduled trip to the States, I heard myself casually, half-seriously asking Sammy if she would ever like to come too—just for a few days, only if we could sort medical insurance, and provided we could find someone to have the kids . . .

I think she started packing before I could finish the sentence.

●　●　●

Sammy and I were thrilled to find that the movement in America was multiplying fast. Fuelled by word of mouth and the publication of *Red Moon Rising*, prayer rooms were popping up everywhere, from a brewery in Missouri to the US Naval Academy in Maryland (the prayer slots were apparently particularly well regimented there).

We heard about an atheist businesswoman who stepped into a prayer space in Tulsa, Oklahoma. "I didn't believe in Jesus or God or much of anything," she confessed, and yet, "I was rocked to the point of no longer being able to stand on my own two feet. I sat there shaking, desperately trying to hide my tears, shocked because I'd given up on God and yet I was instantly (and to my own surprise) a believer in Jesus Christ." We had witnessed one or two dramatic epiphanies like these at the start of the movement in Europe, but now they were beginning to occur in America too. Someone wrote from a prayer room in Tennessee to report that "our church has been changed forever . . . Dozens are coming back to Jesus, or are being saved or filled with the Holy Spirit."

"I sat there in the prayer room shaking. I'd given up on God and yet I was instantly (and to my own surprise) a believer in Jesus."

We were moved by the story of a man with an AIDS-related illness who was admitted to a hospice in Brooklyn, New York. Preparing to die, he requested pens and paper, explaining that this was how he'd learned to pray in his local prayer room. Reports like these from the length and breadth of the States left us shaking our heads in amazement. Broken people were learning to pray in Brooklyn, non-Christians were encountering Christ in Tulsa, soldiers were learning spiritual warfare in Maryland, and entire churches were being revived in places like Tennessee. The movement was clearly flourishing in fertile soil four thousand miles from home.

A pastor called Gary Schmitz heard that I was in Kansas City and asked to see me. We arranged to meet in a coffee shop. You can spot a traditional Midwestern pastor a mile off. Smart hair, plaid shirt, tank top, and chinos. Standard issue at all traditional seminaries. We shook hands and he thanked me for my book. He told me that his church was doing 24-7 prayer. "How's it going?" I asked casually.

"Pete," he said, staring at me intently and beginning to weep, "we are being *undone*."

After years pursuing a programme-driven approach to ministry in a traditional denomination, Gary had been close to burnout, on the verge of quitting. In desperation he announced plans for a week of 24-7 prayer at his church in Missouri, secretly assuming that he would have to fill most of the hours himself. But the time slots filled up so fast that Gary didn't even get to use the room. They decided to add a second week of prayer. So many people began to encounter God in that room that they soon added a third week. They couldn't quite believe it when they passed the one-month mark.

Gary showed me an email he'd received from a member of the congregation. "My husband says that his antennae tune in better in the prayer room," it said. "People can't get enough of the place. The most common remark is 'one hour is not enough.'" Gary's church continued praying night and day for three months, a quarter of the year and twelve times longer than they originally thought possible. It was a time of deep renewal for the entire church, and especially for its re-energised pastor.

Through the simple act of making a little space for God, and with minimal human interference, remarkable things were taking place in the community of Deerbrook, in many similar prayer rooms around America, and in countries across the globe. These wonderful stories had nothing to do with our brand or model. It's God who shows up in prayer rooms, God who mobilises prayer, and God who answers those prayers too.

The Big "If"

It had taken 150,000 men at least seven years to construct the temple in Jerusalem according to plans drawn up by Solomon's father, King David. But having completed this vast project, Solomon must have been acutely aware that all this effort and expense were going to be wasted unless God now deigned to come and inhabit the work of their hands. And so, on the eve of its opening, the king spent the night in the temple begging the Lord to show up. Eventually, God appeared to Solomon with a wonderful reassurance: "I have heard your prayer and have chosen this place for myself." You can imagine the relief in Solomon's heart! Then God added an extraordinary promise which has echoed down the years ever since:

> When I shut up the heavens so that there is no rain, or
> command locusts to devour the land or send a plague among
> my people, if my people, who are called by my name, will
> humble themselves and pray and seek my face and turn from
> their wicked ways, then I will hear from heaven, and I will
> forgive their sin and will heal their land.
>
> 2 CHRONICLES 7:13-14

The most important words in this famous promise are some of the smallest and easiest to miss: *when, if,* and *then.*

First, God says *when*—not if—things go wrong. In an agrarian culture, a drought or a plague of locusts could be a cataclysmic national, social, and economic disaster, equivalent to a banking crisis or a recession today. God does not promise to eliminate such crises from the lives of his people or to make us immune from the disasters that afflict the wider culture. In fact Jesus assures his disciples, "In this world you will have trouble" (John 16:33). We tend not to turn that particular promise into a range of greeting cards.

Second, God says that when such troubles come, he will hear us *if*—not when—we turn to him for help. Sadly, it is neither inevitable nor automatic that we will respond to the problems of life with the humility of prayer. God knows, and history shows, that our human instinct in the face of any crisis tends to be independence rather than intercession. We are self-help addicts. God tends to be our last resort when all else fails, and rarely our first port of call. In the UK there are at least three major denominations on the verge of extinction as I write. Two of these organisations are currently trying to rebrand and restructure their way out of their terminal decline, which of course isn't working. But the Salvation Army received a prophetic word that if they would "turn to God and seek him in prayer, he would hear from heaven and send the rain." In response to this simple, biblical exhortation, they gave themselves to a year of 24-7 prayer. During those twelve months the tide began to turn, many Salvation Army churches started to grow again, and the rains of renewal fell upon the ranks of William Booth's army. Again and again we see that there really is a big, fat, screaming "if" hanging over the people of God in every generation: Will we, or will we not, turn to God in prayer when the inevitable troubles come?

Finally, God makes an incredible promise to Solomon which echoes down the millennia. When the crises come, if we will turn to him in prayer, *then* he promises three far-reaching blessings:

- *To hear our prayers*—a promise of miraculous intervention
- *To forgive our sins*—a promise of salvation for the lost and sanctification for the church

> **There's a big, fat, screaming "if" hanging over the people of God in every generation: Will we, or will we not, pray when trouble comes?**

- *To heal our land*—a promise of reconciliation, restoration and deep social transformation

God offers a big, holistic promise of salvation for individuals, societies, economies, and the environment. Whenever God's people restore the proper ecology of creation by returning humbly to dependency upon their Creator in prayer, his life begins to overpower sin's destructive influence at every level. The new creation begins to bud and bloom in every sphere of society. Wounded nations are made whole, poisoned creation is renewed, broken economies are repaired, dying cultures are revived, fractured relationships are reconciled.

When we hear stories about revival in places like the Outer Hebrides, it's natural to long for a similar awakening today. But if the focus of all our prayers is such a revival, then we are praying way too small. God's purposes may begin with a revived church moving in supernatural power, proclaiming the gospel as we should, and baptising the crowds. But that is not the endgame; revival is just the start. Once the church is back to normal, pulsing with life, God's great project is to see creation remade. He is busy building a new heaven and a new earth, which inevitably begins with a renewed church. From there the project extends to change the world and "heal the land."

Whenever we stop saying "no" to God's plans and start saying "yes," his kingdom comes. It's as simple and sensible as that. Economics, politics, the arts, education, and enterprise may well be the tools God uses to heal the land, but the impetus is repentant integrity. Humility is the heavenly algorithm for social transformation. The rusty hinge of human history turns out to be the bended knee.

Indonesian Revival

In our time, one of the most remarkable demonstrations of the power of this promise to transform an entire nation has arisen in Indonesia. In 1998 this fourth-largest nation on earth was devastated by the Asian economic crisis, alongside violent ethnic rioting on the streets, with a death toll running into thousands, widespread student demonstrations, and ultimately the resignation of their President Suharto after thirty years in power. As the nation teetered on the brink of anarchy, Indonesian church leaders took hold of God's promise in 2 Chronicles 7:14 and began to establish 24-7 prayer watches, mainly on the top floor of office blocks because they were forbidden from constructing church buildings.

Humility is the heavenly algorithm for social transformation. The rusty hinge of history in every generation is the bended knee.

They prayed with extraordinary tenacity and faith, repenting and seeking God humbly, claiming his promise of healing for the land. Gradually, as they prayed, the volatile situation in their nation began to stabilise. The rioting died down, the economy rallied, and a new optimism dawned. What's more, the Indonesian church began to experience a powerful revival. They had turned to the Lord in prayer, claiming God's ancient promise to Solomon, and he had heard their prayers, forgiven their sins, and brought remarkable levels of healing to their troubled land.

One night, several years after those first prayer rooms were launched in Indonesia, I saw the results firsthand in Jakarta's Gelora Bung Karno Stadium, where I had the enormous privilege of joining 80,000 others for a day of prayer and fasting. The vast crowd that night was connected by satellite with other similar gatherings around Indonesia, so that an estimated 3 million people joined in that prayer meeting—surely one of the biggest in world history. These numbers would be amazing anywhere in the world (almost unthinkable in the complacent West). I had to keep reminding myself that it was taking place in the world's largest Muslim nation.

I was asked to say a few words and invited the crowd in the stadium simply to raise their phones, glowing in the night. It was a breathtaking sight: a vast glittering galaxy of stars shining, as the apostle Paul says, in the darkness of "a warped and crooked generation" (Philippians 2:15).

It was the biggest crowd I'd ever addressed—a very long way from my solitary encounters with God in that first prayer room.

As I held my phone aloft, it began to buzz. Friends who were watching online or on the live television broadcast began messaging me, just to see if I'd been stupid enough to leave my phone signal on. We are a generation that is connected as never before, and this surely gives us unprecedented opportunities to work together and pray together for God's kingdom to come on earth.

The next day I flew to North Sumatra, to visit a church in the city of Medan. It had started with 119 people in 1993 and had grown to more than 40,000 members in less than twenty years. Today it plants a new congregation every twelve days, has translated the Bible into the dialects of five unreached people groups, and runs a medical clinic caring for thousands of sick people. The pastor explained that the tipping point in this explosive growth could be traced back precisely to the moment they had joined with other churches around the nation in establishing their own 24-7 prayer watch.

"We started 24-7 prayer in November 1999," said the pastor. "That was when everything took off. That was when the revival really began."

Hearing the date, I was momentarily lost for words. Slowly I explained that we had also begun our 24-7 prayer watch in 1999, just eight weeks earlier. So had Mike Bickle in America.

Grinning widely, the pastor offered to show me and my friends their place of 24-7 prayer. Tucked away on the top floor of a Medan shopping centre, we found two women sitting in the middle of a sparse, simple prayer room, one playing guitar while the other prayed, rocking back and forth like a head-banger at a silent disco or a Hasidic Jew at the Western Wall. It was an unimpressive room, hospital-green and empty, but the presence of God was tangible. In fact, one member of our team stepped across the threshold and fell face down to the ground, apparently knocked off her feet, overpowered by the manifest presence of God. We all knew in that moment that the pastor was right. The revival of the Indonesian church and the transformation of Indonesian society was being fuelled by an invisible network of unimpressive powerhouses like these, a hidden circuit board across the land, quietly conducting God's power and light.

The revival in Indonesia was inspiring, but we were about to witness one of the most extraordinary, brain-frying answers to intercessory prayer much closer to home.

• • •

In the US state of Arizona an accountant called Deb Welch made a momentous decision to leave her well-paid job and coordinate a year of 24-7 prayer throughout the Grand Canyon state.[1] Just thirty-four days into this initiative, the Super Bowl was due to touch down in Arizona's University of Phoenix Stadium. One of the newly mobilised intercessors received a terrible premonition about the event: In a dream she saw the stadium filled with blood. Taking the nightmare seriously, Deb dispatched a small team of prayer warriors to the stadium to pray pre-emptively against disaster.

On the day of the game, Deb joined almost 100 million viewers watching the biggest sporting event in America, but her nerves had little to do with the fate of either the New York Giants or the New England Patriots. The contest passed uneventfully, Tom Petty and The Heartbreakers performed at half time, the Giants surprised everyone by defeating the Patriots, and Deb breathed a sigh of relief. In fact, she felt a little foolish for having needlessly dispatched that well-meaning team of intercessors to pray at the stadium.

But then came the news.

Media outlets began reporting that, behind the scenes at the Super Bowl, a bloody massacre had been averted. A disturbed thirty-five-year-old named Kurt William Havelock, furious at having been denied permission for a Halloween-themed horror bar in nearby Tempe, had mailed a series of rambling threats to media outlets the day before the game. The *Los Angeles Times*, *New York Times*, *Phoenix New Times*, and

Associated Press had all received chilling missives from Havelock pledging "swift and bloody" revenge and even vowing to "slay your children."

On the Day of the Super Bowl

Havelock drove himself to the University of Phoenix Stadium, armed with an AR-15 semi-automatic assault rifle and 200 rounds of ammunition. He had retained one final note on his person: "Do Not Resuscitate."

Havelock had no way of knowing that he was parking his car that day in the exact location where a random group of Christians had gathered to pray against bloodshed. Armed to the teeth and intending to kill as many people as possible, the would-be mass murderer unexpectedly experienced something that he would later describe in court as "a change of heart." He broke down in tears and phoned his father. "He was sobbing hysterically," his dad recalled. "He said, 'I've done something terribly, terribly wrong.'" Havelock ultimately handed himself in to the police without a shot being fired.

> **"The critics of Christianity do not see in how many people . . . the flood of evil is restrained and in how many wild habits are tamed by reason of the gospel."**
> —ORIGEN

Somehow Deb's sensitivity to the Spirit and the intercessions of her little prayer team seemed to have helped disarm a potential killer, almost certainly saving many lives and averting an atrocity that would have been witnessed by almost 100 million people in real time, billions more online, and on the front page of every newspaper around the world the next day.

Militant Prayer

More than a thousand years ago Origen pointed out that "the critics of Christianity do not see in how many people . . . the flood of evil is restrained, and in how many wild habits are tamed by reason of the gospel."[2] It's easy to forget that the vast majority of miracles that take place in our daily lives are invisible: secret daily breakthroughs that protect our children, enlighten our politicians, or change the hearts of men like Kurt William Havelock. Jesus tells us explicitly to pray for deliverance "from evil," presumably because we are not automatically safe. Deliverance from evil will occasionally be dramatic and obvious—a healing, a miraculous escape—but mostly it will mean merely that the truck driver applied his brakes just before you came round the corner yesterday, or an antibody was quietly activated to defend your health last night, or an unkind comment was drowned out by a police siren this morning. Life brims over with such mundane miracles, mostly taken for granted although they constitute the majority of God's blessings in our lives. This is why it is vital not just that we pray with gratitude but that we pray regularly and with vigilance, remembering that our intercessions "restrain the flood of evil" at least as much as they activate evident blessing. Many terrible things happen in our world. This is undeniably true. But Origen reminds us that things could be infinitely worse were it not for the myriad of daily interventions by the people of God and the bulwark of Christian intercession at work behind the scenes. Far more of our prayers are being answered than we will ever realise. We are congenitally blind to the goodness of God all around. Our eyes can only be opened to see the world as it truly, objectively is by nurturing a daily attitude of gratitude.

In God's promise to Solomon, and stories like those from Arizona and Indonesia, we see that intercessory prayer is a form of partnership with God. The Bible teaches that the power of this human-divine partnership is integrated into the design of creation. Adam and Eve's willpower was able to defy the will of God. Thousands of years later, when Jesus stood in another garden and prayed, "Not my will but yours be done," the darkness and death of that first garden was repelled, banished by God's light and life. Whenever prayer is reduced to a clumsy technique for getting God to mutter a reluctant "Amen" to our selfish desires, it is merely wishful thinking in a religious disguise. But when prayer is an "Amen" to God's desires, it is profoundly Christian and powerful beyond measure. As Jesus says, "I will do whatever you ask *in my name*" (John 14:13, emphasis added).

The Swiss theologian Karl Barth illustrates the power of this partnership of wills in the strongest possible terms, saying that we actually "participate in the reign of Christ" through prayer: "In him . . . we then find ourselves at the very seat of government, at the very heart of the mystery and purpose of all occurrence."[3] Imagine that the president or prime minister calls your mobile phone tomorrow. As you recover from the shock, he calmly explains that, in the interests of greater democracy, the government has decided to include the opinions of an ordinary, representative citizen in certain important decisions relating to national security. A powerful computer has chosen your name at random from a list of the entire electorate. He therefore asks if you would be willing to come and sit with his executive to share your unique thoughts, insights, and opinions on behalf of the people. I'm pretty sure that although you might be nervous, you would find the time, in fact you would cancel anything, to attend. It would be one of the greatest honours of your life.

> **"We participate in the reign of Christ through prayer. . . . In him we then find ourselves at the very seat of government."**
> —KARL BARTH

As a Christian you have received an even greater invitation. The King of Kings requests your presence "at the very seat of government." He offers you a place on his executive so that you can influence his actions on behalf of the people. It is an unspeakable honour, and yet we are often too busy, or too disbelieving, to accept the invitation. The Bible is clear that our opinions and choices really can shape history, that our prayers really do make a difference in the world. For example, Abraham successfully negotiated with God to spare the cities of Sodom and Gomorrah (Genesis 18:16-33). King Hezekiah was told by the prophet Isaiah that his death was imminent, but his prayers seem to have persuaded God to change his mind and grant another fifteen years (2 Kings 20:6). Moses stood on a rocky hill overlooking a battle between Joshua and the Amalekites, and whenever he held his hands aloft in prayer, the Israelites advanced. But whenever Moses dropped his hands exhausted, the Amalekites began to triumph (Exodus 17:8-13). Jesus assures his disciples, "Whatever you bind on earth will be bound in heaven, and whatever you loose on earth will be loosed in heaven" (Matthew 18:18). The apostle Paul says that we are seated with Christ "in the heavenly realms" (Ephesians 2:6). Behind every battle on earth, it seems, there is a parallel conflict waged "against the powers of this dark world and against the spiritual forces of evil in the heavenly realms" (Ephesians 6:12).

The Highland Warrior

These heavenly priorities were powerfully illustrated in the life of a little-known Scottish prayer warrior called James Matheson. He lived in a tiny Highland village called Clashnagrave, five miles north of Dornoch, in the years 1805–1875. During the Crimean War he would intercede every night, sometimes all night, for the local soldiers, members of the 93rd Highlanders, away fighting for their lives on the front lines. It is said that James Matheson always prayed in a particular place beside the river that ran past his house, and for many years after his death you could still see the hollows worn away by his knees in the ground by that stream.

As James Matheson prayed relentlessly in Scotland, far away in Crimea there were occasional reports of a ghostly figure moving about the trenches at night. These apparitions were, no doubt, dismissed by all but the most superstitious as a mere figment of their terri-fied and exhausted minds. But then at the end of the war, the 93rd Highlanders returned to Scotland and attended a special communion service in the village of Creich. When James Matheson entered the church, those war-worn soldiers turned and gasped. Here before them stood the man they had seen in those distant trenches, night after night, a ghostly figure bringing strange comfort amidst the horrors of war. Somehow James Matheson, interceding so earnestly in Scotland, had appeared amongst the very people for whom he had been battling so fiercely.

It is a mysterious tale, yet not an entirely unfamiliar one. Jesus himself was initially mistaken for a ghost upon the water. Moses and Elijah somehow appeared by his side on the Mount of Transfiguration. Peter walked through locked doors. Philip was transported by the Spirit from the desert road to Gaza and reappeared in Azotus preaching the gospel (Acts 8:40). People like James Matheson in Scotland, Deb Welch in Arizona, Susanna Rychiger in Switzerland, Donald McPhail in the Hebridean awakening, and the church in Indonesia have learned how to pray with a perseverance and passion that alters material reality.

One of the marks common to such intercessors is that they don't just say polite prayers submissively. They tend to wrestle against God with an audacity that brings breakthrough. Their prayer times often seem to move beyond the recitation of liturgy, the quiet absorption of Scripture, and the enjoyment of worship music—valuable as such things can be—to actively laying hold of the purposes of God with a violent insistence. They have learned to enter his throne room expectantly, to make their requests forcefully, to insist upon an answer with a tenacity easily mistaken for defiance. In his classic book *The Soul of Prayer*, P. T. Forsyth endorses the importance of this kind of prayer: "Lose the habit of wrestling and the hope of prevailing with God, make it mere walking with God in friendly talk; and, precious as that is, yet you tend to lose the reality of prayer at last."[4]

> "Lose the habit of wrestling and the hope of prevailing with God, . . . and . . . you tend to lose the reality of prayer at last."
> —P. T. FORSYTH

Travailing in Prayer

We know that Jesus sometimes chose to pray "in a loud voice" (e.g., John 11:43; Luke 23:46). We are also told that the early church interceded with such power that the room in which they were meeting physically shook after they had "raised their voices together in prayer to God" (Acts 4:24). Every part of the world in which revival is being experienced prays together in this way. In Nigeria, in China, in Indonesia, from South Korea to South America, Christians raise their voices together and pray simultaneously and aloud. Perhaps this is not merely a cultural preference but a biblical norm. If we are to pray like Jesus and the early church, we will undoubtedly sometimes pray quietly, we will sometimes use set prayers, and we will sometimes pray alone. But we will also at other times pray, with raised voices, freely and with others in unison.

Many of Donald McPhail's fellow intercessors during the Hebridean awakening were women who truly knew how to prevail in prayer with authority. One of them described how "the breath of the Spirit would come and it was like being in childbirth . . . We would fill up and fill up and fill up with the breath of God, and we would be in agony, and suddenly there would be relief as the new soul was born. Then the weight would come again and we would fill up again and again and others would be born into the kingdom."[5] Those Hebridean prayer meetings were clearly neither reserved nor respectable, and yet they had power to usher in breakthrough as men and women were born again through the preaching of Duncan Campbell and the travailing prayers of these spiritual midwives.

Perhaps such models of prayer sound overemotional or weird. But the apostle Paul describes the Holy Spirit praying for us "in wordless groans" (Romans 8:26), creation "groaning as in the pains of childbirth" (Romans 8:22), and "we ourselves, who have the firstfruits of the Spirit, groan inwardly as we wait eagerly for our adoption to sonship, the redemption of our bodies" (Romans 8:23). There is, it seems, a lot of prayerful groaning going on in heaven and on earth!

I remember running the youth programme at a large Christian festival where a meeting had just finished. Young people were rushing around, skateboarding and chatting. Someone came to me very concerned about two girls who were sobbing uncontrollably, almost screaming, in the corner. I asked a responsible woman to sort it out, but when she walked over to the girls she too broke down in tears and began crying! Nonplussed and slightly annoyed at such immaturity, I walked towards the group. But when I got close enough to discern their words, I stopped in my tracks. These girls were not hysterical; they were crying out to God for a friend who didn't know Jesus. Their hearts were breaking before God with a compassion that challenged me profoundly.

How little we know about travailing and prevailing with God in prayer until "one becomes actually aware of receiving, by firmest anticipation, and in advance of the event, the thing for which one asks."[6] I suspect that many of our prayer meetings today are less effective than they could be because we merely ask but we don't expect. The great English poet John Donne, who was Dean of St. Paul's Cathedral in the early seventeenth century, described such prayer in shocking terms:

> Earnest prayer hath the nature of Importunity; we presse, we importune God . . . Prayer hath the nature of impudency; we threaten God in prayer . . . And God suffers this impudency, and more. Prayer hath the nature of violence; in the public prayers of the congregation, we besiege God, says Tertullian; and we take God prisoner, and bring God to our conditions; and God is glad to be straitened by us in that siege.[7]

Jesus seems to describe a similar attitude in his parable of the persistent widow. She received an answer to her prayers because she refused to accept "no" for an answer. Elsewhere he advocates an attitude of expectancy bordering upon presumption before God: "Whatever you ask for in prayer, believe that you have received it, and it will be yours" (Mark 11:24).

In a world such as ours, torn and bleeding as it is, there must surely be times when we too "wreak violence on heaven."[8] Dark spiritual forces have been loosed on the earth which must be disarmed if we are to free captives from their tyranny. We believe, of course, in the kind of quiet prayer that changes us, but we also believe in the violence of prayer that can change the world. Endless hours listening to worship music or meditating on the Bible may be delightful and even worthwhile, but won't ultimately in themselves advance the kingdom, save the lost, or destroy global evils such as human trafficking.

Jesus models a mystical militancy: wrestling with the devil in the wilderness, rejoicing as he sees Satan fall from heaven, shouting his rebuke to the storm, casting demonic spirits into the abyss. He might well be viewed as a little extreme by many of his churches today. Contemplative prayer and quiet conversation with God may not always be enough. If we truly want to see the kingdom of God return to this enemy-occupied world, we cannot avoid a certain aggression in prayer any more than a soldier can avoid his gun, or a boxer his fists, or a theologian great tracts of his Bible.

> **Quiet prayer can certainly change us, but the kind of prayer that changes the world is more "Fight Club" than golf club.**

Duncan Campbell, the preacher who had been deployed so powerfully by God in the Hebridean awakening, was later also used in a similar revival across the water on the Isle of Skye. On one occasion he locked himself away in the local minister's study to pray. This was in a part of Skye that hadn't yet been touched by the movement. Suddenly the minister, out in the field, heard a startling cry. It was Campbell bounding towards him across the moor. "It's coming! It's coming! We've got through at last! We are over the top!" Sure enough, the revival broke through in that community that night.

It was through this type of prevailing prayer that a Super Bowl disaster had been averted in Phoenix, that James Matheson had interceded for the lives of Scottish soldiers in Crimea, that churches in Indonesia had turned the tide in their nation, that our son had been delivered from a drug overdose, and that Susanna in Switzerland had laid hold of God's miraculous provision.

• • •

On our visit to America, Sammy and I heard so many extraordinary testimonies emanating from US prayer rooms. There was clearly a pressing need for an American office. But, in spite of Floyd's kind invitation, we remained a little unsure about Kansas City as the best location. In fact, various American friends raised their eyebrows when we mentioned it as a possible base, feeling that 24-7 Prayer would be more suited to somewhere edgy and influential, like New York City or Los Angeles. Others remarked that since Mike Bickle's International House of Prayer (affectionately known as IHOP) was already in town, Kansas City could, they said, be the single most confusing place in the entire continent for us to set up shop.

I could see their point. Without Floyd's invitation to the city and the dramatic spiritual warfare around that first meeting with him, we wouldn't have been considering Kansas City for a single second.

With such doubts bouncing around my jet-lagged mind, I woke that first morning in Kansas City and grabbed the devotional book by our bed. Whispering my usual prayer for God to speak, I looked across at Sammy still sleeping next to me. "Lord, is this crazy, or is this you? Is Kansas City really the right place to be based? And why can't I shake this insane idea that we should be the ones to come? Are you really calling us here for a season when Sammy is still so unwell?" It was one of those moments when I had my finger to the wind wondering what God was doing, asking where he was heading, not wanting to get it wrong.

I found the Bible reading for that day. It was the story about Peter walking on the water. Here was my namesake, being asked by Jesus to get out of the boat and take significant steps of faith. It seemed relevant. But the accompanying commentary was a home run—a direct word from God: "When the Lord calls you to come across the water," it said, "step out with confidence and joy. And never glance away from Him for even a moment."[9]

"That sounds like a big, fat green light," said Sammy a little later, sitting up in bed beside me and sipping a cup of tea. "Maybe the Lord really is calling us to come across the water, Pete!" There was an excitement in her eyes I hadn't seen in a long time. "Let's not worry about my health, or about who'll look after 24-7 in Europe, or about money, or the kids." It all sounded completely irresponsible and fun. "Let's just focus on Jesus like Peter getting out of the boat. Surely he will make everything OK!"

USA Today

We had invited various friends to come together later that day to talk and pray about establishing 24-7USA. It turned out to be a very strange group indeed. There were Adam, Nate, David, and Travis, the young men who had accompanied Floyd on his fateful trip to England. But there was also a New York City DJ, a Hollywood sound engineer, a narcotics cop, and a female firefighter from California. There was a big-fisted building contractor we'd first met in Spain, an Oklahoma film-maker in shades and a Stetson, a well-known Kansas City prophet, and a worship pastor from a Florida megachurch who had wept so much reading *Red Moon Rising* that he'd actually climbed under the desk in his office to hide.

I scanned the room's maverick assortment of personalities. Was this really, I wondered, the best team God could muster for establishing a movement of prayer, mission, and justice in the world's most powerful nation? I caught Sammy's eye, and she flashed an uncertain smile back at me. Maybe we were getting it wrong. Perhaps we were setting ourselves up for failure, attempting to make waves in America when we should be home surfing them in Europe instead.

My thoughts were interrupted by a man noisily entering the room, waving a newspaper and beaming from ear to ear. "You guys seen *USA Today*?" he asked. "Check out the cover photo in the Life supplement." He held it aloft, and we gasped to see a large picture of a 24-7 prayer room in Florida. "I don't know how it happened," he laughed, "but

1.8 million Americans just found out about us. We're front-page news, baby!"

I laughed—we all did—and raised my hands in surrender. It was the final confirmation I'd needed. The Holy Spirit seemed to be preparing a way for us after all. This really was his invitation, his timing, and yes, even his team. There had been just too many coincidences. Small things like my Bible reading that morning. Big coincidences like the way we'd returned to Cape St. Vincent at the precise moment Al Qaeda had attacked this country. And massive coincidences like the way Hudson and Misha had both been struck down and miraculously delivered when Floyd first asked us to come. And now, on the day we had gathered in response to all these promptings to consider the spread of prayer rooms in the USA, God had somehow put us onto the cover of the nation's second-largest newspaper. Never before. Never since. Only then, on that particular day.

I looked around the room again at that random mix of people, all shaking their heads in amazement and passing the newspaper from hand to hand. The vision of that global army replayed in my head, and faith began to rise.

We didn't have money. We didn't have a strategy. We were a weird bunch of people. But we did, it seemed, have the favour of God. Hadn't he always hand-picked nobodies like us?

Sammy was looking at me, grinning. Slowly she shrugged in good-natured resignation and nodded her head. We were going to need a place to live, a school for the kids, a visa for America, a bunch of money, a gifted team to support Phil Togwell back home in England, a new team here in the States—and the significant matter of medical insurance for an uninsurable condition. Humanly it seemed almost impossible. Yet we now knew for sure that God really was "calling us to come across the water." And with that certainty came a deep assurance that he would defy all odds. He had been one move ahead of us all along; he could surely be trusted to protect Sammy's health and to provide for all our other needs as well.

SELAH

"The Lord is not slow in keeping his promise, as some understand slowness. Instead he is patient with you, not wanting anyone to perish, but everyone to come to repentance."
2 PETER 3:9

Think of someone known to you who is "perishing" without Jesus. Now pray for them to "come to repentance," remembering that you are not so much pleading with God, or fighting against him, but standing with him against enemy powers. Is there a particular biblical promise you could "claim"? If possible stand, move around, raise your voice. Dare to pray specific, measurable prayers.

Once you have a sense that your prayers have been heard, begin to thank God for his answers as if they have already happened, with faith and expectancy.

"For no matter how many promises God has made, they are 'Yes' in Christ. And so through him the 'Amen' is spoken by us to the glory of God."
2 CORINTHIANS 1:20

7

BLUE CAMP 20

· LITTLE SANTA FE ·

*Faith is not the clinging to a shrine but an endless pilgrimage of
the heart. Audacious longings, burning songs, daring thoughts, an
impulse overwhelming the heart, usurping the mind—these are all a
drive towards serving Him who rings our hearts like a bell.*

RABBI ABRAHAM JOSHUA HESCHEL

Transitioning from the south coast of England to the American
Midwest, we reduced our possessions to the size of four cheap suitcases
and found a place to rent on the Old Santa Fe Trail where it crosses
the state line between Missouri and Kansas. The night we arrived, my
watch broke. Time stopped. We entered liminal space. A new season
was about to begin.

Gradually I noticed the strain lifting from Sammy's face. At last we
were able to talk, to process the things we had lost in recent years. We
went to gigs in Lawrence, Kansas, and ate buffalo wings so spicy they
burned our lips. We frequented independent coffee shops in Westport
and laughed as the kids learned new words in pitch-perfect Midwestern
accents. Slowly I felt the weights lifting from my own shoulders too.
There was work to be done, for sure: establishing the 24-7 office, com-
pleting a book for the publishers, occasionally travelling to speak at
carefully selected events around the States, commissioning a new Boiler

Room in Canada, Skyping regularly with the other 24-7 leaders back home, and training new ones in Kansas City. But most of all I sensed that we'd been led here by the shepherd of our souls simply to rest: "He makes me lie down in green pastures, he leads me beside quiet waters, he refreshes my soul" (Psalm 23:2-3).

We drove an old Ford Econoline van, fully pimped out with shag-pile carpet, tinted windows, a wooden dashboard the size of a dresser, and a row of fairy lights the whole length of the interior. The kids quickly nicknamed it our Scooby-Doo van. In it we explored the city, searching out the forbidden fruits of Jack Stacks Barbecue, Chuck E. Cheese, and the Cold Stone Creamery.

One time that fall, somewhere on the outskirts of the city, we happened upon a vast field of migratory geese. Hudson, who had just turned six, ran towards them screaming until gradually, reluctantly, the grazing birds rose as one. The entire sky seemed to boil black, undulating in time to the wild conducting of an exhilarated infant, suddenly awestruck by his own dominion.

The winter came and brought unknown ice storms, which took out the power and magically coated everything in glass. We woke one morning to find that every twig on every branch of every tree was miraculously exhibited like a wonder of science in its own miniature test tube. We studied sticks and leaves and blades of grass with awe that day. When the wind blew a little, the trees sighed and chimed.

At the top of our street we discovered an old cemetery dating back to the days of the Wild West. Between the graves you can still see furrows worn away by the wagon wheels of 300,000 pioneers who migrated this way between 1821 and 1880, heading south and west, bound for Santa Fe, New Mexico, in search of gold and souls and cattle. Those gnarly old boys back then apparently knew this place at the top of our road by a nickname. They tagged it "Blue Camp 20." "Blue" after the nearby Blue River, "Camp" because, well, that's all it was: a temporary settlement on the edge of the wilderness. And "20" because it was conveniently situated twenty miles—a day's walk—from the town of

Independence, where the Santa Fe Trail began. Blue Camp 20 had been the first stop on the way from somewhere to somewhere else. It was a transitory haunt of vagabonds, the point of no return.

The trek from Blue Camp 20 to Santa Fe was 700 miles, through arid plains, deserts and mountains, traversing treacherous Comanche and Apache territory. One particular adventurer, William G. Johnston, paused a night here in 1849, no doubt preparing himself mentally as well as practically for the unknown trials to come. "At six o'clock we reached Blue Camp Twenty which marks the separation between civilized and uncivilized life. Beyond were the vast plains . . . little known to the white man—the home of the Indian—land of the Buffalo."[1]

By the time we set up home on this wild frontier, things had become far more familiar to the white man than either the buffalo or the Indian. This section of the legendary old pioneer trail had become a benign, tree-lined suburban street with wide lawns and a range of seasonally appropriate flags hanging above the porches. The only thing that could get you scalped around here these days was failing to put your trash out on the correct day in the correct way. It was a very long way indeed from those years gone by, when teamsters trudged and rumbled their way down the hill, cussing and spitting, without a thought about remote-controlled garage-opening devices and automatic lawn-sprinklers.

Inevitably, some of those old pioneers reached Blue Camp 20 and stopped pioneering. They decided they liked the place better than the prospect of 700 miles on foot, dodging rattlesnakes and holding onto their scalps for dear life. So they settled down and built themselves businesses serving the passing trade: liquor and provisions, girls and religion, shoeing horses and fixing wagons for the steady stream of fur traders, gold speculators, mercenaries, and missionaries striking out from here for Santa Fe.

Inexorably the campsite became a settlement and the settlement became some kind of shantytown. And they renamed it, of course. Who wants to be the mayor of a campsite? With more than a touch of irony and no imagination whatsoever, the settlers rebranded Blue Camp 20 as Little Santa Fe; a miniature version of their original destination. An "Amen" before the prayer is spoken.

The settlers were so successful that by the 1850s the camp at Little Santa Fe had grown to boast a post office, two general stores, an inn, a shoe shop, a drugstore, a blacksmith, and a saloon. Little Santa Fe was booming. It would be the smallest of evolutionary hops to Starbucks, Walmart, and the Supercuts hair and beauty salon with walk-in tanning facilities.

● ● ●

The nights we spoke with tongues of fire,
The days we walked out on the wire,
We were young and we were not afraid . . .
JOHN MARK MCMILLAN, "TONGUES OF FIRE"

It was Christmas Day, and I had left the house with a full belly to walk the block, to get a little fresh air and a quiet opportunity to pray. At the top of the road I found myself staring at those grassy wagon ruts running through the cemetery. My heart seemed to know something about this place that my head had not yet discovered. Perhaps it was the peculiar maudlin mood conjured by a grey Christmas Day after dinner, or maybe it was age and stage of life. But the simple story of Blue Camp 20 was stirring me deeply. Christmas lights twinkled in the windows of the houses, and dusk was falling fast, but I lingered there a while, wondering why this little piece of quaint local history was exercising my soul.

Slowly it dawned on me that Blue Camp 20 was a parable, a picture, a prophecy for my own life. We'd come across 4,000 miles, through years of prayer, into so many nations, driven by a very big vision—our own Santa Fe. We had always been certain that if we would just pray hard enough and obey radically enough, eventually we'd see the kingdom come. But so many of the friends with whom we had pioneered this far, dreaming of glory, had been slowing down lately. They seemed to be getting sensible, finding their own equivalents of this frontier camp, settling for a smaller version of the vision that had once fired our souls.

But it was deeper than that. Who was I kidding? It wasn't *them*, it was *us*. Secretly I was struggling profoundly with the same temptations to stop pioneering, to settle down for an easier life. There were weeks when I'd read the Ikea catalogue more than the Bible. Even the automatic garage-opening devices came to hold a certain allure. Somehow the world I'd been trying to change had begun changing me. I'd always had a thirst for adventure, but it had been the craziest five years imaginable; it had been heaven, but it had sometimes also hurt, and I simply wasn't sure I could face any more pioneering. Prayer had spread all over the world, but my wife had nearly died too many times, we had no money, and I was deep-bone tired. Surely the 24-7 movement could continue without us?

Like those early pioneers, we had stopped off here at Blue Camp 20 simply to rest and replenish before striking out again on the next leg of an arduous journey. The plan was not to settle down. The plan was to return to Europe once we were recovered and things were established here in America. But since arriving in Kansas City, I had begun to notice that American pastors get paid a good deal more than they do in Europe. In the Midwest, when you tell people you're a pastor, there's a pretty good chance they'll shake your hand and look you in the eye like you're a brain surgeon or a barrister. They rarely change the subject with a look of mild embarrassment the way they do back home. Maybe we could settle down here and stop pioneering. Let others lead in Europe. Would it really be wrong to serve the Lord with a bit more cash, a bit more kudos, and a lot less rain? Doesn't the Father want the best for his kids?

Another secret temptation was to quit ministry altogether. We seemed to have touched down in Kansas City slap-bang in the middle of a vitriolic church split. Leaders had fallen out and everyone in town seemed to have an opinion. It wasn't our fight, but people seemed to expect us to take sides. Was this really what the kingdom looked like?

Christians competing, hating and hurting one another? Petty politics? Intensity and gossip instead of joy? Maybe we should abandon church work altogether. We could start a business and make some money (for Jesus, of course)! It's one thing to make sacrifices for your own life, but was it fair to make them for our children's futures too?

This played heavy on my heart. One way or another, in ministry or the marketplace, the temptation to bail out, to play it safe and settle down—to turn Blue Camp 20 into our own Little Santa Fe—was stronger than anyone knew.

And no one ever needed to know. Surely I could surf the stories of the last five years for the next fifty without taking any more risks? It would be humility. It would be maturity. It would be wise. Was it really so wrong if we just hunkered down in a new, smaller, more realistic version of the preposterously large vision God had given me on the cliffs of Cape St. Vincent?

The dream had been to see an army of young people praying as if everything depended on God and living like it all depended on them, planting radical new churches, challenging injustices, daring to believe that they could change the world. Five years of non-stop prayer had been a great start by anyone's standards. It had been a wild ride, but maybe it was time to get a proper job, a sensible dream, and an automatic garage-opening device.

Pray as if everything depends on God and live as if it all depends on you.

I've thought about this a lot. Most people pioneer at least once in their lives, when they're young and idealistic and gung-ho to make their mark on the surface of the earth. They start a business, start a band, start a family, move to another town. But gradually "the worries of this life and the deceitfulness of wealth" (Matthew 13:22) constrain the blood-rush of youth. We tame the wild and call it wise. And if we're not careful, before we know it, we find ourselves looking back on a particular year or programme or conference as the spiritual highlight of our lives.

We shake our heads in amusement at the youthful naïvety of it all, we tell the stories again and again and reminisce about the unbridled passions and ambitions that once fired our pristine souls.

Haran

The essential thing in heaven and in earth is . . . that there should be long obedience in the same direction; there thereby results, and has always resulted in the long run, something which has made life worth living.

FRIEDRICH NIETZSCHE, *BEYOND GOOD AND EVIL*

It's easy to pioneer when you're too young to know what it will cost you, when you feel immortal and invincible and the whole of life is an adventure waiting to begin. But pioneering a second time is hard. Abraham was one of the few who never settled down—even in his old age he lived "like a stranger in a foreign country . . . For he was looking forward to the city with foundations, whose architect and builder is God" (Hebrews 11:10).

Abraham's journey had actually begun with his father, Terah, who "took his son Abram [as Abraham was originally known] . . . and together they set out from Ur of the Chaldeans to go to Canaan." Why did Terah never make it 600 miles to Canaan? Because "when they came to Haran, they settled there" (Genesis 11:31). Now, the name of the place where Terah settled, and stopped pioneering, may be significant because his other son, Abram's brother, was also called Haran and he had died. So when we read that Terah settled down in a place called Haran, it's possible that he'd named his resting place after his own dead son.[2]

It's a common human tendency to settle in our grief, to redefine the geography of our lives according to the contours of our pain. And of course, when we are bereaved and hurting, it's important to stop for a while and lament our loss. It's not healthy to continue as if nothing is wrong. But neither is it healthy to make disappointment our permanent domain.

• • •

Dusk had settled silently on the Old Santa Fe Trail. Christmas windows were twinkling in the gloom. And outside in the cold, crepuscular stillness, I stood alone in the cemetery at the top of our road. The bones of the settlers lay buried beneath my feet, but my eyes were drawn to the furrowed tracks of those who'd kept moving, kept pioneering, pursuing their original dreams. In the hush of that winter dusk, I could almost hear their carts rumbling, shaking the bones beneath my feet, calling me on. Like Abram leaving Haran bound for Canaan, these faceless travellers had renounced the soft comforts of Little Santa Fe, setting their faces resolutely towards the real thing.

Gently and lovingly, I was being invited to move on from Haran, from the trauma of the battle for Sammy's life. Yes, it had been terrifying, and the ravages of repeated epileptic seizures continued, but she was alive, we were in America, and there was still a world out there waiting to be won. Slowly and deliberately I knelt down, a lonely figure in a cemetery at dusk on Christmas Day. It was a simple enough thing to do, but as I did so tears of relief welled up in my eyes.

> By an act of faith, Abraham said yes to God's call to travel to
> an unknown place that would become his home . . . an unseen
> city with real, eternal foundations—the City designed and
> built by God.
>
> HEBREWS 11:8-10, MSG

Unless Your Presence

All God's people are called to pioneer. God spoke to Moses when he was a very old man and said, "Leave this place . . . and go up to the land I promised on oath to Abraham" (Exodus 33:1). Abraham's lifelong journey was Moses' journey too, even now in his old age, and it is ours. Then comes one of the most surprising verses in the Bible: "I'm about to give it to you," says God, "and it's going to be brilliant. Go take hold of everything you've been journeying towards and dreaming about for forty years. This is it! It's time to enter the land that I promised to Abraham. I'm going to give you victory. But," he adds, "I'm not coming with you" (see Exodus 33:1-3). You don't find that quoted on many Christian Twitter feeds: "You're on your own," saith the Lord.

At transitional moments in life, God tests our hearts, as he did for me that day in Blue Camp 20. Why? Because he knows that the choices we make at the crossroads determine our future direction and destiny. The priorities we establish in the gear-change moments of life set our trajectory for years to come. And of course, the choices that matter most in life are not functional, strategic, or territorial, but relational. When the time finally comes to leave home, or to get married, or to bank your first pay cheque, or to relocate, or to deal with a terrible diagnosis, or to retire—these are times when God invites us to prioritise his presence very particularly.

God tests our hearts in life's transitional moments, because the priorities we set at gear-change times can fix our course for years to come.

It's possible to step into all the things you have ever prayed for, and in that precise moment to lose the intimacy with God you enjoyed during all the years of waiting and wrestling. Conversely, you can live with the disappointment of unanswered prayers—for healing, for a husband, for a prodigal to return—and yet know the presence of God with you in the midst of your yearning. Frustrations can be the greatest blessings of our lives, blessings the greatest test.

So the question I must ask myself is this: If God were to answer every single one of my deepest heart's desires tonight as I sleep, so that I wake up tomorrow to the greatest outpouring of blessing I could possibly imagine—messages from friends to say that they are turning to Jesus, phone calls from loved ones whose sicknesses have been instantly cured, a letter in the mail to say that I am inheriting a fortune from the estate of an unknown relative, strongholds that have plagued me suddenly losing their power—if God were to promise to do all these things, but then add that I will never again experience his presence the way I do right now, what would I say?

Of course we all immediately say that we would choose his presence. Like the keen kid at Sunday school, we know that the answer is always Jesus. But is that really the truth?

And if God were to see a flicker of hesitation and offer you an alternative path, a rocky road on which many of your deepest prayers will not be answered and certain disappointments will plague you to the grave, but on which he promises to be your companion every step of the way, would you choose that path so quickly?

The answer is, of course, that we would ultimately choose the higher path. Nothing is worth trading for the presence of Jesus. But if we are honest, the decision is not nearly as easy or obvious as we might want it to seem.

So God presents his people with precisely this choice, and old man Moses takes a deep breath and says a wonderful thing: "No deal!"

> If your Presence does not go with us, do not send us up from
> here. How will anyone know that you are pleased with me
> and with your people unless you go with us? What else will
> distinguish me and your people from all the other people on
> the face of the earth?
>
> EXODUS 33:15-16

Ultimately it is only the presence of God that distinguishes us from everyone else. We drive the same cars, speak the same language, watch most of the same movies, but we are temples of the Holy Spirit. This is what sets us apart in the culture: We are carriers of the presence of God.

Encounter Culture

All God's saints pass through Blue Camp 20 eventually. Jacob wrestled with an angel in a place called Peniel. Joseph fled the advances of

Potiphar's wife and endured dark years in prison before his dreams came to pass. Peter denied Christ before he preached that great Pentecost sermon. Jesus endured forty days in the wilderness being tempted with food, security, and pride.

Ultimately Blue Camp 20 is not just a place of testing. It can also mark a season of spiritual encounter. We are told that Jesus left the wilderness "in the power of the Holy Spirit" (Luke 4:14). Jacob left Peniel having "struggled with God and with humans and . . . overcome," carrying a blessing for generations to come (Genesis 32:28). It's perfectly possible to settle for our current level of spiritual experience, but we are given the opportunity to strike out again into the wilderness seeking a deeper place of relationship with God than ever before.

We tend to assume that Blue Camp 20 is the frontier from which we can pioneer into new territory geographically, or into new effectiveness professionally, but ultimately it is the place of testing from which we can pioneer into a deeper intimacy with Jesus than ever before. We wrestle with God at Blue Camp 20 not to overcome God, but to come close to him in greater intimacy. We lay down comfort at Blue Camp 20, not out of asceticism but out of anticipation of greater treasures to come. We pioneer from Blue Camp 20 not to achieve something for God, but to receive something from him—a deeper fellowship with him in his death and resurrection (Philippians 3:10-11). As Jacob insisted to the angel: "I will not let you go unless you bless me" (Genesis 32:26).

The heart and soul of true Christian faith is not dogma, not culture, not behaviour, but a series of encounters with the living God. When the apostles were accused of turning the world upside down, their explanation was simple and defiant: "We cannot help speaking about what we have seen and heard" (Acts 4:20). They didn't resort to apologetics and clever arguments to prove that they were right; they didn't play politics to strike a deal; they simply testified to the compelling evidence of personal experience. As Christians we are witnesses to sights and sounds and experiences of God that compel us to speak. We have encountered something too wonderful to contain.

Contemporary culture often sneers at those who lay claim to mystical experience. It arches an eyebrow when those in positions of power claim to hear God. One former British prime minister was warned to keep his Christian faith quiet. "We don't do God," his press officer cautioned. Yet encounters with God are woven like a golden thread into the fabric of history, marking the lives of many of the most sensible and influential people who have ever lived: artists, scientists, philosophers, and politicians alike.

Blaise Pascal's Encounter

Blaise Pascal was one of the greatest mathematicians, physicists, and engineers of all time. While still in his teens he invented the first mechanical calculator—a precursor to modern computers. He created at least two new fields of mathematical research. His Law of Probability is still used by economists today. His name has been lent to a unit of pressure and a programming language. He even developed the first bus route for Paris. But the defining moment of Pascal's life came on 23 November 1654 between 10:30 and 12:30 at night. Often described as his "Night of Fire," we only know about it because of some words written secretly on a slip of paper and sewn into his jacket, discovered at last by a curious servant after the great man's death:

The heart and soul of true Christian faith is not dogma, not culture, not behaviour, but an encounter with the living God.

> *Fire.*
> *God of Abraham,*
> *God of Isaac, God of Jacob,*
> *not of philosophers and scholars.*
> *Certainty, certainty,*
> *heartfelt joy, peace.*
> *God of Jesus Christ.*

That mysterious encounter with God changed Pascal's life. Thereafter he turned his intellect towards theology and philosophy. His book *Pensées* is widely considered a masterpiece of prose. It includes Pascal's famous "wager" in which he argued that it makes sense to assumed God's existence because if you are wrong your loss will be merely finite, and if you are right your gain will be immeasurable.

Harriet Beecher Stowe's Encounter

One Sunday in 1851 a young mother in Brunswick, Maine, was receiving communion when she saw a disturbing vision of an old slave being whipped to death. Deeply troubled, she walked her children home from church and skipped lunch to record what she had seen. The words poured from her pen until she ran out of paper and continued on brown grocery wrapping. Harriet Beecher Stowe later explained that it felt as if God had been writing *Uncle Tom's Cabin*, one of the bestselling books of all time and one of the most potent creative gifts to the abolitionist cause in America. Eleven years later when she met Abraham Lincoln, he goaded her good-naturedly: "So you are the little woman who wrote the book that started this great war!" Millions have read *Uncle Tom's Cabin* and know the important part it played in the fight against institutionalised slavery in America. What fewer people realise is that its gripping final scenes were inspired by a eucharistic epiphany one Sunday in Maine.

Martin Luther King's Encounter

One night after a particularly threatening phone call, Martin Luther King Jr. got out of bed, made coffee and bowed at his kitchen table. He was worried about his family, and the burden of his responsibilities weighed heavy on his shoulders. "Lord," he prayed aloud, "I am taking a stand for what I believe is right. The people are looking to me for leadership, and if I stand before them without strength and courage, they will falter. I am at the end of my powers. I have nothing left. I have come to the point where I can't face it alone." Later he told his wife, "At that moment, I experienced the presence of the Divine as I had never experienced Him before." Martin Luther King Jr was imbued with a new sense of confidence through that encounter. In fact, his wife would later recall that it was a turning point, after which he became willing and able to face anything.[3]

Of course, most encounters with God are less dramatic than those of Blaise Pascal, Harriet Beecher Stowe, and Martin Luther King Jr. Generally, God speaks to us in the mother tongue of our own particular psychology and circumstance. Everyone encounters him differently at different times. There is no formula. Abraham waited ninety-nine years for his epiphany, while David was anointed unexpectedly one day in his teens. Isaiah was mysteriously transported into heaven, but Anna simply stared into the face of a baby and "knew." Blind Bartimaeus received his sight, but Saul was blinded to see. An encounter with God may be dramatic, as it was for Paul on that Damascus Road, but for most it's a gentler, Emmaus Road process, more like the gradual dawning of day than fireworks in the night. It doesn't really matter how you encounter the Lord, but it does matter eternally that you do.

> **"I experienced the presence of the Divine as I had never experienced Him before."**
>
> —MARTIN LUTHER KING JR.

⸙　●　●

Having encountered God alone in the graveyard at Little Santa Fe, I rose from my knees and walked down the hill to enjoy the rest of Christmas with Sammy and the boys, knowing for sure that the coming year would bring us fresh adventures. I'd resolved to keep pioneering, whatever the price, and where there had been heaviness and weariness I now found joy and new faith for the journey ahead.

Not long after this significant decision, an old friend arrived in town for a visit from England that would prove pivotal for the next chapter of our story. I met Brian Heasley at the airport in the Scooby-Doo van and took him straight to my new favourite prayer spot: Skies, a revolving restaurant overlooking Kansas City. We ordered drinks, laughing and talking fast, both at the same time. Brian looked the same as ever. Built like a brick outhouse, with a shaved head and trimmed goatee newly flecked with grey, he's the sort of guy you wouldn't want to meet in a dark alley. But meet him in daylight, and you'll see the Irish twinkle and the laugh lines around his eyes.

"Not bad, eh?" I said, regally sweeping my hand across the city below.

"God bless America!" he said, and raised his glass towards the nearest skyscraper.

"Good trip?"

"Bit of trouble at immigration. I thought they weren't going to let me in."

Homeland Security officers are some of the most powerful officials in America, and in the wake of 9/11 they were making sure everyone knew it. When Brian stepped forward to the booth at Chicago O'Hare, a female officer had taken his passport, scanned it into the computer as usual, and then raised her eyebrows as she looked at the screen. "Well, you've been a naughty boy, Mr Heasley," she said.

Brian groaned inwardly. It wasn't fair that his criminal record could be available to a complete stranger at the click of a button after all these years and on the other side of the world. He'd served his time. God had forgiven him, but perhaps the world never would.

"So what's the reason for your visit?" she asked suspiciously.

Brian explained that he was no longer a criminal. In fact, he had become a pastor and was coming to the States to meet with a publisher about a book he'd been commissioned to write for the 24-7 prayer movement. It must have sounded a little unlikely from this Irish ex-con who still looked more punk than monk, and she asked if he could prove his involvement with 24-7. Brian reached into his bag for the manuscript, completely forgetting that the cover design was a large radioactive symbol. "Um, sorry about the logo," he stammered. "It's not what it looks like. It's about the power of prayer."

Unsmiling, the officer glanced at the manuscript, looked back at the screen, and then lifted her gaze to study Brian's face. Eventually, with a sigh of bemused resignation, she stamped the Irishman's passport and welcomed him to America.

"Well, I'm glad you made it," I laughed. "They're obviously lowering their standards."

Brian grinned, leaned back in his seat, and began sharing news of life back home. Maybe it was the jet lag, but he got really honest really fast, describing his inner struggle with the fact that so many of our once-radical friends in England seemed to be selling out and settling down. Successful pastors were getting bored and quietly starting businesses on the side with dreams of getting rich. Brian had been asked to join in with one or two of these start-ups. Other friends, he said sadly, were just getting a little cynical. One was having an affair.

"To be honest, I've been wrestling with temptations to take it easy—just sort of coast," admitted Brian. "It's easy to get sucked into the world's way of thinking. And when your friends are all expecting to become millionaires, you're terrified of missing out. But God's been speaking to me about Abraham and how he kept pioneering."

It was moving to realise that my friend had been wrestling with his own Blue Camp 20, 4,000 miles away. "Ultimately," he said with a sigh, gazing out at the vast urban sprawl, "I signed up to change the world. I never wanted to be like it."

Anam Cara

We sat there in silence, surveying the lengthening shadows. A neat circuit board of streetlights began to glow in the gathering dusk below. Skyscrapers stood tall, glittering gold and silver in the sun's last rays like elegant, sequinned ladies at a cocktail party. And all the while, Skies kept revolving slowly, eventually bringing Arrowhead Stadium into view.

"Ever been?" asked Brian.

"Not to a game," I replied. "Almost impossible to get tickets for the

Chiefs. But yeah, I was there in October for one of Billy Graham's last ever gigs. I wanted the kids to hear the great man while they still could."

Billy Graham had preached his heart out that night. He was old and frail, and for the first time in more than sixty years of ministry, he'd preached alone, without his lifelong buddy, George Beverly Shea, leading worship by his side. The poignancy of his loss had caught me off guard. On the way to the stadium that night, I'd been informed about some very serious moral failures by two well-known, well-trusted Christian leaders. The news had affected me deeply. One of the men was known to Brian and me personally. He had abandoned his wife to run off with his secretary, leaving a whole network of churches distraught. The other man was a respected prophet, an international statesman whose words had shaped literally thousands of lives, including my own. I'd looked up to both men, and I had trusted them.

I had arrived at Arrowhead Stadium that night carrying disappointment. Was this whole thing just a big show? Who could I really trust? The high-profile performers shifting units on the stage? The grinning pastors with their coachloads of deferential guests? Who was I kidding? I couldn't even trust myself.

In the shadow of these dark thoughts, I glanced at our boys, lit up with excitement, sitting on the edge of their seats, swinging their legs, wide-eyed at the magnitude of the stadium and the thousands of people and the fact that it was well past their bedtime. Did the trajectory of ministry mean that I would one day disappoint my sons the way these two spiritual fathers had just failed theirs? Did we all become hypocrites in the end?

It was a gloomy train of thought, and the Enemy was no doubt whispering a few lies, but my reverie was quickly interrupted by the eruption of applause as Billy Graham shuffled forward to speak. The old man raised his hands, and I could see on the giant screens that they were shaking.

"Why's he doing this?" I wondered. "Why isn't he tucked up at home with his wife, drinking cocoa and watching TV, like any other self-respecting octogenarian?" A night in Kansas City was hardly going to make him any more famous. Billy Graham had preached to more people live than anyone else in history. He had been the confidant of successive world leaders. He was old and frail and sick. He had every right to retire. So why was he here tonight?

I began to realise that the great evangelist was with us on that bitterly cold night, simply because he was gnarly and determined and true. It was nothing but beautiful, bloody-minded faithfulness to the call of Jesus; an old-fashioned sense of duty, an ardent resolution just to "do the work of an evangelist" (2 Timothy 4:5) with every breath he was to be granted. The old man on the platform had remained faithful to his wife over six decades. He had also clearly remained true to lifelong friends like George Beverly Shea. And along the way he had dignified the high office of Christian leadership with humanity and integrity. His message to me that night was not his sermon—I can't remember a single word of it. It was the gift of his life. Billy Graham's shaking hands and the breath steaming from his mouth as he preached reassured me eloquently that it really is possible to keep pioneering with integrity all your life—not to sell out, burn out, or settle down, but to run the race beautifully and to finish it well.

The familiar voice echoed around the stadium. I squeezed Sammy's hand and then, glancing at our wide-eyed boys, I made them a simple, silent promise.

● ● ●

Sitting in Skies, I reminisced a little about Billy Graham, and then, a little more hesitantly, I told Brian about wrestling with God at Haran, about Blue Camp 20, about my difficult decision not to settle down. The ancient Celtic monks had a phrase—*anam cara*—to describe a person they deemed a "soul friend"; I think, perhaps, in that moment I found one of mine.

We stared out of the window as darkness fell. The silence was easy. My mind wandered from Arrowhead Stadium to the cemetery at the top of our road. I thought of Abram leaving Haran. I remembered standing on the cliffs of Cape St. Vincent shaking like a leaf. "Here's to pioneering," I said eventually. We chinked glasses and Brian said, "Amen." And so did God, because within a month of that toast he had called Brian through a series of miracles into the wildest adventure you can possibly imagine: pioneering in ways that would propel the whole 24-7 movement out from our prayer rooms and onto the very front lines of missional engagement.

> Your friends were once strangers. Somehow at a particular time, they came from the distance toward your life. Their arrival seemed so accidental and contingent. Now your life is unimaginable without them.
>
> JOHN O'DONOHUE, *ANAM CARA*

SELAH

Let us run with perseverance the race marked out for us, fixing our eyes on Jesus, the pioneer and perfecter of faith.
HEBREWS 12:1-2

Lord Jesus, you know how weary I get, how hurt I've been, how easy it would be to downgrade my dreams, to play it safe in Blue Camp 20. Grant me a steely perseverance. Don't allow me to settle for anything less than your very best for my life. Teach me to run in step with your Spirit, at your pace, by your side, all the way to Santa Fe. Amen.

May I have the courage today
To live the life that I would love
And waste my heart on fear no more.
JOHN O'DONOHUE, "A MORNING OFFERING"

MISSION

GOD'S PRESENCE IN THE CULTURE

. . . for all nations . . .

ISAIAH 56:7

Mission begins with a kind of explosion of joy. The mission of the Church in the pages of the New Testament is . . . like the fallout from a vast explosion, a radioactive fallout which is not lethal but life-giving.

LESSLIE NEWBIGIN, *THE GOSPEL IN A PLURALIST SOCIETY*

8

STRANGE ANGELS

AMERICA · IRELAND · ENGLAND · SPAIN · UGANDA

God makes his saints out of fools and sinners
because there is nothing much else to make them out of.
FREDERICK BUECHNER, *THE FACES OF JESUS*

There was one last conversation I needed to have with Brian Heasley before he returned to England. It would involve asking a question so outrageous that I'd been putting it off all week. I knew that his answer, one way or the other, would have enormous implications for the future of the entire 24-7 mission. What neither of us knew, however, as we drove in the Scooby-Doo van towards Kansas City International Airport to catch Brian's flight home, was the number of miracles awaiting the outcome of this one awkward exchange.

We were seated in a Lone Star Steakhouse beneath a giant pair of bull horns the width of a truck. It was now or never. "Brian," I began, taking a deep breath, "we need someone to go and lead our work in Ibiza; to establish something permanent on the island the whole year round—not just summer teams."

Brian's fork had frozen, halfway to his mouth.

"Look, we haven't got any money. We wouldn't be able to pay you a bean. In fact, we don't really have any infrastructure on the island at all, so I don't know where you and Tracy and the boys would actually, um, live." It was a lousy pitch, but I didn't know how to stop. "It's a messed-up sort of place, as you know: drink, drugs, sex on the streets, you name it. Terrible place to raise teenagers."

Brian was looking at me quizzically. "You do know," he said, placing his fork very carefully on the side of his plate and staring at me with a wry smile, "that I'm the senior pastor of a growing church in a beautiful Norfolk town, and I'm not entirely unpopular with my congregation?"

Suddenly I felt stupid. Why would anyone abandon a fruitful ministry, with a house and a salary, in a church that loved him, in a pretty, rural English town in which his two sons were happily at school and where his wife's family all lived close by—why would anyone leave every shred of security in order to start from scratch, on a wing and a prayer, without a house or a church or a community or a word of Spanish or even an income? What responsible father would risk the happiness and safety of his beautiful wife and two young, impressionable sons in the debauched party capital of Europe?

Andrés

I was about to back down, apologise, and tell Brian that if he knew anyone who might be interested to let me know, when an image flashed through my mind. It was a picture I'd seen of a dreadlocked, tattooed Venezuelan called Andrés, a male stripper at some of San Antonio's seedier nightclubs. Our team had recently befriended Andrés, they had prayed with him, he'd experienced the power of the Holy Spirit and had given his life to Jesus. We had introduced Andrés to one of the only Spanish-speaking churches on the island, expecting that they would welcome and nurture this brand-new brother generously. Initially they had been kind, giving him a place to stay, while making it clear that they disapproved of his appearance, his tattoos, and the way he dressed.

Andrés knew that he wasn't perfect and had certainly made some serious mistakes, even after becoming a Christian, but he couldn't understand why Jesus wanted him to cut his hair, to dress formally and cover his tattoos. Hadn't we told him that God's love was unconditional? The truth was that Andrés needed discipleship, but instead, the moment he put a foot out of line, he was shunned and rejected by the only church in town that spoke his language.

I was sitting here now, trying to ask my friend an outrageous question because of people like Andrés. It wasn't about building an empire, or a brand, or extending our reach; it was about countless lost souls looking for Jesus without knowing his name, night after night in the pubs and clubs of this forgotten mission field.

The gospel has always provoked the church just as much as it has challenged the culture. "The Church," as Archbishop William Temple famously said, "is the only society that exists for the benefit of those who are not its members."[1] We are a prayer-fuelled missionary movement, continually discomfited by the consequences of our own gospel.

One of the most significant turning points in Christian history came when the apostle Peter received an appalling vision during his time of prayer. A menagerie of non-kosher animals descended from heaven, and a voice commanded the apostle to do the most offensive, repulsive thing imaginable: "Get up, Peter. Kill and eat" (Acts 10:13). It was a confrontation designed to offend the most deeply ingrained cultural and religious convictions of any devout Jew. Embracing and discipling a Venzuelan stripper was a very minor challenge indeed compared to this. It's surprising that Peter didn't dismiss the voice as a Satanic temptation rather than a divine revelation.

A knock at the door, at that precise moment, interrupted Peter's reverie, summoning him to the house of a Roman soldier called Cornelius. Peter was propelled from his place of prayer to preach the gospel just as he had been on the day of Pentecost. But this time, shockingly, his audience was to be a Gentile household:

> While Peter was still speaking . . . the Holy Spirit came on all
> who heard the message. The circumcised believers who had
> come with Peter were astonished that the gift of the Holy Spirit
> had been poured out even on Gentiles. For they heard them
> speaking in tongues and praising God.
>
> ACTS 10:44-46

It was a breathtaking moment, a paradigm shift, a quantum leap
for the gospel, through which Peter and the other leaders in Jerusalem
came to fully accept that the glories of Christ belonged even to the dirty
Gentiles.

True prayer continues to provoke and propel us out of our holy places
to engage with those who challenge our subconscious cultural percep-
tions and deeply held religious prejudice. To reach the unchurched we
will have to leave the church to visit places and people we might previously have considered "unclean." Peter's experiences in the house of
Cornelius suggest that when we step out in this way, we do not need
to be afraid. Far from being defiled by dirty people and places, we may
well bring cleansing and experience the Holy Spirit moving in surprising ways.

• • •

The harsh way in which Andrés had been rejected presented us with a
simple, stark choice: We either could stop sending missionaries to Ibiza
because the church, at that time, was unable to welcome and nurture
the sort of people we were reaching, or we would have to establish our
own long-term discipling community on the island to care for those
who came to faith. It may sound like a no-brainer, but it wasn't an easy
decision. To this day we still receive criticism for planting missional
communities, even though we spend most of our time and resources
blessing and supporting existing churches—most of whom would welcome Andrés with open arms.

It was also a difficult decision because planting a community in a modern-day Sodom and Gomorrah would be unspeakably hard. This was not the sort of place you could just lay on good preaching and decent coffee and watch the thing grow. It would require an exceptional prayer warrior who knew how to plant a church, run a nocturnal mission, care for people who are utterly broken, and somehow do all this without an income. In short, we needed Brian Heasley.

"Look," he said laughing, "I promise I'll talk to Tracy and we will certainly pray about Ibiza, but you're not exactly selling this to me!" He took a sip of his drink and gazed out of the window. "Mind you, it's interesting—you asking me this now. A

The church is a prayer-fuelled missionary movement, continually discomfited by the consequences of its own gospel.

piece of paper fell out of Tracy's Bible the other day—a word someone had given her years ago about travel. Since then we've been wondering if maybe it's time to move on. Everything's going great in Norfolk, but . . . well, I suppose it's this call to keep pioneering."

When I heard this, I think I breathed for the first time since the conversation had begun.

"A few weeks ago on holiday," Brian continued, "Tracy just turned to me and said—for the first time ever—that she could imagine living somewhere else but that it would have to be sunny! So I actually said to her"—Brian leaned forward conspiratorially—"'How about doing something with 24-7 in Ibiza?' That was the first place that popped into my head, and she made me promise not to mention it to you unless you raised it first."

I gasped. "Lucky I did, then!"

"Look, don't get too excited, Pete; it was only a chat on holiday. Nothing serious. But we will pray about it, OK?"

I dropped Brian off at the airport, whispering a prayer that God would speak to him loud and clear. As I drove away, my thoughts kept returning to Andrés walking forlornly away from the church. It would be tragic to stop sending mission teams to such a needy place. But if Brian said no, I honestly didn't have anyone else I could ask. Where else was I going to find a seasoned pastor, a natural evangelist who loved 24-7 Prayer and knew how to trust God for provision, who also had enough experience with drugs and criminality to be able to relate to the majority of young adults who flocked to Ibiza every year? "O God," I prayed again, "speak to him." Brian's background seemed to me to have prepared him perfectly—perhaps uniquely—to develop our work in one of the toughest spiritual environments on earth.

The Life of Brian

Growing up in East Belfast during "the Troubles" had been tougher for Brian and his brothers than they realised at the time. For them it was normal to have bombs exploding, people disappearing, hunger strikes in the nearby Maze Prison, and a large paramilitary mural at the end of their street depicting masked men with machine guns declaring, "For God and for Country." Their father was a straightforward, mostly self-educated working-class man who taught his four sons not to sing the rebel songs, not to hate, not to take sides. He knew that the troubles in Northern Ireland were tribal, political, maybe even religious; but they had little to do with Jesus, who calls us to love our enemies, to forgive those who sin against us, and to pray for those who spitefully use us.

Billy and Eileen Heasley prayed earnestly every day for their four sons to grow up knowing Jesus—the real Jesus of the Bible—and not to be sucked into the prevailing poison of sectarian violence. Nearly every morning they invited Brian and his brothers to memorise a Bible verse before school, often rewarding them with sweets. "Those childhood Scriptures have followed me," he says. "Through school, into adulthood, even when I was in prison. I just couldn't get them out of my head."

The Heasley family rarely had a fixed income and learned to rely upon God to provide for all their financial needs. It wasn't easy, but it certainly taught them to trust God for everything. On one occasion, when the family car had broken down, Brian's big brother announced, "I believe God is so powerful he can give us a new car *in fifteen minutes*." Billy must surely have glanced nervously across at Eileen and checked his watch, but within five minutes (not fifteen) there was a knock at the door and a gleaming silver Simca parked in the drive. "I've got a wee car for ye here, Billy," said the man on the doorstep. That's the kind of miracle a kid doesn't forget in a hurry.

When Brian was eight, his dad secured a position pastoring a church in England. The whole family somehow squeezed into the small car with all their luggage and moved across the Irish Sea to begin a new life in Grays, Essex. Starting at Quarry Hill Primary School with a thick Irish accent was intimidating, and Brian found that most of his new classmates had different-coloured skin, which he'd never seen before. But an older boy—a real bruiser—was assigned to look after him, and Brian soon got to grips with the multicultural environment. Their new house had an apple tree in the garden and, best of all, a park next door where Brian and his brothers spent all their free time building dens, riding bikes, and playing football until Eileen called them in over the fence for tea and homemade cakes warm from the oven. "I guess," says Brian, "if I'd known that my mother was about to die, I'd have paid her more attention. Talked to her a bit more. Played a bit less football. Asked her a few more questions." He pauses. "But she was *eternal*. She was . . ." His voice trails away and eventually he sighs. "A boy needs his mum."

Eileen died suddenly, almost without warning, when Brian was eleven. She had been the centre of gravity, the homemaker, the tender voice amongst five men of varying sizes. Their joy-giver had gone and they barely knew how to grieve. Billy tried his best, but his sons were becoming wilder, hurting in their own different ways. Brian began hooking off school to visit London, where he would stare in awe for hours at paintings by Caravaggio and Rembrandt in the National Gallery. At the age of seventeen he was finally kicked out of college and decided to run away to Ireland, hoping perhaps to reawaken childhood memories of a happier place and time.

When he arrived in Cork, a busker urged him to visit Skibbereen, the most southerly town in Ireland, where you can sit on the rocks and sometimes, he said, hear the angels playing harp. After a few pints of Guinness, Brian believed him and set off, but the angels weren't playing that day in Skibbereen and he was merely picked up by the police for stealing food. Bizarrely, the officers dispatched him to a Hare Krishna community that promised to feed travellers, and so it was that Brian found himself living on an island on the Fermanagh Loch with a bunch of bald vegetarians in orange robes, chanting and dancing around in circles. The monks were kind but weird, and eventually Brian could take it no more. He returned to Essex with a heavy heart. There had been no angel harps in Skibbereen, no enlightenment amongst the Hare Krishna, and there was no mother to welcome him home.

> There had been no angel harps in Skibbereen, no enlightenment amongst the Hare Krishna, and there was no mother in Belfast waiting to welcome him home.

Having failed to find answers in Ireland, Brian began looking for comfort elsewhere. He stormed out of home on his eighteenth birthday and was soon whacked out on drugs. His weight fell to just 125 pounds. He attempted to rob an electrical goods store armed with a claw hammer and moved into a party-squat with a disreputable crowd. "They'd very kindly bring me a line of speed on a mirror and say, 'Morning, Brian, here's your breakfast.' We were all just trying to get back to that buzz we'd had at the start."

When the police released a photo-fit likeness of Brian, he fled to Amsterdam and spent a few miserable weeks there on the run. Eventually he returned home to Essex and decided to surrender himself to a passing police car. It was probably the least dramatic, most gentlemanly arrest for armed robbery in history. Not like *NYPD*, *Breaking Bad*, or *America's Most Wanted*. Strolling up to the policeman, Brian introduced himself as a wanted criminal. "Oh right, well look, you'd better just hop in the car," said the officer apologetically, opening his back door. "Let's pop you down to the station, shall we?"

Brian was charged with armed robbery and sent to Chelmsford Prison for attempted theft. "Stick yer chin out, son," said the Scottish guard kindly to the terrified new teenager. "That's it! And yer chest too. Act like you've done it before." Brian was escorted brusquely through a series of steel doors, dressed in a new blue remand uniform but still wearing his own shoes (a small victory), on the way to spend his first night incarcerated at Her Majesty's Pleasure.

The sound of men crying and even howling that night echoed eerily around the nineteenth-century penitentiary. Brian soon discovered that these were the groans of new inmates enduring drug withdrawal. He learned to bury his head under the pillow to shut out the sound. That's how he still sleeps to this day.

The following morning, a giant with a broken nose, a man who had stabbed three people, was staring at him. "Why," growled the man suspiciously, "do I know you?"

Chin out, shoulders square, try not to look afraid.

By now the giant was studying Brian's features, a little too close for comfort.

Suddenly he jabbed Brian in the chest. "Heasley!" he cried triumphantly. "Quarry Hill Primary School. Remember? Teacher made me show you round on your first day. Funny little Irish kid, you was back then. Don't you remember? I was the big boy what looked out for you."

Brian grinned with relief as much as recognition.

"Welcome," said the giant, holding out his hand. "I guess you'll be needing me to look out for you in here too, eh?"

Somewhere outside those forbidding walls, an Irish preacher must surely have been on his knees, praying hard for his son at the start of his first day in prison: "Lord, would you protect my boy in there . . . Would you help him not to be too scared today . . . Please teach him what he needs to learn . . . Help him to make friends—the right kind of friends."

It seemed only yesterday that Billy had been praying such similar prayers for the same frightened little boy, waking up for his first day in another uniform at Quarry Hill School. And of course, inside Chelmsford Prison, God was answering Billy's prayers, reenlisting the same guy again—a violent, broken-nosed giant to protect a very lost sheep.

• • •

Later that week, Brian's dad became his first visitor. "I could see that it was breaking him up inside to be talking to me like that, across a barrier, in the visiting room." Brian looked into the eyes of his father on that first visit, and felt deeply ashamed. "It finally dawned on me that this man who had once held me and had watched me grow must have dreamed dreams for my life. And this—the visiting room at Chelmsford Prison, having been kicked out of college, drug abuse, simmering aggression, armed robbery—this was not the dream that a young father dreams for his son. It was too easy to blame it all on the loss of my mum, but no one made me terrorise a shopkeeper with a claw hammer. Other people lose their mothers without doing the things I did."

Brian pauses, and when eventually he continues, it's in a whisper. "I wanted a prodigal moment with my father when he came to visit me that day. But it didn't happen. You don't hug and cry with a man like my dad. And you definitely don't hug and cry in prison. You learn to lock all those feelings away in your cell."

Back in his cell, Brian read the Bible voraciously. Even at night when the lights went out, he would lie there with his head under the pillow, blocking out the screams, remembering verses he'd memorised as a child. Brian's shame was deep, and his prodigal journey was to be long and painfully slow. In fact, there were to be three further terms in prison—sentences for threatening behaviour, violent disorder, theft and fraud—before he finally, fully "came to his senses and said . . . 'Father, I have sinned against heaven and against you. I am no longer worthy to be called your son'" (Luke 15:17, 18-19).

Slowly, God began to put Brian's life back together. He turned up at a church in a rural Norfolk town called Diss as an ex-con on probation, after his fourth term in prison, and found himself invited to Sunday lunch—accepted, not condemned. That wonderful church loved Brian unconditionally, and gradually he began to find healing and restoration. His childhood faith came alive. Before long he was offered a job as the youth pastor. He met Tracy, a beautiful girl who seemed to like him and eventually agreed to become his wife. And then, a full decade after arriving at the church as an angry, broken man newly released from his fourth stretch in prison, Brian Heasley was asked to become its pastor.

•   •   •

It seemed to me that God had been preparing Brian over many years for the extreme challenges of a mission field like Ibiza. I prayed like mad that he and Tracy would agree. Where else in the world would we ever find an experienced pastor, steeped in the Scriptures, with such an unshakeable faith in God's ability to provide for every material need through prayer, whether it was a car in the driveway or a guardian angel in prison, who could also relate to those caught up in the destructive cycles of casual violence, criminality, alcohol poisoning, and drug abuse? Little did I know that as Brian and Tracy sought God about Ibiza, they were about to receive some of the clearest, most dramatic guidance I have ever known.

The Transvestite Prophet

One of the first things Brian did on returning to England was to buy a book about Ibiza. Feeling a little jet-lagged, he took it upstairs and lay on the bed. "Lord, is this Ibiza thing you?" he whispered.

At that precise moment his reverie was shattered by a blast of music from the room next door. "Whoa!" sang the voice. "We're going to Ibiza!" Brian's niece, knowing nothing of her uncle's dilemma, had just randomly chosen to play an old hit from The Vengaboys. Then she played it again. And again. And again.

Brian laughed. "OK, maybe. But if you don't mind, I need a bit more than a dodgy dance track, Lord."

On Monday a mentally ill, homeless transvestite turned up unannounced to see Brian in the church office. He was wearing tights under filthy, ripped jeans, and a touch of eyeliner. He smelled terrible. But Brian really didn't mind; people like this were his favourite part of pastoral ministry. Without knowing anything at all about Brian's dilemma, the man looked him in the eye and said, "I've got a house for you, Brian. It's in Ibiza. You should go there!" He didn't have anything of the kind. It was just a random comment from an addled mind that somehow spoke directly into the specific question Brian was privately asking the Lord.

God certainly seemed to be speaking, but so far it had been through a confused transvestite and a cheesy dance-floor anthem.

God certainly seemed to be speaking, but so far it had been through a confused transvestite and a serendipitous rendition of a cheesy dance-floor anthem. Neither could be considered conventional or reliable means of guidance for major life decisions involving small children and potential financial jeopardy. It was enough, however, to persuade Brian and Tracy to visit Ibiza, to spy out the land discreetly without alarming the church, their family, or the kids.

Their first appointment in Ibiza was with the headmaster of its only English-speaking school. He listed, with great relish, all the famous people whose children attended the school, and the Heasleys quickly felt intimidated. Eventually he paused and inquired about their reasons for relocation. But before Brian could explain that he was a globe-straddling rock star and that his wife worked in international finance for a Russian oligarch, Tracy said very simply, "We'll be missionaries. With an organisation called 24-7 Prayer."

Brian held his breath. A complete stranger suddenly seemed to hold their entire future in his hands, and he was clearly trying to formulate a decorous way of telling them that penniless missionaries weren't quite the clientele he was looking for on the PTA. But instead, at that moment, an older lady stepped forward. She had been sitting quietly in the background, and now introduced herself as the owner of the school. "I've heard of 24-7 Prayer," she announced, beaming at Tracy appreciatively.

The headmaster looked surprised, and so did Brian. "We would be delighted," she said, extending her hand and shooting a glance at the headmaster, "to offer your sons places at this school."

Every traffic light seemed to be turning green, but it was all happening too fast. Brian and Tracy decided to go for a walk on one of the island's fifty beaches. They selected Playa d'en Bossa, which stretches for two kilometres of golden sand with beautiful views of the Old Town. Barefoot and holding hands, Brian and Tracy set out walking between the sun-loungers on the sand and the crystal-clear sea lapping at their toes.

"OK, I'm going to pray something a bit weird," Brian announced after a while. "Lord, if you want us to come to Ibiza, please give us just one more sign: Let us bump into Aunty Anne while we're here."

Tracy's aunt happened to be holidaying somewhere on the island that week, but they had no idea where. With fifty beaches and 6 million tourists a year, the chances of bumping into her were infinitesimal, so they had deliberately not told her about their visit.

"OK, but what happens if we *don't* see her?" asked Tracy, realising how unlikely it was. "Does that mean we're *not* supposed to come?"

Before Brian could respond, a gust of wind blew a beach ball out from the crowded ranks of sunbathers. It bounced right in front of Brian and Tracy, pursued by a generously proportioned lady in her fifties wearing a black bathing suit. "Tracy?" the woman screamed. "Brian? What on earth are you doing here?"

On the flight home Brian and Tracy reviewed events with a measure of awe. It had all started weeks earlier with Tracy's fairly innocent announcement about wanting to live somewhere sunny, triggered by the rediscovery of a fourteen-year-old prophetic word about travel and movement. In response Brian had immediately suggested Ibiza, priming them both for the unsolicited conversation with me.

Next there had been the Vengaboys track at the precise moment Brian asked God about Ibiza: "Whoa! We're going to Ibiza!" Even their name, "Venga," is the Spanish word for "come on!"

Next, a couple of days after that, God seemed to have spoken prophetically through a homeless transvestite, who barely knew what he was saying.

Then, in Ibiza itself, they had been offered places at an exclusive school thanks to the surprise intervention of a stranger who just happened to know 24-7 Prayer.

Finally, there had been the instantaneous answer to Brian's prayer for a specific sign at Playa d'en Bossa, in the shape of Tracy's Aunty Anne emerging from a crowded beach in pursuit of a beach ball blown by a random gust of wind at the exact moment when her path would cross theirs, and immediately after Brian had prayed to meet her amongst thousands of tourists on this particular beach at this precise moment. The mathematical probabilities were mind-bending.

When they landed in England, they collected their baggage and boarded the airport transit train to the car park. "What do you think?" Brian finally asked. "Do you feel like God's speaking?"

Tracy was giggling, pointing up at the advertisement for a travel agency, immediately opposite them in the train: "Plane Obvious," it said. "The way to go is 24-7."

* * *

That evening Brian quietly slipped out to the church prayer room with his friend Albert. The story of the last few days soon came tumbling out.

"So what do you think?" Brian asked.

"What I think," said Albert, grinning, "is that God's shouting at you!"

"What do you think?" Brian asked another friend later that night on the phone.

"It's so clear that if you don't go now," said the friend, "it'll be an act of disobedience."

The next day Brian and Tracy Heasley said yes to Jesus. They made the decision to leave the comforts of their home, their church, their jobs, their incomes, their children's schools, and their country in order to pioneer an extreme mission, for which they had, it seemed, been perfectly prepared.

• • •

I flew back to London from Kansas City for the fifth anniversary celebrations of 24-7 Prayer. Floyd McClung came with me and spoke powerfully about the call to keep pioneering in prayer, mission, and justice. "You're a prayer movement, for sure," he told the gathered crowd, "but you'd better get ready, because you're becoming a mission movement too."

Brian and Tracy cheered. Others looked less sure. One of our leaders later threatened to resign, concerned that we were getting distracted away from intercession. But the movement from prayer into mission was unstoppable. It just kept happening, whether we liked it or not.

Kacunga

We heard about a prayer room in Uganda where God had simultaneously given several people the same strange word: *Kacunga*. It turned out to be the name of an island—one of 3,000 on Lake Victoria, a vast inland sea connecting Uganda with Tanzania and Kenya. Having located it amongst the eighty-eight Ssese islands in the Kampala District of the lake, Paul Masindende and a troupe of valiant prayer warriors set out from their prayer room excitedly, wondering what they would find on the island God had named.

Pray with ambition. Pray with adventurous imagination. There is no better measure of the person you are becoming than the way you are praying right now.

It was a long journey by land and by boat, but at last they arrived and discovered an indigenous community of illiterate subsistence fishermen who had never heard the name of Jesus. The Kacungans were eking out a life on the island with no electricity, no hospital, no school, no church, a 90 per cent HIV infection rate, and a 99 per cent belief in witchcraft. The Holy Spirit had, it seemed, directed the Ugandan group very specifically to a community that was desperately needy and totally unreached by the gospel.

A church was planted in a day on an unreached island through a single strange word spoken by the Holy Spirit in a distant prayer room.

The islanders welcomed their unexpected visitors warmly, and were astounded to hear how God had singled them out from all the other islands on the great lake. When they heard the gospel he'd sent to them, fifty of the Kacungans immediately believed and received Jesus. A church was planted amongst an unreached tribe in a single day—all because of a specific, unexpected word from the Holy Spirit in a prayer room far away.

• • •

At our fifth birthday celebration in London there were many thrilling reports such as this one from Uganda. And then there were two separate prophetic words from trusted voices, both telling us to prepare for another five years of prayer. It was a sobering moment. We'd always said that we'd stop whenever God did, and that had sometimes been quite a reassuring prospect. But now the Spirit seemed to be telling us to prepare for a decade of non-stop prayer. This was about to become a significant chunk of our lives.

I looked around the room nervously. There was a sobriety on many of the faces I knew so well. Then slowly I watched them pledging themselves to strike out again from Blue Camp 20, whatever and wherever it might be for them. Together we set our sights once more on Santa Fe.

Somewhere in the crowd a young father found himself so stirred that he went home to his wife and together they quit their jobs, sold their house, packed their two young children with everything they owned into a VW campervan, and began travelling. Scot and Misty Bower would spend the next five years on the road touring Europe, blown by the wind anywhere the Spirit sent them, encouraging and equipping 24-7 communities wherever they happened to be.

Somewhere else in the crowd, a girl called Carla kissed a musician called Steve for the first time. She was there because she had surrendered her life fully to Jesus five years earlier in the very first 24-7 prayer room. Now she was doing anything she could to help out around the office. But the Spirit of God was moving in Carla's life, raising her up from office work to become one of the great global champions of the movement. On that day in London, however, she was falling in love with the man who would become her husband.

With marriages being made, careers being jettisoned, and prophetic exhortations to continue for a decade, the stakes were being raised significantly. We were growing up fast; it was sobering and it was fun. God was connecting and commissioning people in remarkable ways. Then, standing in front of that large crowd, I asked Brian and Tracy Heasley why on earth they were giving up a safe life leading a growing church in a picturesque Norfolk town to go to Ibiza without any security at all. I knew that Brian had many great things he could say in answer to that question. Things about growing up in Belfast, losing his mum, and spending time in prison. Stories about the extraordinary ways in which God had called them to Ibiza through a homeless transvestite and a chance encounter with a lady in a bathing suit pursuing a beach ball. Observations about Abraham in Haran and Andrés in Spain and the need to keep pioneering for the sake of a generation that is "harassed and helpless, like sheep without a shepherd" (Matthew 9:36).

Brian could have said so many inspiring things in answer to my question. Intelligent things. Things that might be strategic in drumming up a bit more support. It was a soft pitch of a question, and all he needed to do was hit a home run. He opened his mouth to answer, but nothing came out. And then Brian Heasley, the hardened ex-con, the seasoned pastor, began to weep. He stood in front of that great congregation and simply lost it. Tracy held his hand tight, and he cried.

The room fell silent. Everyone felt the holiness of the moment; the cost of the cause. And then we prayed for them, commissioning the Heasleys by crowd-surfing them above our heads to the back of the room. It was a way of lifting them to the Lord, promising to uphold them in prayer as they embarked upon the next great adventure of their remarkable lives.

> Then I heard the voice of the Lord saying, "Whom shall I send? And who will go for us?"
> And I said, "Here am I. Send me!"
>
> ISAIAH 6:8

SELAH

When he looked out over the crowds, his heart broke. So confused and aimless they were, like sheep with no shepherd. "What a huge harvest!" he said to his disciples. "How few workers! On your knees and pray for harvest hands!"
MATTHEW 9:36-38, MSG

- Do I dare to ask Jesus to break my heart for the lost souls all around me?
- Do I know anyone who is "harassed and helpless" right now?
- With whom could I share the hope of the gospel today?

We have to love our neighbour because he is there . . . He is the sample of humanity which is actually given us. Precisely because he may be anybody he is everybody.
G. K. CHESTERTON

9

PORKY THE PIRATE

SPAIN · ENGLAND · GERMANY · USA
JAPAN · BULGARIA

It has always been my ambition to preach the gospel
where Christ was not known, so that I would not be building
on someone else's foundation.

ROMANS 15:20

It's eight o'clock in the morning on the seventh day of July when the first rocket is fired and six unfortunate bulls are released into the cobbled streets of Pamplona, Spain. Hundreds of young men wearing white trousers with red waistbands run ahead of them, trying to avoid getting trampled, skewered, or gored to death. This is the way of things. Stags rut on the hills, wolves howl at the moon, gorillas beat their chests in the jungle, and young men with college degrees run ahead of six crazed bulls in Pamplona.

The popularity of this dangerous rite of passage, and of bullfighting in general, can be traced back to 1926 when that manliest of writers, Ernest Hemingway, issued a testosterone-fuelled dare to successive generations of young men, defying them to prove their manliness in this, "the most beautiful thing I've ever seen [which] takes more guts and skill and guts again than anything possibly could."[1]

A few years ago, my friend Bob arrived in Pamplona to make a film about "the running of the bulls," and stumbled upon a completely surreal scene, unimagined by Hemingway on his wildest bender. Bob found thousands of naked joggers—no bull in sight—with shoes on their feet, fake horns on their heads, and absolutely nothing in between. It was the annual protest by animal rights groups, known simply as "The Running of the Nudes."

Like a seasoned pro, Bob thrust his camera in front of the first two men he could find and asked what they were doing.

"No idea, mate!" they cried in Australian accents.

"Where are you going?"

"Search me."

"But . . . but you're naked," said Bob.

"Yeah," they laughed. "When in Rome . . ."

"Pamplona . . ."

"Look, mate, we came to see the Running of the Bulls and found all these naked people heading that way." They pointed enthusiastically at several hundred bottoms. "We didn't really think about it. We got here, got undressed, and got involved."

And with that they were off again, running with the herd wherever it happened to be going.

●　●　●

It's easy to get caught up in the hype of life, swept along with the crowd, never really pausing to wonder, "What am I actually doing this for?" "Where am I heading?" and "Why?" The apostle Paul warns us explicitly not to "run like someone running aimlessly," but rather to "run in such a way as to get the prize" (1 Corinthians 9:24-26). The writer of Hebrews uses similar language: "Let us run with perseverance the race marked out for us, [by] fixing our eyes on Jesus, the pioneer and perfecter of faith" (Hebrews 12:1-2).

Life doesn't have to be particularly complicated or confusing. Unlike those naked Australians, we can know precisely where we are heading and why. The Bible gives us our bearings around two simple alignments: On the vertical plane, Jesus commands us to love God with all our hearts and minds and strength; on the horizontal plane, he commands us to go and love our neighbours as we love ourselves. "Do this," he says, "and you will live." Purpose and meaning await every single person on the planet in obedience to these two great commandments, but how are we to do them?

First, Jesus invites us to *come*. "Come, follow me" (Matthew 4:19). "Come . . . all you who are weary" (Matthew 11:28). "Come with me by yourselves to a quiet place and get some rest" (Mark 6:31). We approach Jesus primarily through prayer and worship. We learn to sit with him, listen to him, and love him. This vertical axis has been the subject of the first half of this book.

Second, Jesus says *go*. Go into all the world. Go make disciples. Go preach the gospel. Go heal the sick, feed the hungry, pick a fight with injustice. Go make a difference. This horizontal axis is the subject of the second half of this book.

The prophet Isaiah discovered this correlation dramatically on the day that he "saw the Lord, high and exalted, seated on a throne." He heard the seraphim singing "Holy, holy, holy," saw the temple filled with smoke, and felt it all shaking. It was an awesome experience. And yet God was not absorbed in the spectacle; neither was he gazing at himself in the mirror as the angels worshipped. Instead he was looking outwards, actively surveying the earth, consumed with our problems, even crying out in desperation, "Whom shall I send?" (Isaiah 6).

A House of Prayer for the Nations

When Jesus denounced the temple for its inadequacy as "a house of prayer for all nations," he was not condemning it so much for a lack of prayer (there were regular times of prayer in the temple each day), but rather for failing to turn those prayers outwards to be a missional and hospitable blessing to "the nations." His message was unequivocal: A house of prayer that is inaccessible, unwelcoming, and disengaged from the lost is failing to be a true house of prayer, no matter how many hours of intercession and worship it might clock up along the way. Those who pray continually without engaging missionally are simply missing the point, "like someone running aimlessly," like those Australian tourists caught up in the hype of Pamplona without any real sense of direction or purpose. If we claim to have our eyes fixed on Jesus and yet fail to focus on the profound needs that break his heart, we are hypocrites.

Those who pray continually without engaging missionally are missing the point.

When King Herod rebuilt the temple in the years just before Jesus' birth, he enlarged and enclosed its outer court, creating a vast, cloistered plaza, paved with marble and surrounded by Corinthian pillars thirty-seven feet high. Anyone from any nation was permitted to enter this part of the temple. Significantly it was here, in the "Court of the Gentiles," that Jesus overturned the tables of the money-changers. He was enraged by two particular violations of the temple's true purpose: the scandalous way in which pilgrims were being *exploited* in the Gentile courts, and the way the Gentiles were being *excluded* from the rest of the temple.

Exploitation. Ancient records reveal that 226,000 animals were sold and slaughtered in the Court of the Gentiles during a single Passover festival in AD 66. It was little more than a noisy slaughterhouse. And in the middle of this chaos, hundreds of traders were overcharging the crowds of earnest pilgrims—Jew and Gentile alike—as they purchased animals for sacrifice. The authorities may well have been complicit in the racket (more on this later), so Jesus had good reason to be furious at the way honest pilgrims from many nations were being exploited in his Father's house.

Exclusion. The temple architecture was laid out a bit like a Russian doll: Every area enclosed another. Within the Court of the Gentiles stood the Court of the Women, within which lay the Court of the

Israelites, open only to Jewish men. Within that stood the Court of the Priests, which in turn enclosed the Holy of Holies, accessible only to one specially selected priest just once a year. This brutal hierarchy of progressive exclusion—on the basis of ethnicity, gender, and ordination—seems to have enraged Jesus just as much as the commercial exploitation and corruption of the temple trade. Pilgrim foreigners coming from afar to worship the King of Kings were being excluded from God's presence in the very place intended for their blessing.

In 1871 an archaeologist dug up a stone plaque from the Court of the Gentiles. Carefully inscribed and originally inked in large red letters, it said:

> NO FOREIGNER IS TO GO BEYOND THE BALUSTRADE AND THE PLAZA OF THE TEMPLE ZONE. WHOEVER IS CAUGHT DOING SO WILL HAVE HIMSELF TO BLAME FOR HIS DEATH, WHICH WILL FOLLOW.

Jesus must have known—and hated—this sign. Its forbidding red letters precisely spelled out the very religious apartheid he had come to destroy. His mission was, in part, to pull it down, to fling wide the gates of the Holy Place, to welcome every tribe and tongue into God's presence, and to welcome God's presence into every tribe and tongue. Jesus had come to bring life, not to threaten death; to give grace to the Gentiles, not to exclude them with the law.

Jesus came to abolish the temple's exclusive hierarchy of racial, sexual, and religious apartheid.

So Jesus stood in this cacophonous courtyard, perhaps pointing at that forbidding sign, and bellowed out the prophecy of Isaiah: "Is it not written: 'My house will be called a house of prayer for all nations?'" (Mark 11:17). His listeners knew the verse and its context perfectly. Isaiah was anticipating a joyous day when "eunuchs . . . foreigners . . . and exiles" would be gathered to God's temple in complete acceptance (Isaiah

56:4-8). The temple was meant for everybody. Instead its rulers were self-seeking and xenophobic, even issuing death threats to any eunuch, foreigner, or exile who tried to get too close to God.

Access All Areas

The message of Jesus is that God has broken out of the Holy of Holies and is now to be found in the barn, at the party, in the workshop, at dinner with sinners, up the mountain, in the crowd, asleep in the boat, on death row, in the morgue, in the garden, on the beach cooking breakfast. The "Lord of all the earth" (Psalm 97:5), who had once apparently been cloistered away somewhere for some, is now everywhere for everyone. Ladies and gentlemen, Elvis has left the building.

When Jesus died on the cross, so too did the purpose of the temple. At that moment, a ninety-foot curtain separating its Holy Inner Courts from those of the women and Gentiles ripped in half, from top to bottom. The sacrificial Lamb of God had taken away the sins of the world once and for all. Jesus' death had superseded the entire sacrificial system; his resurrection had opened a new means of blessing and atonement for the nations. The temple had been made redundant by the cross. No wonder Jesus' last words were the cry "It is finished!" (John 19:30). His own suffering was finished, and the power of sin was finished, but so too was the towering artifice of Herod's temple and the religious bureaucracy it sustained.

• • •

My heart was nearly bursting with gratitude as I boarded the flight home to Kansas City from our fifth birthday celebrations in London. God had done "immeasurably more" than anything we could possibly have asked or imagined (Ephesians 3:20) back in that first little prayer room, tucked away in a forgotten corner of an industrial estate on the south coast of England. Around the world countless souls were praying around the clock. Mission teams were being mobilised. Prayer rooms and Boiler

Room communities were multiplying with a common, compelling vision to change the world through shared lives of prayer, mission, and justice.

One of these Boiler Rooms had been established in an abandoned school near Leipzig, not far from the village of Herrnhut—our spiritual home. In this unlikely place, Moravian refugees prayed non-stop through the eighteenth and nineteenth centuries. And it had been almost exactly five years into this remarkable prayer meeting that the Moravians had sent out their first two missionaries, thereby launching the first great mission movement of the Reformation. It dawned on me that—by commissioning Brian and Tracy at our fifth anniversary event in London, after five years of 24-7 prayer—we were unwittingly following quite precisely in the footsteps of our Moravian heroes once again.

I gazed down at the Atlantic 37,000 feet below, and tried to imagine those gnarly Moravian missionaries crossing this same vast ocean in wooden boats bound for Labrador and Greenland, Pennsylvania, Georgia, and the Caribbean, many never to return. Fired up by prayer and shot out from Herrnhut like rockets, Moravians were the first to convey the gospel to many nations. The Cherokee and Delaware tribes in America, for instance, first heard the name of Jesus from the lips of Moravian missionaries. The Moravians were also the apostles to the Inuit people in Greenland and the tribes of Surinam, Jamaica, Antigua, and Barbados. On the sugarcane plantations of the Danish West Indies, Moravians from Herrnhut baptised 1,600 slaves before any other missionaries arrived on the scene. Along the way they translated the Scriptures and served the poor.

A team of eighteen was sent to evangelise the islands of St. Thomas and St. Croix in the Danish West Indies, but eight of them died from yellow fever. A further eleven volunteers duly left Herrnhut to replace the dead, but four of them died in their first two months on St. Croix. After eighteen months of extreme sacrifice there was just one solitary convert to show for such a great price. Many of the surviving Moravians began to return to Herrnhut in terrible physical shape, three of them being shipwrecked en route.

A full six years after their first two-man team had arrived in the Danish West Indies, Zinzendorf went to visit, wondering whether there would be any survivors or any fruit at all. "Suppose the brethren are no longer here; what shall we do?" he asked his companion.

"In that case, we are here," came the reply.

"*Gens aeterna, diese Mähren!*" replied Zinzendorf ("An indestructible race, these Moravians!") In fact, Zinzendorf found a thriving church of 800 newly converted plantation workers.

The Moravians sacrificed everything for the gospel, and the results were extraordinary. For instance, it was at a Moravian Bible study in London that John Wesley felt his heart "strangely warmed." Before long England would be aflame with the fire that had been kindled in Wesley's heart that night, but first he travelled to Herrnhut for three months to receive personal discipleship from the leader of the Moravian mission, Count Zinzendorf.

In Herrnhut Wesley first witnessed the radical model of mutual discipleship which gave rise to his reforming Methodist Class System (one of the "methods" that would give them their name). It was also during his three-month stay amongst the Moravians that Wesley caught the vision for unceasing intercession. And so on New Year's Eve 1738, John Wesley, no doubt remembering the non-stop prayer meeting in Herrnhut, gathered with sixty friends at Fetter Lane, London, to pray through the night. His journal records what happened next:

> About three in the morning, as we were continuing instant in prayer, the power of God came mightily upon us insomuch that many cried out for exceeding joy and many fell to the ground. As soon as we were recovered a little from that awe and amazement at the presence of His majesty, we broke out with one voice, "We praise Thee, O God, we acknowledge Thee to be the Lord."[2]

Wesley himself was propelled out of that prayer meeting aflame with the Spirit, riding more than 250,000 miles over the next fifty years preaching the gospel. Meanwhile, his brother Charles was inspired to begin writing a canon of more than six thousand hymns. Their friend George Whitefield crossed the Atlantic to stir up the fires of America's First Great Awakening alongside Jonathan Edwards in New England, preaching to crowds of up to 30,000, befriending Benjamin Franklin, and becoming one of the most recognised characters in America.

The Moravian and Wesleyan mission was an astonishing story of global impact, and yet it had begun very simply on that momentous day back in 1732 when just two men, a thirty-six-year-old carpenter and a twenty-six-year-old potter, left Herrnhut after five years of prayer, sent out by Zinzendorf to find a way

John Wesley organised a prayer meeting that changed the course of British and American history.

to reach slaves in the Caribbean. Those two brave men walked 400 miles to Copenhagen and boarded a ship bound for the West Indies. A crowd gathered on the dockside, weeping and waving as they set sail towards an uncertain future. But one of the men cried out triumphantly, across the water from the ship, "That the Lamb may receive the reward for the blood that he shed!"

I sighed, remembering the relatively minor things I had turned into a litany of complaints that day in the cemetery at Blue Camp 20. Then my thoughts returned to the Heasleys, our first two brave missionaries leaving behind every shred of human security; setting out after five years of prayer, bound for a very different island to address a very different form of captivity. Did I dare to believe that God could do again in our day the same wonderful things he'd done back then? Could he use our little Herrnhuts to spark a new missions movement, to reach the unreached tribes of the twenty-first century? Might one of the people we reached become the John Wesley of our time?

What, I wondered, might happen if the Spirit were to invade just one of our prayer rooms anywhere in the world, the way he had come to the one in Fetter Lane, London, at 3 a.m. on New Year's Day in 1739? The sun was rising as we flew west. Gazing out of the window, I watched another plane, far below, pulling a candyfloss vapour-trail across the sky. It was a beautiful sight, but I pulled down the blind, whispered a prayer for the Heasleys on their way to Ibiza, and quickly fell asleep.

• • •

As 24-7 Prayer continued to morph into multiple missional expressions, Sammy and I began to ask the Lord for help. That day at Blue Camp 20, I'd made the difficult decision to keep pioneering, and in London at the fifth birthday celebrations many others had done the same. It was wonderful and exciting, but sobering too. It's one thing to invite a bunch of your friends on an adventure for a year or two, living together on a wing and a prayer, but quite another to commit to a cause over a decade. We'd always said we'd stop when God did, but how does that mindset work once people are signing leases on buildings and quitting their jobs, and moving to other countries? Somehow I knew that the movement needed to be organised—without becoming an organisation.

We began to pray for a little help from some older, wiser heads to come alongside us, tell us when we were being stupid, maybe shoulder a little weight, and cheer us on.

I have no doubt that it was in direct answer to these cries for help that God connected our hearts with an American who was to become a dear friend, mentor, and godfather to the 24-7 tribes. Some day they should make a movie about Jon Petersen's life. It's incredible, and if you want to understand where 24-7 went next, it will help to know a little bit about his wild experiences living on three continents over six decades and surfing at least three successive waves of the Spirit along the way.

1950s and '60s Japan

Born in Yokohama, Japan, to American missionary parents, Jon Petersen grew up speaking Japanese and watching fishermen making the freshest sushi in the world, right there on the beach. The Second World

War had devastated Japan just six years before Jon's birth. A quarter of a million people had died in the nuclear terror of Hiroshima and Nagasaki—half of them in a single day. Japan was traumatised at a level we can barely imagine, struggling with profound questions of identity and faith. Growing up in this context, as a son of the nation that had so recently decimated the only homeland he'd ever known, Jon was wrestling with his own internal questions of identity too. His "third culture" loneliness intensified at boarding school, where his parents ran the dormitory system and insisted (doubtless with good intentions) that he live with all the other children in the dorm, and not sleep at home with them in their adjoining family apartment. Jon felt displaced and confused, as if he had to deny his own sense of belonging. He lived for the holidays when they would regroup as a little family of three, usually in a mountain cabin high above the Japanese snow line. It was there, more than anywhere in the world, that he truly felt he belonged, and to this day, half a century later, Jon still feels happiest up the highest mountain, buried in the deepest snow.

1970s California

At the age of eighteen, Jon was sent to study in America. He touched down in California just as the 1970s "Jesus People" movement was about to explode. Turning up at church on his first Sunday in this bewildering new land, Jon found barefoot hippies from the street and surfers from the beach mingling uncomfortably with the usual congregation in their Sunday best. Smart new carpets had recently been fitted in the sanctuary, and someone had posted a sign, obviously aimed at the hippies, saying "Absolutely No Bare Feet." The pastor, Chuck Smith, flew into a rage and broke that sign in half, rebuking the congregation like a latter-day Jesus overturning tables in the Court of the Gentiles. "Anyone and everyone is welcome in this sanctuary, *with or without shoes*," he said. "No one will ever again take cheap shots or place prohibitions upon those coming to meet with God in this place!"

It was a defining moment for that church: a prophetic act of missional hospitality that would position Calvary Chapel as an epicentre for the movement about to shake America.

Word got out. More and more bare feet dirtied those carpets over the coming months as hippies came off the beach to sit in circles with Bibles in one hand and joints in the other. There were about 700 worshippers at Calvary Chapel on Jon's first Sunday; by the time he left just four years later, there were more than 20,000. The Jesus People movement had begun right there, in that place, in that four-year period, and it was now spreading uncontrollably around the world.

The church had grown from 700 people to 20,000 hippies in four years. The Jesus Movement had begun.

Time magazine put Jesus on its cover. Some 800 Christian communities and coffeehouses were planted within fifteen years. There were revivals on campuses. Artists like Keith Green pioneered modern worship music. Pastors like John Wimber got saved. New ministries were launched.

Walking across his university campus one day, Jon heard the strains of Bach's magisterial *Mass in B Minor* thundering out from the organ in the music hall. Drawn by the beautiful music, he ventured inside to listen, and could hardly believe his eyes. The organist behind this vast sound was a cute, petite brunette, her hands a blur and her feet dancing on the pedals. Her name was Mindy Fox. She turned out to be the granddaughter of Hollywood A-listers Roy Rogers and Dale Evans. Within two years Jon and Mindy were married, serving God together, side by side, reaching out to students, hippies, and freaks.

Giving God a Joint

They moved to New Mexico to work on a Native American ranch mission until they were kicked out for exercising the gifts of the Holy Spirit. They returned to California, where Jon took up a post as a college pastor, but once again he was kicked out for "associating with charismatics." This time he was informed that he had "no discernible spiritual gifts." With this rousing endorsement ringing in their ears, Jon and Mindy moved north to the town of Grants Pass, Oregon. They began a Bible study in a barn with fifteen people. Within two years it was a church of 500 feral hippies—5 per cent of the town's entire population.

Jon and Mindy's new congregation mostly lived off the land, many in teepees and tree houses, weaving their own yarn, dropping acid, and experimenting with sha-manism. One of their first baptism services took place in a Rosicrucian nudist colony in the Siskiyou Mountains. "You had to be real careful where you put your hands," laughs Jon whenever he tells the story. One day a beanpole called Terry, with long hair and long, tie-dyed robes, approached Jon, smiling.

When you're baptising people from a nudist colony, you have to be very careful where you put your hands.

"I just came to Jesus, man," he said.

"Awesome!"

"Yeah, but I need to know what to do now." Terry looked around as if he didn't want to be overheard. He began fiddling with the beads round his neck. "The thing is," he said, "I've got a garden."

"OK," said Jon reassuringly. "God likes gardens!"

"No, you don't understand," said Terry. "It's pretty big, man."

"Yep, that's fine, Terry. The Garden of Eden must have been pretty big too."

"But it's all just marijuana," said the hippie. "Hidden away up in the forest. Like, it's worth about 300,000 dollars. What do I do with it now I'm with Jesus?"

Jon thought for a moment. This guy was farming marijuana on an industrial scale. It was his livelihood. But it was also massively illegal.

"Terry, you've got to burn it. Not just because it's hash and it's illegal, but because it's got your heart."

Later that night, deep in the forests of Oregon, dozens of hippies in kaftans, beads, and overalls arrived at a particular location in pickup trucks, carrying burning torches. Many of them gasped at the sight of the largest quantity of pot they'd ever seen.

Solemnly Terry knelt by his handiwork, praying a prayer to dedicate his marijuana to Jesus. "May it be a pleasing aroma unto thee, O Lord," he said with feeling, and everyone laughed their "Amen!" And then, carefully checking the wind direction and ensuring that no one had accidentally strayed downwind, they offered God the biggest, holiest spliff you can imagine, and went home rejoicing, laughing and free.

Porky

Jon was studying the Bible with a couple of friends in a diner one day when the door slammed open. A strange figure filled the frame, his bearded face caked in dried blood, his clothes ripped. He shuffled drunkenly towards an unoccupied table. Nervously Jon held out his hand towards the newcomer, trying to ignore the food stuck in his beard and the overpowering smell.

"Hey there, my name's Jon."

"Well, hello, Jon," slurred the stranger, ignoring his hand entirely as he settled down at a table. There was an awkward pause. "They call me Porky," he said eventually, fixing Jon with an intimidating stare. "Porky the Pirate."

Trying not to laugh, Jon asked how he'd got himself a name like that. The giant lifted the tablecloth, rolled up the leg of his overalls, and revealed the spout and cap from a drag-racing car where his leg should have been. A homemade prosthetic. Then, with a flourish, he revealed a tube running down through his shirt and overalls into the cylinder. He could pour up to two gallons of tequila in through the gas cap of his keg-leg every morning, and would suck on it all day long through the tube.

Jon's Bible study companions watched nervously as Porky the Pirate began to tell Jon his life story. He had once, he said, been married, had even worked for a while as a respectable professor at UCLA. But everything had changed when the drug-culture guru Timothy Leary visited the campus. For Porky it was a defining moment. He "turned on, tuned in, and dropped out," abandoning his wife and career to party on hallucinogenic drugs. He built an incongruous new life for himself as an expert welder on the local drag-car racing scene. At the circuit one day, a 350-ton wall had fallen and crushed his leg.

Warming to his new friend, Porky invited Jon outside to see his home. It was a caravan resembling a mobile junkyard on the outside, and the inside was wallpapered with pornography cut from magazines. In this unlikely space their conversation somehow turned to Jesus.

The more Jon talked about his faith, the angrier the pirate became. He was educated and clever, sucking relentlessly on tequila, and he clearly hated Christians with a vengeance. He was furious to discover that his new friend was just another Jesus freak. Jon continued to talk about Jesus until eventually Porky erupted, grabbing a double-barrel shotgun from a rack on the wall and pointing it directly at Jon's head. "If you say another thing about Jesus," he snarled in a drunken rage, "I'm gonna pull the trigger." He was wild-eyed, dangerous, and leaking tequila.

> **"If you say another thing about Jesus, I'm gonna pull the trigger." Porky the Pirate was wild-eyed, dangerous, and leaking tequila.**

Jesus promises to give us the right words to say when we're in terrifying situations, "for it will not be you speaking, but the Spirit of your Father speaking through you" (Matthew 10:20). Porky the Pirate was clearly a broken man, not just physically but mentally and spiritually too. And so he sat there in his gallery of porn, pointing a shotgun at his visitor, commanding him to stop talking about Jesus. But somehow, in that moment, Jon knew exactly what to say.

"Well, Porky," he said, looking directly down the barrel of the gun and barely recognising his own voice, "if that's your position then we have a problem. You see, I just can't stop talking about Jesus, and if you shoot me it will trigger a very interesting phenomenon in your life."

"What phemone-mom is that?" growled Porky, stumbling over the word.

"If you shoot me, you will attract the love of God. He will pursue you for the rest of your life. He will break you down."

Porky paused for a moment, lowered the gun, and stared at Jon as if he was seeing him for the first time. "OK, Christian. I'm gonna tell you a story, and then I'm gonna ask you a question, and if you answer me right I won't shoot you." He leaned his head back against a naked photograph, rested the shotgun on his knee, and took a leisurely drag of tequila. Then he launched into a long, sad story about his life and his wife—the terrible things she had done to him, the things he had done to her, and their eventual, inevitable, bitter divorce. Suddenly he stopped talking, his knuckles whitened around the gun, and he fixed Jon with a hard stare.

"Here's the question, Christian. Answer me wrong, and I'll shoot ya." He cocked the gun. "Who was right? My wife, or me?"

Praying silently for wisdom, knowing that his life might well depend upon it, Jon remembered the way that Jesus answered questions with questions. "What's better?" he asked, returning Porky's stare. "To be right or to forgive?"

Porky's features contorted, his muscles stiffened. At last he let out a heavy sigh and put down the gun, clunking it against his metal leg. "I can't get you, Christian," he said sadly. "What you've said is . . . well, it's *eating* me. I need a day to think."

He snatched a picture from the wall, one of the few non-pornographic ones, scribbled something across it, and handed it to Jon. It was a photograph of himself in a Viking helmet, holding a sabre in one hand and a cat-o'-nine-tails whip in the other. "To Jon," he wrote, "the guy who introduced me to God."

Break Down

The very next day a friend of Jon's happened to be driving along the freeway when he noticed a man with a strange metal leg trying to fix his pick-up. His head was under the hood. Jon's friend didn't know that this was Porky the Pirate. He was just a guy who looked like he could use a little assistance.

"Can I help?" he called out, pulling off the road.

"No," barked Porky aggressively.

"Man, you need Jesus!" replied Jon's friend without thinking.

At the sound of the word, Porky the Pirate stood bolt upright, almost banging his head on the hood. He spun round to stare at this Good Samaritan. As he did so he let out a groan.

"I give up," he said, throwing his hands in the air. "Two Jesus freaks in two days! I surrender."

And with that, Porky the Pirate took his metal leg, bent it at the knee, and knelt down awkwardly by the freeway. With cars rushing past and tequila leaking from his foot, Porky surrendered his life wholeheartedly to Jesus Christ.

•   •   •

The Barn Church in Oregon was flourishing, but Jon and Mindy Petersen began to sense that it was time to pioneer once again. God was speaking to them about moving to Amsterdam to work alongside our friend Floyd McClung. And so that was where they raised their children on the edge of the city's red-light district, seeking to shine a little light in its darkest corners.

It proved to be an extraordinary time to touch down in Europe. The Berlin Wall dividing East from West was about to tumble. Not far from Amsterdam, more than 70,000 people were filling the streets of Leipzig, East Germany, every Monday night to pray for a peaceful end to communism. The authorities had announced that the "counter-revolution"—that's what they were calling this prayer meeting—would be put down "with whatever means necessary." This was no idle threat. The communist government in China had just massacred hundreds of "counter-revolutionary" peace protestors in Tiananmen Square. Anticipating similar bloodshed, Leipzig's churches were being converted into emergency clinics. Snipers had been stationed on the roofs, and tanks were patrolling the streets as Christians, clasping candles, marched defiantly through the city, chanting "No violence!"—praying for peace down the barrel of a gun.

By the following Monday, those 70,000 protestors had swelled their ranks to 120,000 as similar prayer rallies sprang up in other East German cities. Just two days after that, on Wednesday, 18 October, the unthinkable happened. The party secretary, who had originally threatened to crush the prayer rallies, suddenly resigned. From that moment there was a certain inevitability to their cause. The revolution had become unstoppable.

A weekly prayer meeting in Leipzig grew to 70,000 people, playing a verifiable role in the fall of East German communism.

Sure enough, exactly a month to the day after the great Leipzig Prayer Rally of 9 October, the Berlin Wall came down. The world woke up to images of young people dismantling the Cold War's ultimate icon, attacking it with sledgehammers, graffitiing the concrete, standing astride it triumphantly. One communist official from Leipzig quietly admitted that they had been ready for any eventuality, but not "for candles and prayers."

A Monday night church prayer meeting in St. Nicholas Church, Leipzig, had grown over seven years to galvanise a generation. Markus Lägel, who was to become the first leader of 24-7 Prayer in Germany, experienced those prayer rallies as a boy. He witnessed the power of courageous and persistent intercession to dethrone principalities and ultimately to change the face of a continent, all without bloodshed or a shot being fired. As Eugene Peterson says, "Prayer is subversive activity [that] involves a more or less open act of defiance against any claim of ultimacy by the current regime."[3]

• • •

As these historic events unfolded in East Germany, Jon Petersen continued to mobilise intercession in Amsterdam. He was praying over a world map one day when the Lord told him to pack his bags and go immediately to Sofia, the capital of Bulgaria, still under the control of a communist, atheistic dictatorship. Jon wasted no time. He packed his bags and boarded the first flight to Sofia.

When he arrived at Sofia airport, Jon noticed a man jumping up and down near the baggage carousel. The gesticulating stranger was making a beeline for Jon, almost ready to burst with excitement. "It is you!" he said. "It is you!"

This one-man welcoming committee explained that God had told him to wait here for a man called Jon Petersen. Vaguely remembering Jon's name from a conference, he had been waiting expectantly at the airport all day. Jon didn't know whether to laugh or yell "Hallelujah!" as he explained how the Lord had spoken to him too that morning, directing him to fly to Sofia without any further instructions.

"Well, I am glad you have come," said the Bulgarian, "because I have arranged a special meeting for you at my house this evening. I have told all my friends that we have a very special American guest speaker flying into Sofia and that you are carrying a message from God for us!"

We often invite the Holy Spirit to come to our meetings, but it's a different thing entirely when he invites us to attend one of his.

Later that night, Jon opened the Scriptures to the gathered group with a sense of awe, knowing that this was a meeting ordained and arranged directly by the Lord. We often invite the Holy Spirit to attend our meetings, but it's a different thing entirely when he invites us to attend one of his. Everyone at the meeting received Jon's message with faith, aware that this was not just an ordinary Bible study; it was a divine encounter scheduled by the Holy Spirit.

The next day Jon went with his new friend to Sofia's Battenburg Square, where they prayed with great conviction for six hours, declaring the same freedom over Bulgaria that had come to so many of its neighbouring countries in Eastern Europe. They made a particular point of marching around the idolatrous white marble mausoleum of Georgi Dimitrov, the dictatorial founder of Bulgarian communism. Then, turning towards the imposing government headquarters which dominated the square, they raised their hands and declared the lordship of Jesus Christ. It was an act of spiritual defiance, buttressed by the authority of a very specific commission from the King.

Within days of that prophetic showdown, the embalmed body of Georgi Dimitrov was stolen from its mausoleum, and the headquarters of Bulgarian communism was destroyed by fire. Bulgaria duly followed East Germany on a peaceful transition towards religious liberty and parliamentary democracy.

Are we to conclude that Jon's prayers singlehandedly triggered the end of Bulgarian communism? Of course not! Countless saints had been praying in Sofia for decades. Bulgarians had been campaigning and protesting relentlessly. Politicians and diplomats had worked hard too. It would be ignorant and arrogant to presume that a few hours of prayer from a couple of people in the central square had made all the difference. But it would also be foolish to dismiss the significance of Jon's prayers in the remarkable events that followed, especially when God had assigned him to Sofia so clearly.

Many years after these events, when I met Jon in Kansas City, his memories of the Jesus Movement in America and the fall of the Berlin Wall in Europe inspired us to pray with greater expectancy. We longed for a similar movement of the Spirit in our time, and his eyewitness accounts reassured us that it really is still possible. A generation can be changed. Thousands can turn to Jesus in a handful of years. Popular culture can be rewired. Oppressive regimes can be dismantled. Not just in ancient history. Not just in the Bible, but right here and now in the West, with people just like us.

• • •

I studied the man sitting opposite me in Skies, the revolving restaurant overlooking Kansas City. Jon's dark hair was receding a little, his goatee was flecked with grey, and his eyes promised to erupt with laughter at the slightest provocation. This unassuming man had grown up in the shadow of the nuclear holocaust in Japan, had witnessed first-hand the rise of the Jesus Movement in the 1970s, had chosen to raise his family in Amsterdam's red-light district at the end of the Cold War, and in the 1980s his prayers had played some part in the destruction of Bulgarian communism.

The writer Donald Miller rightly observes that no one makes a movie about a guy whose dream is to buy a Volvo.[4] To this day the greatest stories of all time are adventures of sacrifice, resilience, and risk. Bilbo leaves the Shire. Schindler defies the Nazis. Andy Dufresne breaks out of the Shawshank State Penitentiary. Lucy steps through the wardrobe. Abram leaves Haran. Two Moravians leave Herrnhut. The Heasleys set out for Sodom and Gomorrah.

To inherit our destiny we must refuse to settle in familiar comforts— whether Haran, Herrnhut, or Blue Camp 20. "Blessed are those," as the psalmist says, "whose hearts are set on pilgrimage" (Psalm 84:5).

If Jon's parents had not left America as pioneer missionaries, he would no doubt have enjoyed a more normal childhood. He might have avoided some of the struggles of being a third-culture kid. But he would have missed out on the adventure of growing up in Japan, the land that he loves passionately to this day, whose language he lapses into whenever he is excited, whose food he celebrates with friends.

If Jon and Mindy had stayed in Costa Mesa, enjoying the comforts of California at the start of the counter-culture, they would never have planted the Barn Church and changed so many lives in Oregon. And had they then settled down to raise their babies in the shade of the giant redwoods instead of pioneering again in Europe, they would certainly have missed some of the greatest adventures of their lives.

We spent many evenings together in Kansas City, talking, laughing, and praying, sharing tales of God's faithfulness and building our friendship. Jon always loved hearing about the growing family of Boiler Room communities, all centred on prayer and committed to making a measurable difference amongst the poor and the lost. I sometimes wondered if it was because they reminded him of that old Barn Church in Oregon and the communities he'd planted in Eastern Europe after the fall of the Berlin Wall. I asked Jon to help with 24-7, and to this day you will find him flying between emerging Boiler Room communities, quietly nurturing young leaders, sharing all that he's learned from the Scriptures over six decades on three continents and three major movements of the Holy Spirit.

SELAH

The wind blows wherever it pleases. You hear its sound, but you cannot tell where it comes from or where it is going. So it is with everyone born of the Spirit.

JOHN 3:8

- Where do I see the Holy Spirit moving most obviously in my community?
- What are the marks of his activity, and who is he particularly using?
- How could I bless what he is doing practically, or, better still, join in?

10
WORD ON THE STREET
IBIZA • OHIO • VANCOUVER • CALIFORNIA

I am not ashamed of the gospel, because it is the power of God
that brings salvation to everyone who believes.

ROMANS 1:16

"Hey, Brian! Remember me?"

Brian did remember—he'd been praying for the security guy from the nightclub all week. They'd chatted and he'd accepted the gift of a Bible, but he'd been drunk at the time, so you never knew.

"Of course! Nice to see you again."

"Yeah, well, you know that book you gave me?"

"Yep. It was a Bible. A New Testament—"

"It's good stuff, mate." The bouncer was grinning enthusiastically, clutching a well-thumbed copy of the *Jesus Loves Ibiza* New Testament, which the 24-7 team had been handing out all summer. "I mean, it's a bit dull in places, but on the whole I thought it was very good."

He offered Brian the book, pointing to some spidery handwriting on one of the pages. "I've made a few changes. Just suggestions. How you can make it better. Up to you."

Brian laughed incredulously. "Let me get this right. You've read the whole of the New Testament . . ."

"Yeah, right."

". . . and you reckon you've *improved* it a bit?"

The bouncer nodded absentmindedly, watching a girl in a miniskirt walk by before offering his "corrected" Bible to Brian once more.

"You do realise that this isn't just any book? We may have put a funky cover on it, but inside it's still just the same old Bible, the Word of God?" Brian could hardly believe he was having this conversation, but he wasn't getting through. As far as the guy in front of him was concerned, he'd taken the time to read the book, he'd got some great ideas about how to improve on it, and he'd kindly offered to help.

Brian took the corrected Bible and decided to be direct with him. "Look, I'm seriously impressed that you read it. I'm really glad you found it interesting, but . . . well, most people do agree that the Bible has kind of passed that whole editorial phase. It's been pretty much untouched since the Council of Trent in 1546."

The bouncer just shrugged and said that he didn't care what the council thought, he was only trying to help. "See what you think about my suggestions." He waved and disappeared into the crowd of young bodies flowing from bar to bar at the end of a long day on the beach, and the start of an even longer night on the town. Brian stood silently for a moment, watching the faces go by. Sometimes he wanted to shake them, to wake them, to tell them that there can be more to life than ten pints of beer, sex with a stranger, and puking on your shoes in the taxi home. He thought about the bouncer's surprising enthusiasm for the Bible and wondered how many others knew the meaning of the story that had unfolded 2,000 years ago, not so far away, just at the other end of the Mediterranean Sea. Did anyone in Ibiza realise how this ancient story had shaped their world—how the town in which they were partying, San Antonio, had been named after St. Anthony, a missionary like him?

Brian sighed. Why should they care? In the broken-hearted words of Jesus, the crowds were "confused and aimless . . . like sheep with no shepherd" (Matthew 9:35, MSG). Every fibre of Brian's being longed for them to find the Good Shepherd in the pages of these Bibles, the way that he had as a child, memorising its verses, and again as a young adult serving time in prison.

Pray, Play, Obey

The mission to Ibiza was growing from strength to strength under Brian and Tracy's leadership, but it was a mission field unlike any other. They loved their new home and could see God's presence everywhere: in the sparkling creativity of the culture and the natural beauty of the island, in the flamboyant fashions, the sheer exuberance of the party scene and its world-class music, in the evident desire to belong to a scene, and even in the spiritual questions people would ask when they were stoned. Brian and Tracy particularly loved to watch the crowds of partygoers on the beach at Café del Mar applauding the sun with liturgical reverence as it sank, flaming, into the sea. It was always a moment of transcendence, stillness, wonder.

But of course there was also a darker side to the culture. As they walked the streets befriending strangers, the 24-7 teams learned to refuse drinks with a smile and to guard their water bottles against the "date rape" drug Rohypnol. They adapted their body clocks to become fully nocturnal—you can't reach hardcore partygoers by inviting them to a Sunday-morning service. But of course, while everyone else seemed to be taking drugs to keep them buzzing all night, the 24-7 team had nothing but coffee and Jesus. They would serve and pray, in any

In approaching any new culture our first task is always to remove our shoes, recognising that we are standing on holy ground.

way they could, with promoters outside bars, with partygoers in various stages of disrepair, even with prostitutes caught between clients. When these unlikely missionaries weren't on duty, they would dance the nights away to the hottest dance-floor anthems, celebrating all that was fun in the culture and wearing the latest and wildest fashions they could afford.

Our presence in Ibiza, and particularly our celebratory approach to mission, had attracted media attention—and some criticism too, mainly from Christians. This seemed strange, because it was really nothing new. Hudson Taylor had scandalised polite Victorian society 150 years earlier by growing a ponytail and donning flowing Chinese robes. "Let us in everything not sinful become like the Chinese," he wrote, "that by all means we may save some" (see 1 Corinthians 9:22). Hudson Taylor understood that all societies host the good, the bad, and the morally neutral. Unlike bigoted colonialists, he believed in recognising, redeeming, and learning from all that was good in a new culture, whilst honouring and adopting its neutral facets, its music, food, dress, language—and even ponytails.

In approaching any new culture our first task is always to remove our shoes, recognising that we are standing on holy ground. We are not bringing the Lord somewhere new, because he is already here. Our primary task, therefore, is to identify God's fingerprints and to trace his footprints in the new environment.

Of course, inevitably we will also spot ugliness. All cultures are fallen, and with our foreigner's eyes these failings may well be particularly apparent and offensive to us. But whenever we do speak out against the evil behaviours embedded in a host culture, we are expected to do so with the "gentleness and respect" befitting a visitor, remembering that "love covers over a multitude of sins" (1 Peter 3:15; 4:8). We have no right to renounce all that is wrong in another person, place, or culture, until we have recognised all that is right, good, and beautiful.

The apostle Paul took this redemptive principle to shocking extremes during his visit to the Greek city of Athens, where "he was greatly distressed to see that the city was full of idols." He could so easily have vented his distress, railing against the Athenians for their paganism, but instead he held his offence discreetly and chose something very surprising indeed to affirm. It is astounding that a devout Jew like Paul, who would have recited the *Shema* since childhood ("Hear, O Israel: the LORD our God, the LORD is one," Deuteronomy 6:4), should now choose to use a reviled idol to point the Athenians to Jesus. But this is precisely what Paul does. "People of Athens!" he says. "I see that in every way you are very religious . . . As I walked around and looked carefully at your objects of worship [note that he doesn't dismiss them as idols], I even found an altar with this inscription: TO AN UNKNOWN GOD. So you are ignorant of the very thing you worship—and this is what I am going to proclaim to you" (Acts 17:22-23).

The "objects of worship" in Ibiza were every bit as obvious and distressing for Brian and Tracy as they must have been for Paul in Athens. But the apostle's radical missionary method challenged them continually to recognise and celebrate what was right in Ibiza and, if possible, to use even its many idols to point its inhabitants towards Jesus.

• • •

"Oh ****! Sorry!"

Brian's reverie was shattered by a girl in stiletto heels knocking the "corrected" Bible out of his hand. He picked it up slowly, smiling once again at the cover: *Jesus Loves Ibiza.* It was true! A security guard at the door of the club had recently taken to reading his copy whenever things were quiet, and his colleagues would sometimes join him for an impromptu, incongruous little Bible study group in the middle of the night. The other big hit that season had been cigarette lighters branded "Jesus, light of the world!" Whenever people asked for a light, the 24-7 team would grin and say, "Yep, sure," whipping out the lighter and adding, "It's Jesus!" It was toe-curlingly cheesy and yet it worked. Everyone laughed and wanted a Jesus flame. This one bad joke had actually started loads of great conversations about things that really mattered.

Our experimental approach to mission in Ibiza had been inspired, in part, by the pragmatism of the Salvation Army who once patrolled the debauched streets of nineteenth-century London. They would carry drunks home on stretchers from the city's many gin parlours, primitive pubs which preyed on the poor, encouraging men, women, and even children to get "drunk for a penny, dead drunk for two pence," and offering them "clean straw" for sleeping off the hangover.[1] Brian's team had started operating a similar rescue service, affectionately known as the 24-7 Vomit Van. They used it to rescue hundreds of people who were dangerously drunk, wasted on drugs, vulnerable to robbery, assault, and even rape. Night after night through the long summer seasons, successive teams had been quietly caring for people in this unglamorous way, often kneeling in the gutter more than they knelt in the serene, candle-scented prayer room. The Heasleys would frequently drive their sons to school in the Vomit Van the morning after a night on duty, and it would still be reeking of bodily fluids. It was dirty, thankless, exhausting work, but they were seeing people saved. Not metaphorically, not just spiritually, but literally, physically *saved*. From sin for sure, but also from alcohol poisoning, degradation, and violence.

Jesus commands us to engage with the needs of the world. Not just to pray from afar, but to live holy lives in the midst of the mess.

Of course, there were plenty of people who thought we shouldn't be supporting drunks, praying with prostitutes, rebranding the Bible, and printing the eternal words of Scripture on cigarette lighters. We could understand their concern: The light of Christ is not a flippant catchphrase, the Bible is not just an ordinary book in need of a trendier cover, and sin is not to be taken lightly. We are told to "flee from sexual immorality" and not to tolerate any "hint of impurity" in our midst (1 Corinthians 6:18; Ephesians 5:3).

Yet Christ himself came very explicitly "not . . . to condemn the world, but to save the world" (John 3:17). He attended at least one party where there was too much alcohol, risked his reputation befriending prostitutes, and didn't seem shocked at all when confronted with a woman who had just been caught having sex with a married man. In fact, he refused to punish her even though the Law said that he should (John 8:1-11; Leviticus 20:10). When the Pharisees questioned the company Jesus was keeping, he told them outright, "I have not come to call the righteous, but sinners" (Mark 2:17).

Jesus commands us to engage with the needs of our broken world—not just to pray from afar, but to live holy lives in the midst of the mess, just as he did. "My prayer is not that you take them out of the world," he told the Father, "but that you protect them from the evil one" (John 17:14). Clearly it is possible to be protected from the evil one even in the jaws of his domain, and in fact it is here that Jesus wants us to remain.

So, yes, Brian knew for sure that "Jesus Loves Ibiza." Jesus loves guys like that bouncer trying to upgrade the Bible. He loves the flamboyant gay community, the businessmen trying to make a fast buck, the pushy club promoters, the West African drug dealers pretending to sell watches, the sex workers emerging from public toilets requesting condoms and prayer, and yes, even that drunk girl in the stiletto heels who had just knocked the Bible from Brian's hand.

●　●　●

In the 1970s, when the Catholic missionary Vincent Donovan returned home after thirty-five years church-planting amongst the Masai tribe in Africa, he famously discovered "an exotic tribe called the young people of America." As he began to apply the missionary principles he'd developed amongst the Masai with Western young people, the results were remarkable: "Do not try to call them back to where they were," he was advised, "and do not try to call them to where you are, beautiful as that place may seem to you. You must have the courage to go with them to a place that neither you nor they have been before."[2]

As they walked the streets of San Antonio and grew to love the island and its culture, Brian and Tracy realised increasingly that they had not been brought to Ibiza just to convert people to their own way of thinking, but rather to befriend and accompany them on a journey of mutual transformation into the likeness of Christ. Here in this strange new place and amongst these strange new people, they were finding Jesus and being changed into his likeness in ways that they could never have been changed had they stayed back home. "Christ in you," says the apostle Paul, is "the hope of glory" (Colossians 1:27).

It never took very long to find the glory in the dirt. All around them they discovered surprising acts of kindness, gained new insights, enjoyed sparkling creativity, even from the most messed-up people they met. Brian and Tracy never forgot that they had in part been guided to Ibiza by the unwitting prophecy of a homeless transvestite, the lyric of a cheesy dance track, and a middle-aged lady in a swimsuit. And so, of course, it became a sort of game to spot Jesus moving in the most surprising ways and to hear the whisper of God emanating from the mouths of the unlikeliest people.

When we adopt this posture—seeking to love and honour God's presence in other people—they tend to return the favour. They begin to recognise Jesus in us too. A mutual grace grows, and we welcome one another, more and more, into Christ's likeness. The onus for initiating and developing such relationships must always rest with those who have the most grace to give, but it can become a reciprocal process. For too long evangelism has been a one-way performance, a soliloquy delivered from an elevated platform by an actor, hoping for applause. But Jesus shows us how to bring good news relationally, as a mutual movement towards beauty, an intimate invitation to dance.

We are sent out not just to preach but to listen, not just to witness but to worship, not just to save others but to get saved ourselves.

We are sent out as missionaries to build relationships that are real, not just to preach but also to listen, not just to witness to Jesus but to worship with the lost, not just to save others but to get saved our-selves. Our own journeys of salvation and spiritual formation will thereby become intertwined with those to whom Christ is sending us. Our posture becomes one of humble confidence, in which we dare to acknowledge that the other person has insights we do not yet possess, and that our understanding of Christ is currently incomplete, inad-equate, and in some parts probably just plain wrong without them. We go to the lost and make space for them to preach to us, to teach us, to minister to our unbelief. This requires stillness and humility, a deeply anchored assurance in the gospel, and the ability to ask gently disruptive questions.

When my friend Paul was studying theology, he was set an essay entitled "What Is Church?" He decided to go out into the street and ask normal, non-religious people to help him answer the question. He fell into conversation with a man in a café who described himself as a pagan. This man told Paul firmly that there was absolutely nothing any Christian could possibly do to make him ever want to step inside a church.

Paul listened carefully, asked a few more questions, and made a couple of notes. They continued talking until, after about twenty min-utes, the pagan asked Paul what he was writing down.

"Oh, just the stuff you're telling me: that you wouldn't go anywhere near a church no matter what we ever did."

"Right," said the pagan. "Yes, that's true." Then he paused, studying my friend's face. "But I think I would probably come to church if it was with you."

Paul had simply listened with respect. It hadn't been a method or a technique for evangelism. And yet, by asking questions for twenty minutes, he had broken through a lifetime of hardened prejudice.

This gentle approach was familiar to the team in Ibiza as they spent time each night talking with ordinary people in the street. By doing the jobs that no one else wanted to do—over years and not just months—Brian and Tracy gradually established a formidable credibility for the gospel on the island. No one dared to accuse us of being naïve do-gooders any more. In fact, local club owners and promoters came to consider 24-7 as Ibiza's unofficial fourth emergency service, often phoning Brian for help with distraught customers. At the annual end-of-season party, as wild an occasion as you might imagine, the island workers started to give an unsolicited "offering" to help fund the 24-7 mission. By blessing and respecting those that others might curse, evangelism had stopped being something we were doing *to* them or *for* them. It had become something we were truly doing *with* them wherever they were on their own journey of faith.

• • •

Our theology seemed to be turning full circle. By withdrawing in prayer to prioritise the presence of God, we had been propelled out onto the front lines of mission, not just in Ibiza but elsewhere around the world. And now, as we gave ourselves to mission, God seemed to be drawing us back into the paradigm of prayer and worship. We learned to encounter his presence in the places to which he was sending us.

In the forest of faith and doubt, honest prayer can be the clearing in which we meet, heart to heart, with those of other tribes.

We were discovering, I think, that prayer is more than a preliminary to evangelism; it can also be an effective form of missional engagement in its own right. People who don't want to be preached at almost always still want to be prayed for. People who don't believe in God may still believe in the power of prayer. In the dark forests of faith and doubt, honest prayer can be the clearing in which we meet, heart to heart, with those of other tribes.

One of the most breathtaking and tragic examples of this missional principle took place thousands of miles from Ibiza but in a similar cultural context: amongst partying students in a debauched American fraternity house.

Divine Appointment

When a church in the town of Bluffton, Indiana, launched a 24-7 prayer room, they had little idea just how powerfully God was about to use them to impact the lives of students at the local university, just across the state line in Ohio. A few weeks into their season of prayer, a girl called Aimee[3] was chatting to her friend John at the university when she realised that her slot in the prayer room was looming. "Oh, I've got to go," she said. "I've got an appointment with God!" Noticing John's understandable surprise, she plucked up the courage to ask if he would like to join her. And so, a little later that day, John found himself stepping into a place of continual prayer.

He was blown away completely and unexpectedly by the presence of God. "During that hour," he wrote, "I accepted Christ and I cannot tell you how life-changing the experience has been for me." John began to return regularly to the prayer room, and the Holy Spirit started to work deeply in his life. He'd grown up with an abusive dad, but as he spent time discovering the Bible's teaching about God as a good Father, he would often leave the prayer room with a sense of peace he had never before known.

One day John noticed a simple card stuck to the prayer room wall requesting prayer for "THE LOST." His mind turned immediately to the thirty-three frat brothers with whom he lived. "I couldn't get them off my mind and Aimee explained how, now I was a Christian, I had been called to tell others about the great love I'm experiencing. So she prayed that I would have boldness and courage to do this at school."

John began to pray diligently for his friends by name, asking that each one of them might encounter the love of the Father. Almost immediately he began to be given opportunities to share his newfound faith with members of the fraternity. One of them heard the gospel and gave an immediate response that, yes, he wanted to become a Christian. Overjoyed, and using the simple prayer he'd learned from Aimee, John welcomed his friend into the kingdom of heaven. Just two days later, someone else announced that he, too, would like to do the same.

Those two conversions triggered a domino effect. Another member of the fraternity gave his life to Christ just a few days later, and then another and another. "It was a little bit crazy," recalls John, laughing. "Every couple of days one of the guys would come and ask me to pray with him, or tell me that he had already surrendered his life to Jesus on his own. I can't tell you how exciting it was to watch salvation spreading like a contagious virus through our house."

By the time everyone departed for Christmas, just less than six months after John's first encounter with God in the prayer room across the state line, he'd led thirty-two of his thirty-three frat brothers to Jesus. Almost two per week for half a year. Every single member of that fraternity had now encountered Jesus, except for one particularly stubborn housemate called Tim. During the Christmas holiday, however, Aimee—whose invitation for John to join her in the prayer room had sparked this mini-revival in the first place—invited Tim over for dinner. He really never stood a chance. By the end of that night, Tim had also surrendered his life to Jesus. All thirty-four frat brothers—the entire house—had turned to Christ in less than six months.

This story would be remarkable if it ended there. But Tim began to pray for his parents to come to know Jesus too. There was an unusual urgency and passion to the way he prayed for their salvation. "Little did we know how perfect God's timing was in all of this," recalls John. Just twenty-seven days after Tim placed his faith in Christ, and a few days after his first Christmas as a Christian, he was involved in a fatal automobile accident.

It was impossible to process the news. Tim had died so suddenly, his whole life ahead of him, still so young. The fraternity was thrown into a state of deep shock. His parents' grief was beyond articulation. They looked ashen on the cold January day of their son's funeral. The church was packed with mourners, every eye fixed on the polished wooden box standing brutally alone at the front. Songs were sung, and then the pastor tried to describe Tim's short life. Tim had been a Christian for less than a month, the pastor said, but he would now spend all eternity with the Lord Jesus Christ.

The earnest prayers that Tim had prayed for his parents were to be answered at his own funeral. Following in their son's recent footsteps, they surrendered their lives to Jesus. So too did fifteen of Tim's high-school football teammates. In total, over the six months up to and including that tragic day, fifty people had come to Christ. "Very truly I tell you," said Jesus, "unless a grain of wheat falls to the ground and dies, it remains only a single seed. But if it dies, it produces many seeds" (John 12:24).

"Lord, let me know how transient I am," prays the psalmist (see Psalm 39:4). "We were born only yesterday and know nothing," laments the book of Job, "and

Fifty people came to Christ in six months thanks to an unstoppable chain reaction that had begun in a prayer room.

our days on earth are but a shadow" (Job 8:9). Seven hundred years later, the apostle James is equally depressing: "You are a mist that appears for a little while and then vanishes" (James 4:14). The tragedy of Tim's story reminds us of life's fragility. But it also reveals the irrepressible and incomparable hope we have in Christ:

Where, O death, is your victory?
Where, O death, is your sting?

I CORINTHIANS 15:55

The New Testament pulses with this energy and hope. It calls us to proclaim the good news of the gospel with a sense of urgency and opportunity. "I tell you, open your eyes and look at the fields!" cries Jesus to his followers. "They are ripe for harvest. Even now . . ." (John 4:35-36). The apostle Paul echoes this same sense of urgency: "Now is the time of God's favour, now is the day of salvation" (2 Corinthians 6:2). "I am compelled to preach," he says a little later. "Woe to me if

I do not preach the gospel!" (1 Corinthians 9:16). And the very last words spoken by God in the Bible maintain this pace: "Yes," he says, "I am coming soon" (Revelation 22:20). Tim's story reminds us that personal evangelism is always urgent. When Jesus sent the twelve disciples out on their first evangelistic mission, "they preached with joyful urgency" and "didn't even have time to eat" (Mark 6:12, 31, MSG). The apostle Peter says that we must "always be prepared" to share our faith. The Greek word he uses here, *ephistēmi*, is not used anywhere else in the Bible and literally means "be on standby" (1 Peter 3:15).

No one knows how much longer they have in this life—how many breaths, how many beats of the heart, how many opportunities to say yes or no. But we will certainly all stand before our Maker soon enough. And on that day we'll be held accountable for the decisions we have made, and especially for the ways in which we have stewarded and shared the riches of the gospel. After just twenty-seven days as a Christian, Tim will have at least seventeen others rejoicing by his side. And after more than twenty-seven years as a Christian, I am ashamed to admit how few there may be because of me, how many gospel opportunities I have squandered because I was merely too scared, or too busy, or too uncaring to speak.

Many people will say, "Lord, look at all the impressive things I did for you, the churches I built, the miracles I performed, the injustices I fought." But he will simply look each one of us deep in the eyes and distil everything we've ever said and thought and done down into a single, simple question: "Did we ever know each other?" (see Matthew 7:23).

Aimee will answer immediately and without blinking, "Yes, Lord, *of course* we knew each other!" And he will smile and welcome her inside. It's as simple as that. She knows Jesus. That's why she kept "an appointment with God" in the prayer room, and dared to invite John along too. From that one simple act she triggered a small revival. Thanks to Aimee's witness and the persevering prayers of her church, an entire fraternity turned to Christ in six months, their house was totally transformed, and

Tim will spend all eternity with Jesus, as will his parents and fifteen of his high-school friends. I have a hunch that, on the day when at last Tim sees Aimee again, he will throw his arms around her neck, throw back his head, and howl, "Thank you!"

Contagious Holiness and Unconditional Acceptance

From a fraternity house in Ohio, to the pubs and clubs of Ibiza, to Porky the Pirate's porn-lined caravan in California, Jesus Christ sends us out with a sense of urgency to a dying world, to speak his words and shine his light in the weirdest, darkest places. The very environments that some Christians avoid for fear of corruption seem to be the very places that he most wants to be. Two thousand years ago Jesus interacted repeatedly with the type of people and situations that should, technically, have made him religiously unclean, and yet, as Craig Blomberg writes:

> He does not assume that he will be defiled by associating with corrupt people. Rather, [he believes that] his purity can rub off on them and change them for the better. Cleanliness, he believes, is even more "catching" than uncleanness; morality more influential than immorality . . . The unifying theme that emerges is one that may be called "contagious holiness."[4]

The contagious holiness of Jesus means that it is possible to dwell in the darkest, dirtiest places without being negatively affected and, in fact, that in these environments we can make a positive difference. Of course, we need to be discerning and wise. None of us is immune to sin.

Cleanliness is even more catching than uncleanness, morality more influential than immorality. Holiness is contagious.

"Be alert and of sober mind," counsels the apostle Peter, because "your enemy the devil prowls around like a roaring lion looking for someone to devour" (1 Peter 5:8). Before immersing ourselves in environments of extreme temptation, we should think carefully and seek the counsel and support of wise friends. Clearly, if you're coming off drugs, you will need to avoid your old haunts for a while. If you're struggling with lust, you're probably not called to evangelise the porn industry. If you're an alcoholic, don't take a job in a bar.

But Blomberg argues that Jesus engaged with sinners very deliberately because his missional method was "transformation by means of acceptance."[5] When we accept people as they are and where they are, they can be changed to something new. They can be healed (generally quite slowly) by the contagious effect of holiness. This relational, non-defensive, interactive ethos, which was displayed throughout Christ's ministry, offended the Pharisees. It also challenges the idea that a person must always "repent" before they can be received by Christ. In fact, it's the other way round: we repent because we have been received.

We aren't accepted by Jesus because we apologise for our sins on a particular day at a particular time. It's the other way round: we apologise in response to acceptance. Paul says that it is "while we were still sinners" that Christ died for us.[6] So we have already been accepted. Similarly, the parable of the Prodigal Son describes the father outrageously embracing his ritually (and literally) unclean son. Holiness has nothing to fear from the dirt. The traditional idea that we must articulate a coherent confession in order to activate Christ's forgiveness may well be unbiblical. The flow of the gospel is this: The Prodigal Son is embraced and reinstated before he properly apologises. "I was hugged," he might testify, "until I cried, held so close that the excrement wiped off me onto his white robes, listened to until I had no more lies inside me, accepted until I was changed."

Christ's response to a Samaritan woman with five husbands is a case study in transformation through acceptance. As a righteous Jew he probably shouldn't have engaged this despised foreign woman in conversation, and certainly shouldn't have allowed himself to be alone with her. Most definitely he should not have asked her for a drink. But he reaches out to her, showing radical acceptance to someone who has been rejected again and again. Jesus certainly doesn't gloss over her sin—in fact, he deliberately exposes her shame with a provocative question, neither pretending nor condemning. Eventually he commissions this despised woman as his witness, sending her home to share good news with the entire town. At no point has the Samaritan woman formulated the kind of apology we would generally prescribe as a condition of conversion, let alone a commission to preach.

Jesus calls us to accept people unconditionally, whether it's on a university campus in Ohio, or at a club in Ibiza, or with a challenging colleague at work. We are called to love people indiscriminately, not as a technique for "saving their souls," not as a manipulative exercise in "friendship evangelism," but because we like them and consider them lovelier by far than all their ugly choices.

Vancouver

A beautiful embodiment of this principle of *transformation through acceptance* emanates from a Boiler Room run by the Salvation Army in Vancouver's infamous Downtown Eastside. This radical community in one of North America's poorest postcodes once prayed non-stop for three-and-a-half years. Everyone who visits the 614 Community, even just for a day, can see how deeply they have embraced their neighbourhood, and that the motivation and methodology at the heart of their mission is nothing more complicated than love. Aaron White, who co-leads the Boiler Room there, explains his motivation very simply: "The people we love are being left to die from AIDS, drug overdoses, violence, or just plain old poverty."

When Aaron and Cherie's son Noah was born, they decided to invite their entire neighbourhood to help them dedicate him to the Lord. A small crowd gathered in Crab Park beside Vancouver Harbour, respectable family members mingling with recovering addicts, prostituted women, the lonely elderly, those who were mentally vulnerable, and homeless men with dirt under their nails. Aaron and Cherie passed their newborn baby around this maverick circle, asking each person in turn to hold him and to give little Noah their personal blessing. Some of them, especially some of the men, held back, feeling too dirty to touch the baby, too unreliable to be entrusted with holding him, too sinful to speak anything good over his pristine life. They tried to exclude themselves from praying. But Aaron and Cherie were adamant, insisting that everyone should touch the little boy and give him their own unique benediction. "Some of the men wept as they held our baby and prayed their stumbling prayers over him," recalls Aaron. "In fact, years later, some of them still talk about that moment with tears in their eyes."

Aaron and Cherie entrusted their precious, perfect baby to all those broken people that day because they believe in transformation through acceptance. It wasn't a gimmick or a technique. They were seeking to give dignity, recognising relationship, invoking goodness, and practising the power of contagious holiness in a simple yet radical way.

Campus America

The story of contagious holiness sweeping through that fraternity at Bluffton University emerged at a significant time. Students had always been integral to the 24-7 movement. Prayer rooms have always found fertile soil on campuses around the world. Our very first prayer room had primarily been populated and led by students, as had the summer mission teams heading out to places like Ibiza. To this day we recognise that campuses are the single most strategic key to mobilising this generation and reaching the next.

But God was about to turn up the volume on campus in a big way, initiating one of the most exciting and difficult chapters in our journey so far.

It began when we were living in Kansas City. I was invited to speak in Redding, California, at the famous Bethel Church and at one of their early Jesus Culture conferences. I'd flown there with my friend David

Blackwell, the wiry epicurean from Chicago who had accompanied Floyd on that fateful trip to England.

Students at the conference had flooded forward at the end of the talk, requesting prayer. But as we began praying for them, David's hands had become extremely hot. The Holy Spirit had started working particularly powerfully, visibly, through him.

Early the following morning, I was woken by a voice. One moment I was fast asleep, the next I was flung bolt upright, adrenaline pounding through my veins, with the words that had woken me still echoing in my head: "Campus America," the voice said. "Call Campus America to pray."

My heart was pounding. The hotel room was dark, and I glanced across at David in the other bed, wondering if he'd heard the voice too, but he was still fast asleep. Trying not to wake him, I pulled on my jeans and a T-shirt, grabbed my journal, and crept out of the room, blinking in the bright lights of the corridor. "Campus America," the words were still reverberating in my mind. "Call Campus America to pray."

I had rarely heard the Lord so unmistakably: "Campus America. Call Campus America to pray."

Finding my way to the hotel lobby, and nodding at the night receptionist, I began scribbling notes furiously in my journal. What, I began to wonder with mounting excitement, was the Lord planning? And how on earth were we going to galvanise American students to pray? And why was God speaking to us about it? There were so many other great student ministries out there, far better resourced, with a far bigger reach and way more experience than us.

Eventually, I stumbled back to the room with pages of journal notes and my neural pathways still buzzing. Nothing, it seemed, could ever be quite the same again. Finding my roommate still asleep, I snuck into the shower. That was when God spoke to me a second time. This time it was just four words, almost laughably mundane: "David's had a dream."

I got out of the shower excitedly, wrapped a towel around my waist, and stepped out into the bedroom to find that David had woken up and was writing in his journal.

"So what did you see?" I asked, as casually as I could.

"Huh?"

"In your dream. The dream you just had. What did God show you?"

David stared at me with his mouth open. "How did you know I had a dream? I just woke up and I'm trying to write it down. I don't want to forget it. I never normally dream. How did you know, Pete?"

"Um, God told me," I said, trying to sound relaxed, when really I was freaking out inside. "I bet it was something to do with students, too."

This time David let out a little yelp of surprise. "That's exactly what it was about."

"Students and college campuses, right?"

"Yes! Pete, this is crazy. Would you mind telling me what's going on round here?"

At last I allowed myself to laugh. "Come on then," I said. "Don't keep me in suspense. Tell me what you saw—every detail—and then I'll tell you what's been happening with me."

David began describing his dream. He had been standing, he said, in a busy foyer area. It was the lobby of a sporting arena, and he could tell that a college football team was preparing to play. He had noticed an old friend from high school, a guy called Donni West.

"Donni West," David repeated. "Remember that name."

Donni was standing alone to one side, wearing all the correct kit for the game, clearly about to play. Yet he seemed vacant, disengaged, totally unprepared for what was about to happen. David began to bombard him with questions, trying to fire him up for the game. As he did so, Donni began to stir, becoming animated and engaged.

The dream continued, and now David found himself on the playing field. The whistle was about to go, and David was psyching up the team like a coach. Then, in the dream, there was a voice: "Call the dead to get into the game."

David stopped talking and stared at me. He repeated the phrase as if I was failing to understand: "Call the dead to get into the game."

"OK, wow!" I said, feeling slow, wondering if I was missing something. Secretly, I was a little disappointed that David's dream didn't seem to connect more directly with campuses.

"No, you don't understand, Pete." David was staring at me intently and began to speak more slowly.

"First of all," he said, "Donni West is dead. He died in our senior year. It was a drugs overdose. Really tragic. He never graduated high school. I haven't thought about him for years and suddenly here he is in my dream and he's playing football but he's not really alive—he's some kind of zombie."

"And God's telling us to get the dead in the game, right?" I chipped in.

"Right! I reckon Donni represents a generation of people like the living dead. Zombies. They've got all the right kit, but they don't know why. They're just going through the motions. But Pete, there's another thing: It was *college* football. Donni was wearing a black-and-gold strip. So it was Purdue . . ."

David was looking at me, laughing, but I hadn't a clue why. I'm British. I know nothing about American football. For me football is soccer, a game involving a foot and a ball. My limited knowledge of American football stops a long way short of college teams and colours. But David is a sports fanatic and had recognised it immediately.

"OK, it's like this," he said good-naturedly. "Purdue is a university based in Lafayette, Indiana. Its football team is pretty good, they have a black-and-gold strip. They're known as 'the Boiler Makers.'"

"Wow," I said. And then, as the meaning of it all began to sink in, I grinned at David and shook my head. "Wow," I said again. *Boiler Makers* seemed to be a reference to our "Boiler Room" communities. And as for Donni West, his tragic life and death made sense of so many of the questions scribbled in my journal. The call to prayer on campus was for the sake of a generation merely sleepwalking through college, with all the right kit outwardly but an inward emptiness. It was a Lazarus cry to raise the dead, to rouse the church, to awake and "get in the game." As the apostle says:

Wake up, sleeper,
rise from the dead,
and Christ will shine on you.

EPHESIANS 5:14

It was my turn to tell David about God's seven electrifying words to me: "Campus America. Call Campus America to pray." We began to wonder how we might obey the unexpected commission God had given us in the night. Might it be possible, we wondered, to plant prayer rooms and even Boiler Rooms on American campuses? Was this to be the shape of our next great adventure, the army I'd seen arising all those years ago as a student on the cliffs of Cape St. Vincent?

"At the heart of the crisis in Western civilization lies the state of mind and the spirit in the universities."

—AMBASSADOR CHARLES MALIK

Our conversation turned to Tim and the prayer room at Bluffton where that entire fraternity had turned to Christ. What might happen, we wondered, if similar gospel movements occurred on other campuses? What if Bluffton, amazing as it had been, was just a sign, a prophecy, some kind of firstfruit of a transformational movement God wanted to roll out throughout the nation? Might this be why God had spoken to us both so dramatically in the night? For the sake of an entire generation of students like Tim and Donni West, whose short lives were suddenly speaking with such urgency to ours?

• • •

Ambassador Charles Malik, one of the authors of the United Nations Declaration of Human Rights, issued a rousing call to universities almost forty years ago at the dedication of the Billy Graham Center at Wheaton College:

At the heart of the crisis in Western civilization lies the state of mind and the spirit in the universities. Christ being the light of the world, His light must be brought to bear on the problem of the formation of the mind . . . Therefore, how can evangelism consider its task accomplished if it leaves the university unevangelized? This is the great task, the historic task, the most needed task, the task required loud and clear by the Holy Ghost himself.[7]

America continues to be the greatest missionary-sending nation on earth, and most church historians trace this legacy back to a single student prayer meeting on a university campus in August 1806. On that day, a group of five Christian students at Williams College in Williamstown, Massachusetts, got caught in a brief summer rainstorm and decided to take shelter in a haystack. They passed the time by praying for other nations. Just as a prayer meeting in Herrnhut had launched the first great missions thrust of the Protestant Reformation in Europe in the previous generation, so this little prayer meeting was to launch something even bigger in the United States. Within ten years that little group of intercessors, under the leadership of Samuel J. Mills, had established America's first Missionary and Bible Societies and was sending evangelists and church-planters all over the world.

Call of the Wilder

One of the first missionary couples to be sent was the wonderfully named Royal Wilder and his wife, Eliza. They raised their children, Robert and Grace, in Kolhapur, India, before sending them back to America for university. Having grown up on the mission field, Robert and Grace began to pray together every single night for their fellow students, that they would not just bottle up God's blessings for their own benefit but strike out to other nations carrying the gospel, just as their own parents had. Those earnest daily prayers were heard and answered by God on a remarkable scale; it is estimated that as many as one in every thirty-five American students of Robert and Grace Wilder's generation went on to commit themselves to some kind of missions work.

This dramatic generational mobilisation found its tipping point in the summer of 1886, when the great evangelist D. L. Moody gathered 251 students at his Northfield base in Mount Hermon, Massachusetts. Robert Wilder, egged on by his sister, effectively hijacked Moody's conference and turned it into one of the most significant gatherings in the history of American missions. With apostolic urgency, he persuaded twenty-one of his fellow delegates—almost a tenth of the conference—to join him in prayer every morning for those millions in other nations who had not yet been given the opportunity to receive Jesus. On the final night of the conference, Robert laid down a specific challenge to the whole confer-ence. Ninety-nine of those present that night solemnly put their names to a document that came to be known as the "Princeton Pledge":

> We hold ourselves willing and desirous to do the Lord's work
> wherever He may call us, even if it be the foreign lands.

Robert's sister had been praying for one hundred to sign this pledge. He hoped she would not be disappointed with ninety-nine. But then, just as he was about to leave the gathering, one more student came running out to ask if he, too, might sign the pledge. Grace's prayers had been heard in heaven and answered exactly.

Robert proceeded to tour America with the Princeton Pledge. Fuelled by his sister's daily intercessions, he visited 162 campuses on horseback, personally recruiting 2,106 of the brightest and the best to give them-selves to the cause of world evangelisation. Many of the greatest mis-sion leaders and statesmen of that generation were first recruited to the kingdom cause on that early university tour. In fact, it was this tour that launched the Student Volunteer Movement (SVM), an extraordinary missionary body which—in its first forty years alone—mobilised more than 20,000 young people to go overseas as missionaries. It was a vast army, but they had an even bigger vision: "The evangelisation of the world in this generation."

The leader of SVM for twenty-five years was a remarkable man called John Mott, one of the original signatories of the Princeton Pledge at Mount Hermon. Mott later also led the YMCA through the war, founded the World Council of Churches, and received the Nobel Peace Prize in 1946 for his lifelong work with students.[8]

The heroic accounts of Robert Wilder and John Mott at the turn of the twentieth century, and Jon Petersen's stories of the Jesus Movement in California during the 1970s, left us in no doubt that America's students can be mobilised by the Spirit of God to change nations. Of course, David and I had no real idea how to "call Campus America to pray." But we did know that the Lord had spoken, and we were determined to obey as best we could, come what may. For the sake of thousands of students like those in that frat house in Bluffton, for the sake of places like San Antonio in Ibiza and Vancouver's Downtown Eastside, for the sake of a sleepwalking generation wasting their precious lives, we knew it was time to sound some kind of bugle, to rise up and call the dead to get into the greatest game on earth.[9]

SELAH

My prayer is not that you take them out of the world but that you protect them from the evil one.
JOHN 17:15

- What might contagious holiness mean for me this week?
- If God's embrace and acceptance is more powerful than sin, why is it so hard to accept his acceptance and love?
- To whom might I show unconditional acceptance today?

JUSTICE

GOD'S PRESENCE IN THE POOR

". . . but you have made it a den of robbers."

LUKE 19:46

*So this we believe: a kingdom of justice and righteousness has begun,
and it is making its way into people's lives and denting structures
that continue to oppress and dehumanise. Such work is seldom
done in the corridors of power nor in the halls of the great. Often
it is in the many small acts of integrity and goodness that many
faceless men and women do every day . . . It is this daily practice
of hope which keeps most of us going, keeping the monsters at bay
as humbly and powerfully we are caught up in the kingdom fire
and the stubborn grace that shines at the heart of existence.*

MELBA MAGGAY, *TRANSFORMING SOCIETY*

11

BOY'S TOWN

MEXICO • USA

Cannery Row's inhabitants are, as the man once said, "whores,
pimps, gamblers, and sons of *****," by which he meant everybody.
Had the man looked through another peephole he might have said,
"saints and angels and martyrs and holy men," and he would have
meant the same thing.

JOHN STEINBECK, *CANNERY ROW*

It's midday on Halloween, in the Mexican border town of Reynosa.
Kelly Tietsort is sitting near the entrance to Boy's Town, a red-light
compound ruled by the cartel. She's watching children playing football in the street. Prowling predators drive slowly through the gates.
It's almost 90 degrees Fahrenheit. A horse and cart clatters past, stirring up dust. Music blares out from an open window. There are no
shadows.

A trucker with an Alabama licence plate winds down his window
and acknowledges the guard. With a nod, he's ushered inside to cruise
the block and take his pick. Kelly notices the *Vote Republican* sticker on
his bumper as it disappears through the gate. "I mean, how do you even
pray for a guy like that?" she says, to no one in particular.

A beautiful woman with dark skin and long raven-black hair is leaning against the door of her room gazing lazily out onto the street. She's
maybe seven or eight months pregnant and wistfully watching one of

the children kicking a ball as tall as his knee. Kelly knows that the boy's picture—an 8-by-10-inch framed portrait—sits on a table within the woman's apartment. The boy may never know that she is his mother, that the baby curving in her belly will one day soon be his half-brother or sister. It's best that he doesn't know. And as for her, at least she has the picture.

Stories of quiet tragedy seep through the pores of this place. Kelly watches Crystal watching the boy and sighs a sort of prayer. Breathes in the air, hot as a furnace. Boy's Town has its own unique smell: the aroma of jalapeno peppers and roasting pork from the neighbourhood *taqueria* mingled with noxious wafts of fetid sewage and Fabuloso, a potent pine-and-lavender cleaning fluid used to wash floors, sluicing out in rivulets to the gutter.

This dark shrug of a place—a walled shantytown within a city— has hidden itself away beside the Rio Grande just west of the Hidalgo Bridge for as long as anyone can remember. In the 1840s American troops crossed the river here to occupy the region, bringing with them dollars for liquor and girls. Some say it all started then. Nowhere holds a grudge like a border town. Today this tired, ramshackle block of unrestricted prostitution is controlled by warring factions of the Mexican mafia. Dollars drive south across the border in BMWs and Buicks and beat-up trucks. Many of the men who come here for sex were first brought here as teenagers by their fathers. And their fathers were brought here by their fathers.

As for the women, inside these twenty-foot concrete walls daubed in graffiti and crowned with barbed wire, there are at least three generations for hire: grandmothers, mothers, children. From one to another it all goes on as it always has.

A pickup is leaving the compound. He's pulling out slowly past the tarot reader's kiosk set in the wall by the gate. He's got a Texas registration. Expressionless face. A stray dog trots in front of the vehicle and he sounds his horn angrily, a long, loud blast cutting through the stifling heat, but the stray just saunters past unperturbed.

A grey Crown Victoria Saloon purrs past Kelly a little too slowly. The driver's got spiky hair and Robocop reflector shades. He throws her a sideways grin as he passes. She immediately looks away.

"O God," she groans, "what am I even doing here? I mean, Lord, haven't you got anywhere *nicer* where a girl can go completely insane?"

A minute later the guy in the Robocop shades passes by again, but this time he stops, winds down the window, and asks if she needs a ride. Kelly declines. He asks where she lives.

"Not here," she counters.

"OK, OK," he says, laughing, and drives off.

But a couple of minutes later he's back, and this time he pulls right up to block Kelly's line of escape.

"What are you doing here?" he demands.

"Me?" she says as casually as she can, though she's terrified and preparing to run. "Oh, I'm praying." What else would she be doing? What else would anyone be doing at midday on Halloween in a red-light zone in a border town in Mexico?

"O God," she sighs, again. "He's right. What *am* I doing here?"

• • •

Kelly first caught sight of Boy's Town—its giant red neon "Lipstick" sign, its billboard advertising various women with exotic names, its single gated entrance and exit—on a Spring Break missions trip. "What is that place?" she'd asked innocently enough. And so it had begun.

"We don't go there," the pastor replied with a shrug, "and they don't come here. It's been there for ever. They do what they do and we do what we do."

He folded his arms, but Kelly was angry. "No!" she wanted to cry. "We can't just ignore a place like that. Surely that's why we're here. Not to play religious games. Jesus wouldn't have ignored Boy's Town, and neither should we."

A part of Kelly's heart remained at the gates of Boy's Town when she returned home to Tulsa, Oklahoma. She found herself praying for it—a sort of compulsion, a splinter under her skin. Again and again she asked the Lord to do something, to intervene, to send someone, to rescue the mothers, grandmothers, and daughters trapped within its concrete walls. Boy's Town just wouldn't go away.

Prayer without action is just religion in hiding.

Eventually she went to see her pastor, Roger Nix, and he listened carefully. He didn't shrug or tell her to forget it. Instead he suggested that she should go back with a few others to pray around the place. This she did. And then, the following year, Kelly finally relented to the insistent whispers of God. If she didn't become the answer to her own prayers, she would go crazy. No one else was going to do it. Prayer without action, she figured, is just religion in hiding.

Kelly had no team, no husband, no income, no experience, and no real plan, but she did have an unshakeable sense that the Holy Spirit had placed this unlikely, unglamorous place on her heart. She made arrangements, raised a little financial support, handed in her notice at the coffee shop, and began to say her goodbyes.

Just two weeks before Kelly's scheduled departure, she was out with friends at a farewell dinner in a Mexican restaurant when her mother called. It was ten o'clock at night. "Kelly, it's serious . . ." Her mother's voice was barely more than a whisper. "It's Rick . . ." She paused. "Kelly, I'm so sorry. Your brother was killed today."

Everything stopped. Nothing was making sense. Rick was a successful doctor at the University of Texas Medical Branch. He was her big brother, father to two boys. What could possibly have happened? And had her mum really just said "killed"? Kelly was still trying to process the words when the second blow landed.

"Kelly, he was shot dead. By Erick." Erick was her ten-year-old nephew. Erick was Rick's own son.

Kelly collapsed, hardly able to breathe or believe what she was hearing. Her mother's familiar voice seemed to be echoing from a distant room; explaining shakily how Rick had arrived to collect the boys from his ex-wife and had phoned her to say he was waiting in the car outside. Erick climbed into the seat behind his dad with eighty milligrams of Prozac in his bloodstream and a .45 pistol in his backpack. He shot Rick in the back, through the car seat, five times, while his mother watched from the house. No apparent motive.

Kelly's world began to implode. Her pastor insisted that she should put her plans for Boy's Town on ice. "Wait six months and see how you feel," he said kindly.

But something rose up within Kelly. She was hurting, but she was also angry and adamant. "My brother's still going to be dead in six months. And everything's already packed in my car. Thanks but no thanks. I'm good to go."

Kelly wasn't inclined to put her life on hold for half a year. Endless shifts in a Bible Belt coffee shop were not going to stop the pain or bring Rick back. The tragedy of her brother's death and her nephew's homicide had, if anything, accentuated her resolve to heal a little pain for someone somewhere if she possibly could. That, and the desire to escape all the sympathetic, prying eyes. Mexico seemed as good a place as any to grieve.

Sure enough, Kelly found a kind of numb comfort in the anonymity of Reynosa. Most of its inhabitants were processing some kind of loss. Her own crazy story seemed almost mundane in this messed-up no-man's-land of a place. Everyone had their own tales to tell of arriving with nothing, knowing no one, running from somewhere or someone, all the while hoping for something else, some place else entirely. No one moves to a border town like Reynosa with a plan. Everyone is either hiding or trying to leave. All 600,000 of them. It's a mezzanine floor, a city of ghosts, temporary for as long as anyone can remember. In Reynosa Kelly could be normal.

Kelly began to patrol the walls of Boy's Town, praying for its women and its users, its pimps, dealers, bar owners, sex workers, and innocent children, all eking out a life inside. She lapped the compound like Joshua around Jericho, again and again, several times every week. But after fifteen months walking in circles, sleeping in a storage container and working without a team or a fixed income or any contacts at all inside those forbidding concrete walls, Kelly began to wonder if she was going crazy.

"I hate this!" she yelled at God one day. "I have no friends here. I don't know what I'm doing. I don't know what to tell people. I feel trapped. All I do is talk to you, and . . ." She hesitated, but was too angry to be polite. "And you're not helping. Those sleazeballs in their cars just keep rolling in and rolling out, night after night. My prayers aren't working. What possible difference can I be making, just walking round and round in circles?"

• • •

It was around this time that I met Kelly. "I blame your book," she said, waving a dog-eared copy of *Red Moon Rising*. There was something strong and fiery about the petite brunette in front of me. Behind her big brown eyes and easy smile there was a spark, an inner grit that had compelled her to pick a fight with injustice in the most dangerous, least glamorous place she could possibly find. I grilled her with questions, and she started to describe her dream of establishing some kind of Boiler Room for Boy's Town: a praying, caring community that could rescue and redeem broken people, discipling them and sending them out to bind up the hearts of others. "My dream is to see women who used to be prostitutes and men who used to be drug dealers sharing their stories of redemption. One day I want to see the broken men and women of Boy's Town restored and sent out to the nations."

Kelly was impressive, but when she told me about her brother's death and the multiple tragedies surrounding that loss, I became troubled. Was her mission to Boy's Town, I wondered, just some wild, self-destructive reaction to post-traumatic stress? Was she safe? Was she sane? No one should move to a place like Boy's Town without training and a team. That's just common sense. And even with a team and training, no one should embark on an extreme mission while grieving deeply. This was obvious to everyone on the planet—except Kelly. Here she was, defying common sense and the advice of her pastor, ministering in Boy's Town regardless of what anyone said, asking for support from the 24-7 movement.

"How do I know you're not just a little, um, crazy?" I ventured.

She laughed and admitted that it was a question she had often asked herself.

"I mean, isn't it dangerous?" I asked. "Walking round a place like that every day, a single girl, on your own?"

She nodded.

"Kelly, you do realise that you could get attacked, assaulted, abducted in there?"

She shrugged and let out a sigh. "Obviously, I know that it's violent. My heart is often pounding. I don't know who the bad guys are. And because I'm wanting to get girls out, I guess I'm a threat to some folks' income. But, well, Jesus said he would never leave me nor forsake me. So I figure he's gonna look after me. He's gonna make it OK."

Her simple faith was beguiling, but it was also colossally naïve. But before I could assemble the necessary words to make this clear, she continued in a much smaller voice. "Pete, I have a recurring dream . . ." She seemed to be letting me into a place that was holy. "I'm an old lady. Old and wrinkly. And I'm walking the streets of Boy's Town. The place is different. People know me. They smile at me." She looked at me with a shy smile. "I guess it means that I'm going to become an old, wrinkly woman. It's kind of a promise. They're not gonna kill me. The Lord is going to protect me. He's going to use me to change Boy's Town."

I stared at Kelly, wrong-footed by her innocence. Her dream seemed remarkable because it was long-term and local. The young woman in front of me seemed willing to lay down the rest of her life if necessary for just a few dirty streets, a couple of hundred broken people, a seedy shantytown in the armpit of a violent Mexican border town.

Kelly's courage reminded me of Jackie Pullinger, the pioneer missionary to Hong Kong, with whom I had worked in another walled city in another generation on another continent far away. *Thank God*, I thought, *no one ever managed to talk any common sense into Jackie.*

Kelly clearly wasn't going to abandon Boy's Town if I asked her to leave. She'd be there whether we helped her or not. And so I took a deep breath and offered to do whatever I could to recruit people to join her. I also promised to pray for her. And then, as something of an afterthought, I suggested that she might also try praying the words of Isaiah 62 prophetically over Boy's Town, inserting its name in place of Jerusalem and Zion:

Because I love [Boy's Town], I will not keep still,
Because my heart yearns for [Boy's Town], I cannot remain silent.
I will not stop praying for her until her righteousness shines like
    the dawn.
ISAIAH 62:1-2, NLT

• • •

And so it was that Kelly came to be sitting there that day beside the gates of Boy's Town at midday on Halloween, holding a scrap of paper on which she had printed the words of Isaiah 62. She was quietly praying these words over the people she saw passing: over Crystal with her long dark hair, watching her two-year-old son playing in the street, over the man pulling his donkey across the potholed road, over the deadpan Texan who'd nearly just run over a dog.

The grey Crown Victoria Saloon pulled up on its third lap, blocking her line of escape. The driver in his Robocop reflector shades wound down the window and called out, "What are you doing here?" and Kelly told him she was trying to pray.

"Why?" came the bemused reply. "Don't you know what kind of place this is?"

"That's exactly why it needs prayer."

Her heart was racing. Was this how it happened? Was she about to get attacked at last? Abducted?

"Oh, that's good," he said. "Yeah, I pray too." He paused and leaned a little out of the open window. "They call me Kilo." No prizes for guessing why. "What does it say on your paper?"

"Uh, it's from the Bible," stammered Kelly.

"Here, give it me." He was holding his hand out the window.

Nervously Kelly walked over to the car and leaned down to hand him the extract from Isaiah. Kilo was young. Early twenties at most. "You wanna know why I'm here?" she said, hardly recognising her own voice. "I'm here because Jesus loves you, Kilo. He loves the women who work in Boy's Town. I believe he wants to change this place."

Had she said too much? Hard to tell when you're staring at your own reflection in a pair of Robocop shades.

"You make me nervous," he said eventually. "You talk as if you *know* something. As if you have the *right* to say these things."

She took a deep breath. "Can I pray for you?"

Kilo hesitated before slowly nodding. Kelly reached inside the car to place her hand on his shoulder. The old boy watching from across the road chuckled. He thought he knew exactly what was happening, but he was wrong. Kelly knew how it looked, but she simply didn't care. This was her first proper connection, in fifteen months, with anyone from Boy's Town. She wasn't going to miss it for the sake of a little pride. Jesus had risked his reputation in similar ways.

Kelly prayed a simple prayer, asking God to reveal his love to Kilo. As she did so, an extraordinary thing happened: A single tear rolled down from behind the Robocop shades. "Jesus is after you, Kilo," she grinned. "He wants to give you a whole new life."

Kilo became Kelly's first friend in Boy's Town. He'd been running bars and girls since the age of sixteen. Now, at twenty-four, he was a wide boy, a businessman, a proprietor, and a pimp. He had a couple of dubious establishments in Boy's Town and a nine-year-old son 350 miles away in Houston, Texas. At last Kelly had a face, a name, a story behind the walls she'd carried in her heart for such a long time.

Our prayers prepare the way of the Lord. We ask and he comes with healing in his wings.

Cautiously Kilo began to introduce Kelly to his friends. She e-mailed her supporters back in Tulsa to share the exciting news. This was the breakthrough they had been praying for. Here at last was the "man of peace" who could maybe open the doors of Boy's Town.

Back in Tulsa, the church began praying for Kilo by name, daring to believe that he could become the first of many to surrender his life to Jesus.

A few weeks later, just before Christmas, Kelly's pastor came to visit. Roger Nix had been praying specifically for Kilo ever since the news of that first encounter at Halloween. As he walked through Boy's Town with Kelly, Roger mentioned that he was hoping to meet Kilo. But Kelly laughed. She hadn't seen him in maybe six weeks. She thought perhaps he was avoiding her.

At that precise moment, a grey Crown Victoria Saloon came rolling into view.

Beautiful Here

Standing between one of his bars and the row of rooms he rented out to women, Kilo admitted a little sheepishly that he'd been reading his Bible every day since he first met Kelly. He especially liked the Gospel of John. "Since you prayed," he said with a sigh, "Jesus has been chasing me!" Once again, he allowed Kelly to pray with him.

"I'm not sure if words can contain the work of Jesus in this place," she wrote shortly after that encounter, "but I want to tell you it's beautiful here . . ."

> The streets of Boy's Town are littered with evidence of the previous night's activities (used condoms, empty beer bottles) and the doorways are darkened by women who have been stripped of their humanity, mere robots programmed to do only one thing. They don't feel anything anymore, partly because they're strung out on God-knows-what, and partly because they have to turn off all their feelings in order to survive another day.
>
> But things are changing here. I walked these streets sixteen months ago and found cold, empty stares. Today I walk the same streets and women come out of their rooms, pimps and drug addicts stumble out of bars, and they all want to talk. It has nothing to do with the fact that I've been walking these streets and everything to do with the fact that Jesus has been walking these streets with me. It's amazing, but our prayers really do prepare the way of the Lord. We ask and he comes with healing in his wings.

Three months after this triumphant testimony, on 29 March at 6 p.m., Kilo was killed. He had just turned twenty-five. The newspapers said it was a motorbike accident, but no one believed them. The word on the street notched Kilo's death down to another cartel killing. Drugs. Girls. Whatever. Kelly cried herself to sleep that night, replaying their various conversations and remembering the significant steps he seemed to have taken towards the Father in the 149 days since Halloween. Had it been enough? She had lost her only friend in Boy's Town. His eternity was sealed way too soon. Bitterly Kelly remembered all the heady praise and thanksgiving of the previous weeks. Boy's Town was no longer beautiful. She wept into her pillow, devastated and grieving for her friend, wondering how many ways and how many times a single heart could break.

●　●　●

Let my heart be broken by the things that break the heart of God.

This famous prayer was penned by Bob Pierce, the founder of World Vision, more than half a century ago and it remains one of the most dangerous prayers you can ever pray. It is hard for those who love God to be comfortable and content while his heart is breaking. He grieves for the lonely elderly, for the girls in Bangkok bars with numbers on their dresses, for the mother who woke up this morning in a refugee camp without food for her children, for the father in the city taking anti-depressants with his tea. The Messiah is "a man of sorrows . . . acquainted with grief" (Isaiah 53:3, NKJV). He is the Good Shepherd who leaves the ninety-nine sheep in comfort to find the one in peril. His eyes scan the earth relentlessly, looking for those true disciples willing to "share abundantly in [his] sufferings" (2 Corinthians 1:5). Abundantly. Not just occasionally. Not just notionally. Not just a bit.

One of the most dangerous prayers you can ever pray: "Let my heart be broken by the things that break the heart of God."

Kelly knew for sure that God's heart breaks for Boy's Town: for its prostitutes, pimps, and drug dealers, for its users and the people it uses. Night after night Jesus must surely be sitting there in its strip clubs and brothels, bound and gagged, awaiting the person who will finally come to speak his words and do his deeds of love. In the famous words attributed to Teresa of Ávila:

Christ has no body now on earth but yours; no hands but
yours; no feet but yours.
Yours are the eyes through which the compassion of Christ
must look out on the world.

Tonight there will be teams out on the streets of Ibiza rescuing people in
the Vomit Van because of Brian Heasley, a rural pastor with a criminal
record whose heart was broken by God in prayer. That's Kelly's story
too. For more than a century, the cries of prostituted women have risen
to God from Boy's Town. From generation to generation he has heard
their cries, shared their tears, and asked his people again and again,
"Who will go?" It's not God who ignores the heart-cries of the poor, it's
us: you and me, our brothers and sisters, his people around the world.
Imagine the rejoicing in heaven, therefore, the day a petite brunette
from the buckle of the Bible Belt responded to the Father's cries and
allowed her heart to break with his for Boy's Town.

The simple key to fighting injustice and unlocking your highest
destiny is the word *yes* addressed to God. Perhaps he is waiting for you
in a prayer room somewhere even now, or speaking to you through this
book, inviting you to seek his face and to allow your heart to be broken
with his deep concerns. Perhaps he is wanting to wreck your life for
good; longing to give you the commission for which you were born.
There really is only one way to find out!

●　●　●

A team from Kansas City arrived in Reynosa just days after Kilo's death.
Venturing with Kelly into Boy's Town one night, they entered a bar
called La Paloma. Men in dark corners were smoking crack, and no one
needed to ask why there were so many small rooms attached to the main
saloon. Nate, the Alaskan I'd met with Floyd in England, just happened
to be carrying his guitar and was immediately invited to serenade the

entire bar. A little nervously, the clean-cut worship leader, who'd recently been feeling so trapped in Kansas City's Christian ghetto, stood to sing in front of a lifesize mural of a naked lady bathing in a giant martini glass. He looked around the room: men snorting coke, others knocking back beers, women emerging from the anonymous doors, their clients zipping their trousers. Nate began to play the handful of pop songs he could remember. "Hotel California" seemed appropriate. Then, for reasons known only to himself, he broke into "The Lion Sleeps Tonight (Wimba Way)." Finally, running out of secular tunes, he took a deep breath and broke into worship songs. No one seemed to care.

And that is how the team from Kansas City came to be standing in one of the darkest places imaginable, worshipping the Lord Jesus and singing prophetically over men doing crack deals and women locked behind bedroom doors. "Where the Spirit of the Lord is," they sang, "there is freedom."

Is this OK? Kelly wondered. *Or is it just some kind of perverse Christian tourism?* At that very moment a Mexican named Raul sauntered unsteadily over to Kelly, beer bottle in hand and tattoos showing through his tattered shirt. "God sent you," he slurred, as if he'd heard her thoughts. "It's beautiful, what you are doing here, Kelly. God sent you and it is beautiful."

After that, Kelly relaxed. They all did. People started to come in off the street to enjoy the music. Nate stood in front of the naked lady, his eyes beaming, singing his heart out to Jesus.

A pimp came to fetch Kelly. One of his girls was having a breakdown, he said. Sure enough, Kelly found the girl sobbing uncontrollably. Surprised to see a Bible by her bed, she asked about it. This broken soul who was selling herself for sex in order to buy drugs was, in fact, a pastor's daughter, a prodigal child a very long way from home. "You know, in the days before Kilo died," she told Kelly eventually, "he was always talking to me, to anyone and everyone he met, about Jesus."

Now Kelly was weeping too. It was the assurance she had secretly been hoping for, the promise she'd been needing to hear. Perhaps she wasn't wasting her life after all. Perhaps God hadn't let her down. Perhaps, somewhere in heaven's pristine courts, there's a bar-owning, drug-dealing Mexican pimp with spiky hair and Robocop shades, who never did get his life tidied up but at least took a few faltering steps towards Jesus in the last days before he died.

There's a story about the apostle Peter at the Pearly Gates checking everyone into heaven. He's getting increasingly flustered because the numbers aren't tallying with his list. Some people seem to be sneaking into heaven's courts. "It's Jesus," sighs the apostle with a mixture of exasperation and affection. "Jesus just keeps smuggling people into heaven over the back wall."

Kilo might never have ticked any of the conventional, prescribed religious boxes to certify conversion. In fact, he was still dealing drugs and earning money from prostitution when he died. His lifestyle was abhorrent. Kilo was a mess. But maybe he'd snuck into heaven over the back wall after all.

Kelly thought about the thief who died on the cross beside Christ. He never prayed a formal prayer of repentance the way we're told we should. He never got baptised or joined a church or cleaned up his act. Yet Jesus promised him a place in paradise. What an unruly prototype for salvation under the terms of the new covenant. That thief entered eternity just half a pace behind the Lord. What a dangerous precedent to set!

Kelly remembered Kilo weeping when she prayed for him, and the way he'd been devouring the Gospel of John. And now this news that he had been preaching to the people of Boy's Town. She now felt sure that she would see her friend again, that by the grace of God, she'd got to him just in the nick of time. "Truly I tell you," said Jesus, "today you will be with me in paradise" (Luke 23:43).

• • •

Jesus Christ came to earth for people like Kilo and for places like Boy's Town. His mission was unambiguously "to proclaim good news to the poor."

The Gospel of Luke describes Jesus emerging dramatically from a season of prayer in the wilderness, unwashed and unshaven, like a boxer entering the ring, bound for his hometown synagogue. After forty days of intense, solitary spiritual warfare and fasting, he was about to preach the first recorded sermon of his public life. It was to be his inaugural address, a window onto the deepest priorities of his soul. The Bible passage he chose as his text that day (and upon which he had presumably been meditating for the previous forty days) was this:

> The Spirit of the LORD is on me,
> because he has anointed me
> to proclaim good news to the poor.
> He has sent me to proclaim freedom for the prisoners
> and recovery of sight for the blind,
> to set the oppressed free,
> to proclaim the year of the Lord's favour.
>
> LUKE 4:18-19

After reading this passage to the congregation, Jesus preached a startlingly confident, eight-word sermon: "Today this Scripture is fulfilled in your hearing." Here is a man who knows, beyond any shadow of doubt, that the Holy Spirit is resting upon his life for a very specific purpose: for "the poor . . . the prisoners . . . the blind . . . the oppressed."

The call to justice and mercy is the inevitable consequence of a call to walk in the footsteps of Jesus. He lived for the liberation of prisoners and the emancipation of the oppressed, and so must we. There is no other way to be a Christian. Perhaps I am sounding a little too emphatic here, but this really isn't contentious at all. It is biblically, undeniably, and absolutely true that all Christians are called to be messengers of good news to the poor.

Sadly, however, it is entirely possible to resist the challenges of the poor, but only by ignoring vast swathes of the Old Testament and spiritualising Christ's consistent example—in word and deed—of liberation.

The singer Neil Hannon, whose father was an Anglican bishop, wrote a poignant yet witty song about the way in which his deep yearning to believe in God is thwarted by this kind of hypocrisy in the church:

The cars in the churchyard are shiny and German;
distinctly at odds with the theme of the sermon.
And during communion I study the people
Threading themselves through the eye of the needle.[1]

The church of Jesus is called to proclaim good news to the poor. When our lives get too comfortable and begin to diverge from "the theme of the sermon," we become irrelevant—not just to the poor, but also to a world full of people like Neil Hannon who are watching us closely. Conversely, whenever we live by the standards of the Sermon on the Mount, standing up for the meek and speaking out for the oppressed, the world invariably watches and listens carefully. In the year AD 360, the Emperor Julian wrote a letter complaining bitterly about the way in which the church was providing for the weak, despised, forgotten members of his empire:

The church, at its best, has always been radically committed to a gospel that is revolutionary socially as well as spiritually.

These impious Galileans not only feed their own poor, but ours also. . . . Whilst the pagan priests neglect the poor, the hated Galileans devote themselves to works of charity.[2]

The church, at its best, has always been radically committed to a gospel that is revolutionary both socially and spiritually. For instance, Basil of Caesarea (330–379) was a pioneer of monasticism who gave the church many of our earliest written prayers, and yet he also planted a small city called Basiliad in which monks worked with doctors and other professionals to provide food, clothing, shelter, and medical assistance to the poor of Caesarea. Perhaps this was one of the communities that so offended Emperor Julian!

In more recent times, William Carey, best known as "the father of modern missions," campaigned for women's rights and those of lepers. John Wesley launched the first lending banks for the poor. Robert Raikes and Hannah More pioneered free education for all. William Wilberforce fought slavery. Elizabeth Fry campaigned for prison reform. George Müller established orphanages. The seventh Earl of Shaftesbury fought child labour, the oppression of the mentally ill, and many other injustices. William and Catherine Booth waged a vast campaign against every kind of injustice. More recently, in the twentieth century, Amy Carmichael rescued orphans in India, Dr Paul Brand pioneered reconstructive surgery for victims of leprosy, Dame Cicely Saunders established the hospice movement to care for the dying, and Archbishop Desmond Tutu fought apartheid and pioneered reconciliation in South Africa.[3]

All these great men and women of faith clearly understood the profound social implications of the gospel. They knew that the mission of God is bigger than the church. But they also understood the reality of sin and the fundamental necessity of personal salvation alongside social transformation. They are therefore best understood not as humanitarians or social reformers but simply as ministers of the gospel.

Jesus, Justice, and the Presence Paradigm

When our youngest son first spoke to the receptionist at his preschool in Kansas City, she exclaimed, "Oh, that is *adorable*. You're so small and you already have an *accent*!" He just blinked back at her, not understanding. She didn't seem to realise that he hadn't acquired an exotic skill. This was just the way he spoke. Being English is not something my family "does," it is simply who we are. We can't help it!

Justice is similarly essential to God's identity. He can't help it! It is his nature to be unwaveringly just.

The Maker of heaven and earth . . .
upholds the cause of the oppressed and gives food to the hungry.
The LORD sets prisoners free, the LORD gives sight to the blind,
the LORD lifts up those who are bowed down, the LORD loves the
    righteous.
The LORD watches over the foreigner
and sustains the fatherless and the widow.

PSALM 146:7-9

God's love for the afflicted was evident, of course, in Jesus. He didn't just preach about justice; his presence actually *embodied* justice. His life defined the very term. In Jesus Christ we see what the world will one day look like, and how it will one day work, when oppression is finally disarmed and hatred is displaced by love. His earthly ministry was a foretaste of the day when God's glory will fill creation the way it filled his Son.

We have talked elsewhere in this book about "the presence paradigm," which positions life's essential purpose and meaning in the overarching context of Immanuel, "God with us." Our calling as Christians is certainly to seek God's presence in *prayer*, and it is to proclaim God's presence in *mission*, but it is also to recognise his presence in the poor:

> For I was hungry and you gave me something to eat, I was thirsty
> and you gave me something to drink, I was a stranger and you
> invited me in, I needed clothes and you clothed me, I was ill and
> you looked after me, I was in prison and you came to visit me.

MATTHEW 25:35-36

Compassion for the hungry, the stranger, the naked, the sick, and the prisoner is not an optional extra for those with a strong social conscience. It bleeds from the heart of true Christian worship. When we care for the poor, we minister to Jesus himself.

A House of Prayer for Justice

On the day that he cleansed the temple, we read that Jesus entered its outer courts and began to drive out those who were selling. "It is written," he said to them, "'My house will be a house of prayer'; but you have made it 'a den of robbers'" (Luke 19:46). Sometimes this dramatic confrontation is caricatured as if Jesus was merely very annoyed with some dodgy market traders who'd been fleecing a few gullible tourists. The reality was far more serious. Jesus was actually indicting the entire temple bureaucracy for systemic corruption. We know this for sure because contemporary archaeologists have discovered coins minted by the temple at the time of Jesus which proves that its authorities had effectively created their own currency for exclusive use within the hallowed precincts. But this explains why there were so many moneylenders doing business in the Court of the Gentiles. The authorities had probably created their own currency because the Roman money carried a "graven image" of Caesar. But it also enabled them to set their own exchange rates, thereby making as much money as they wanted from those pilgrims desperate enough to pay over the odds for the sacrificial animals that bought them forgiveness or an answered prayer.

No wonder Jesus denounced the temple authorities for reducing the house of prayer to "a den of robbers"—a phrase loaded with prophetic significance. Jesus was quoting the prophet Jeremiah, who stood at the gates of the previous temple and asked, "Has this house, which bears my Name, become a den of robbers to you?" (Jeremiah 7:11). Jeremiah was condemning Solomon's temple for tolerating and even perpetrating injustice against aliens, orphans, widows and the innocent. By using this phrase, Jesus was drawing a direct comparison between Herod's temple in which he was standing, and its doomed predecessor. He was announcing the imminent destruction of an edifice that stood at the heart of Jewish faith and identity. The authorities were alarmed. Quoting Isaiah's words about being "a house of prayer for all nations" had perhaps been an appropriate challenge from the Galilean firebrand. Overturning a few tables had been outrageous, but it was easily fixed. But citing Jeremiah's condemnation of the temple as "a den of robbers" was subversive and politically dangerous. When "the chief priests and the teachers of the law heard *this*" (italics mine), they "began looking for a way to kill him" (Mark 11:18).

Again and again the Old Testament prophets railed against the people of God for two great neglects: turning from God to foreign idols (false worship) *and* ignoring the plight of the poor (injustice). Right worship and social justice were, they maintained, equally important and intrinsically linked. Some people then, as now, clearly considered social justice less important than spiritual worship, but the prophet Amos annihilates any such cant:

> I hate, I despise your religious festivals;
> your assemblies are a stench to me. . . .
> Away with the noise of your songs!
> I will not listen to the music of your harps.
> But let justice roll on like a river,
> righteousness like a never-failing stream!
>
> AMOS 5:21, 23-24

The resounding biblical call to express our worship through justice continues to be an essential and consistent provocation to the 24-7 prayer movement, which could otherwise, so easily, withdraw into cloistered irrelevance. But in prayer rooms around the world, as we seek God, we are continually compelled to engage with the things that break his heart, and conscripted to go out and engage his enemies.

●　●　●

> I used to think I needed to pick sides,
> but now I know it's better to pick a fight.
>
> BOB GOFF

A thousand miles due north of Boy's Town, Sammy and I sat quietly in Skies restaurant looking down on Kansas City. It was our wedding anniversary, and we were reflecting together on the breathtaking events since we had first responded to God's call to "come across the water" to America. Prayer rooms were now proliferating in traditional denominations across most American states. Simple missional communities were getting established the length and breadth of the continent. More and more people seemed to be catching God's heart for prayer, mission, and justice:

- An earnest university professor in Michigan moved with his family from an idyllic farmhouse in the country to establish a community in an inner-city environment scarred by drugs, poverty, and depression, with a radical vision to start a free school.[4]
- A group of students in Santa Barbara, California, converted a duplex on the infamous Del Playa party street into a prayer shed from which they were distributing hundreds of "Jesus burgers" every Friday night.
- A retired oil executive in Oklahoma established a wholesale grocery store in one of the poorest parts of his city where he was now spending his wealth and his years of retirement, working at the checkout. He diligently memorised the names of everyone in the neighbourhood as they passed through his store, and would pray for each of his customers by name as they came to purchase healthy goods.[5]
- A twenty-six-year-old from Ohio State University wrote to say, "I lead a 24-7 Prayer community here in Columbus, Ohio. We're mostly young African Americans, and it's amazing all that God has done. People have been finding freedom from all kinds of sexual immorality and even suicidal depression."
- Kelly managed to purchase some land in Reynosa on the edge of Boy's Town and had recently been granted legal permission to begin constructing a centre for prayer, rehabilitation, hospitality, and employment.

The movement was expanding in its scope, impact, and imagination. There was a steady stream of exciting invitations to share the vision throughout America. At home in Kansas City, Sammy and I had come to love our new tribe of friends, and our kids were thriving in their schools. It was tempting to settle down. But every time I walked up our road to the coffee shop, past that cemetery at Blue Camp 20, I was provoked to keep pioneering.

Europe and the Middle East are the darkest, most challenging, most urgent mission fields on earth today. In America the church is holding its own—at least for now. Everywhere else, it is growing dramatically. But in the Middle East, where the gospel flourished for its first thousand years, violent persecution today is decimating ancient Christian populations. And in Europe, the crucible of Christian faith for its second millennium, ancient denominations are dying. Young people are abandoning the beliefs of their parents. Christendom is dead.

Sammy and I knew that God had launched the 24-7 movement in Europe for a reason. The young people I saw arising that night at Cape St. Vincent were doing so from the countries of Europe and the Middle East. The prayer movement in America was thriving. But if the church in Europe and the Middle East is to be revived, there remains an urgent need for prayer. With a rush of mixed emotions, we realised that it was time to strike out from Blue Camp 20. God was calling us home.

●   ●   ●

There is an aesthetic to life attributable, I suspect, as much to ancillary grace as direct divine intervention. An oak tree grows symmetrically not because God micromanages its development, but simply because he gives nature an inherently beautiful blueprint. The patterns of creation are equally visible whether you look down through an electron microscope at subatomic quantum patterning, or up through an optical telescope at the vast choreography of the stars. When we put Jesus first, walking in step with the Holy Spirit over months and years, unintended patterns start to form from the chaos of our lives. Coincidences occur surprisingly often; disparate voices unexpectedly harmonise. A beach ball blows out from the crowd of sunbathers at a precisely necessary moment. A drunk in a bar is compelled to say that your presence matters, just when you're asking that very question. A compulsion to count your medication, or to board a flight to Sofia, or to move into an apartment you can't afford in the centre of Thun, becomes the voice of God.

But mostly God's interventions are less dramatic than these. Serendipity happens simply (there is nothing "mere" about it) because life's component parts are at last beginning to synchronise, to "work together for good"—constructively and beautifully, in their intended way. Prayers are answered that we never even prayed.

This level of unnecessary blessing on the saints is not, I suspect, a particular reward or a sign of divine favouritism. God is not some kind of pushy parent, continually meddling in everything we do. It's just that life thrives when righteousness abounds. It has been designed to self-propagate easily, in extravagant, unnecessary beauty. Life, it seems, makes life without trying.

It was this inherent symmetry that had, I suspect, placed us on the cliffs of Cape St. Vincent for 9/11. It had stationed Jon Petersen in California for the start of the Jesus Movement, and Kelly by the gates of Boy's Town just as Kilo's car pulled up. This same serendipity now conspired to place us on a flight home to London on the one day in the year when millions of Americans cry a hearty "good riddance" to England.

The boys stared out of the airplane windows waving goodbye to America, gasping in wonder at the sight of the Independence Day fireworks from 30,000 feet. Three days later, back in the UK, I took a train into central London to visit the new Boiler Room facility that had opened while we'd been away. It was a beautiful, sunny day. The River Thames was glittering in the morning light. There was no clue anywhere that this was to be one of the most terrifying days of our lives.

SELAH

A Prayer of George Whitefield for Broken-hearted Preachers

*Yea, that we shall see the great Head of the Church once more
. . . raise up unto Himself certain young people whom He may
use in this glorious employ. And what manner of people will
they be?*

*Those mighty in the Scriptures, their lives dominated by a sense
of the greatness, the majesty and holiness of God, and their
minds and hearts aglow with the great truths of the doctrines
of grace.*

*They will be those who will preach with broken hearts
and tear-filled eyes, and upon whose ministries God will
grant an extraordinary effusion of the Holy Spirit, and
who will witness "signs and wonders following" in the
transformation of multitudes of human lives.*

12

THE FOUNDERY

LONDON • IBIZA • SOUTH AFRICA

Never forget that justice is what love looks like in public.

DR. CORNEL WEST

The train clattered across Grosvenor Bridge on its way into Victoria Station. The sunlight was glinting from skyscrapers, their lines cut sharp into the cornflower-blue sky. My homecoming joy seemed to be resounding around the entire city. Just a few hours earlier, London had won the bid to host the Olympic Games.

I had been looking forward to this day for many weeks, and could hardly wait to see both our new London venue for the first time and my old friend Phil Togwell, still faithfully running 24-7 in the UK. On such a fine morning there was no hint anywhere, no whisper at all in the pristine skies above, nor in the glittering river below, and certainly not in the triumphant newspaper headlines littering the train, of the terror awaiting the evening editions.

I jumped from train to tube, unaware that other men elsewhere in the city were doing the same thing wearing backpacks loaded with homemade explosives. Four suicide bombers had chosen this particular day to destroy three underground trains and to blow the roof off a red double-decker bus, killing themselves and fifty-two innocent people, injuring 700 others. Parents, wives, and children had said casual good-byes that morning, never again to say hello. It was to be the bloodiest attack on London since the Second World War.

It's hard to convey the contortions of disbelief and terror that seized us all that day. One bomb is terrifying. But then there was another. And another. And another. No one knew where or when the next device would explode. The entire city was paralysed with fear and rumour. The rest of the world was watching the story unfold online and on television.

Sammy called; I could hear the fear in her voice. She begged me to get out of London fast before the next bomb went off, before a sky-scraper came down or a plane dropped out of the sky. But of course, I was stuck. The entire capital had been locked down, stations were closed, buses cancelled, airplanes grounded. There was nothing we could do, nowhere we could go.

We sat there in the middle of the hysteria, Phil and I, nervously gaz-ing up at the forest of skyscrapers. It was a beautiful day, and if build-ings were about to fall to the ground, we figured we'd rather be outside than buried below ground in the new subterranean Boiler Room venue. Sirens were screaming, police helicopters buzzing like hornets from A to B. In the end we did the only thing we could, the thing God had been calling us to do for more than half a decade.

• • •

Intercession is often instinctive and always important in the midst of any catastrophe, but at such times we may wonder what possible dif-ference our prayers can make. There are at least four reasons why we sometimes fail to truly intercede in the face of terrible disasters:

1. *A limited worldview.* All too easily we forget, or we doubt, that there is a spiritual reality at work behind the material tragedy unfolding on our screens. We find ourselves believing

in ambulances more than angels, in the power of politicians more than the power of prayer. But the apostle Paul leaves us in no doubt: "Our struggle is not against flesh and blood, but against the rulers, against the authorities, against the powers of this dark world and against the spiritual forces of evil in the heavenly realms" (Ephesians 6:12).

2. *A low self-esteem.* We may also doubt our authority in Christ and the power that can be released by saying a simple yes to his will and no to the forces of evil. The apostle Paul says that God has positioned us alongside Jesus as rulers of the world: "God raised us up with Christ and seated us with him in heavenly realms" (Ephesians 2:6).

3. *Doubts about prayer.* Deep down, we may doubt the power of prayer, questioning its ability to effect change. But the apostle James insists that "the prayer of a righteous person is powerful and effective" (James 5:16). And Jesus, who makes us righteous, and therefore makes our prayers "powerful and effective," elsewhere promises to "do whatever you ask in my name, so that the Father may be glorified" (John 14:13).

4. *Practical questions about how to pray.* Once we have remembered that there really is a spiritual battle, and that we really do have authority to make a difference, and that Jesus really has promised to answer our prayers, we may simply hold up our hands and say, "Yes, OK, fine, but I still don't actually know what to say!" Understanding how to pray for the victims of a terrorist attack in London, or a war in the Middle East, or a tsunami in Asia can be terribly difficult. Many people believe that they *ought* to pray at such times, they probably *want* to pray, but they just don't know *how* to wrap words around so much chaos and loss.

Over the years we have often found it helpful to focus our emergency intercessions at times of large-scale crisis on three particular groups:

1. *People afflicted.* We ask God to *comfort* those who suddenly find their lives torn apart by grief, loss, fear, and trauma.
2. *Pastors and priests.* We ask God to give *courage* to church leaders seeking to bring Christ's presence and hope in the midst of trauma and profound questions of pain.
3. *Peacemakers, politicians, and police.* We ask God to give *clarity* and wisdom to government agencies and NGOs, blessing and supporting their efforts to bring justice, reconciliation, and aid.

Sitting in the middle of the 7/7 attacks on London, Phil and I prayed as best we could. We asked the Lord to bring comfort to the many hundreds of *people affected*, the traumatised, injured, and suddenly bereaved. We prayed for *pastors and priests* as they began the solemn work of counselling, binding up broken hearts, preparing for funerals, wondering what words of hope and meaning they could possibly bring on Sunday. We prayed for *peacemakers*, for the police hunting down the remaining perpetrators, for the government ministers coordinating the emergency response, for the army of exhausted medics tending to the wounded.

Pray the three Ps in a disaster:

(1) People afflicted: comfort.

(2) Pastors: courage.

(3) Peacemakers: clarity.

The Prayer of Lament

The call to intercede at times of tragedy flows directly from the cross of Jesus. In those two intersecting beams we recognise that God identifies with—and participates in—human suffering, but also that he has overcome it. These two axes can also provide a helpful model for intercession.

First, the vertical post of the cross calls us to plant ourselves squarely in the troubles of the world. We choose to engage with the suffering of others—not to ignore it. We cry, "O my God, help! O my God, why have you forsaken us?" Such Good Friday prayers were easy in London that day as terror seized the city. In fact, they were automatic. Before we cry out *for* the afflicted, we should always try to pause to pray *with* them; to wait without any easy answers or guarantees. Intercession, at its most powerful, invariably begins with simple lament: a heavy sigh, silent tears, careful listening to a person's pain without immediately speaking to solve their problem or correct their theology. Lament features in more than half the Psalms and an entire book of the Bible. It is a vitally important, often forgotten expression of prayer.

The Prayer of Authority

Of course, our call to intercede moves quickly from empathy to authority, from the downward trajectory of the cross to its horizontal embrace. Christ flings his arms wide over every human tragedy. His resurrection quivers with defiant hope over every disaster. We are Easter people for whom there are always new possibilities buried within even the greatest troubles. The cross proves once and for all that Satan's worst atrocities can now, in Christ, become God's best opportunities. It is an article of our faith that "in all things God works for the good of those who love him" (Romans 8:28). Unspeakable disasters, personal tragedies, and even terror attacks can somehow be redeemed by the cross of Christ.

> The cross proves once and for all that Satan's worst atrocities can now, in Christ, become God's best opportunities.

And so we pray for his kingdom to come; we declare war on enemy forces; we stand against the evil that has been unleashed; we try to discern God's will in the situation and insist upon its urgent implementation; we wield "the sword of the Spirit which is the Word of God" (Ephesians 6:17); we claim his promises and declare God's truth; we listen to the Holy Spirit and allow him to focus our prayers onto particular people in the crowd. We may also seek out other Christians with whom to pray, forging spiritual alliances, because "if two of you on earth agree about anything they ask for, it will be done for them by my Father in heaven" (Matthew 18:19).

• • •

Phil and I sat there surrounded by the hysteria of 7/7, praying God's peace and healing upon the city. Sirens were sounding, helicopters buzzing between buildings, but my old friend seemed the same as ever: kind, twinkly eyes, cockney accent, and that long, wiry goatee still reminding me of Narnia's Mr. Tumnus. Finally, as the bombs stopped exploding and the initial terror began to subside, we ventured to begin the conversation we'd been anticipating all day.

I began to recount stories from our time in the USA, and Phil responded with equally exciting stories about all the new developments in England. He described a mysterious phone call six months earlier, from a businessman with properties throughout London who wanted one of his buildings to be used as a place of prayer. This Spirit-filled entrepreneur was sensing an urgent need for intercession and integrity right here, in the heart of the world's greatest financial centre, long before anyone knew about the looming financial crisis and the terrifying bomb attacks on the city that day.

"So which one do you want?" he had asked Phil, spreading a map of the city on a table, covered in dots representing his extensive portfolio of potential venues. Phil couldn't quite believe what was happening, but then his eyes fell upon a particular dot situated on the intersection of two well-named roads: Tabernacle Street and Worship Street. "I guess we'd better take a look at that one," he said, grinning.

Although the building turned out to be an unimpressive 1970s-era block of offices, it was right on the edge of the Square Mile—London's financial district. The basement was an extensive rabbit warren of subterranean rooms, stairs, and passageways, with loads of potential for prayer and studio space, offices, and meetings. Eventually, feeling a little shell-shocked, Phil wandered into the neighbouring pub, The Prophet, looking for lunch and somewhere to process.

"So what's with all the religious names around here?" he asked the girl behind the bar.

"Huh?"

"The Prophet pub? Worship Street? Tabernacle Street?"

She'd clearly never given it a second thought. Why should she? But then, just as Phil was about to change the subject, a bespectacled gentleman with slicked-back hair, sitting at the nearby table, spoke up. "Forgive me," he said, "but I couldn't help overhearing your question. It's all to do with John Wesley." His manner was dignified and authoritative. "This is where he was based. The Foundery—the epicentre of Methodism for its first forty years—was just spitting distance from where we are seated now. It was an old cannon foundry originally, before Wesley got hold of it—hence the name."

Phil had certainly heard of Wesley's Foundery. For Methodists and revivalists around the world it is a place laden with almost mythological significance. He'd always presumed it was somewhere buried beneath one of London's tangled back streets, but had never known precisely where.

"So how come you know all this?" he enquired.

"Oh, I do apologise," the gentleman said, extending his hand. "How rude of me. I should have introduced myself. My name is Lord Leslie Griffiths. I am the superintendent minister at Wesley's chapel, the one he built just up the road when the Foundery eventually burned down. My chapel was his base for the last eleven years of his life. People come from all over the world to visit and pray. But of course," he smiled, clearly enjoying the irony, "the real heart of the Methodist revival is actually buried 200 yards down the road."

Phil tentatively explained our vision to establish a centre for prayer, mission, and justice in a large basement we'd just been offered nearby in Tabernacle Street. It seemed trivial compared to the Foundery, but when he heard this, Lord Griffiths became animated. "Tabernacle Street, you say? Tell me, where in Tabernacle Street is your building, precisely?"

They left the pub together and strolled up the road, halting at the Boiler Room door. The minister let out a slight gasp.

"This," he pronounced excitedly, "is the exact site, to the nearest yard, of the Foundery! Your worthy new endeavour is to be based on the precise spot where Methodism was born. Did you call it a Boiler Room? Well, that's appropriate, because the fires of the Great Awakening were certainly once stoked right here!"

We'd picked a building randomly from a city of 8 million people, and it had turned out to be one of the most significant sites in Christian history.

It was another bewildering moment of divine symmetry. Phil recounted the story to me, laughing at the improbability of it all, which made his eyes twinkle even more and his wiry beard quiver. What were the chances, we wondered, of picking a building at random from a city of 8 million people, and finding ourselves here on one of the most significant sites in British Christian history? And having been given the keys to such a place, what did it mean that we were here viewing it, at the precise moment of the city's gravest attack in more than sixty years?

• • •

By late afternoon, most underground lines were nervously reopening, with armed guards at every station. The city continued to contort in shock, but investment bankers and commodity traders were beginning to return to their desks in the skyscrapers surrounding Tabernacle Street. Phil and I could see them through the windows far above us.

Unblocking an Ancient Well

Some 80 million Christians today from more than 133 countries and 80 denominations trace their faith back to the Foundery. This site was the heart of the greatest British spiritual awakening in perhaps a thousand years, an epicentre of world-shaking prayer, mission, and justice—a Boiler Room centuries before we came along. Did we dare to believe that we had been led to this remarkable location, like Isaac to the Valley of Gerar, to "reopen the wells that had been dug in the time of his father Abraham . . . and [to give] them the same names his father had given them" (Genesis 26:18)?

We began to research the history of the Foundery, trying to understand why God had set us down on its doorstep. The more we studied, the more familiar, more familial, those primitive Methodists became.

At the heart of all Boiler Room communities there are certain principles and practices that give shape to everything we do. We had always taken these practices to be distinctively ours, but now, in studying the history of the Foundery, we discovered that all six of our supposedly innovative values had, in fact, been modelled brilliantly by the Wesley brothers, on this very site more than 250 years earlier.

The Boiler Room Rule

The six practices shared by all Boiler Rooms and modelled so powerfully at The Foundery are derived originally from the three great Christian priorities: to love God with all our hearts, to love our neighbours as ourselves, and to love the lost with the gospel (Luke 10:27; Matthew 28:19). The language we tend to use to describe these three priorities comes from our Moravian forefathers: We seek to love God by being "true to Christ," to love our neighbours by being "kind to people," and to love the lost by taking "the gospel to the nations." Whatever language you use, these three loves summarise the universal call of Christ.

Boiler Rooms are distinctive (or so we thought, until we discovered the Foundery) because of the six practical ways in which we try to obey these three great commandments. Our Rule of Life can be depicted for the sake of memorability as a hexagon (the six practices) wrapped around a triangle (the three great commands of Jesus).

A. We seek to be *true to Christ* through:
1. *Prayer and worship.* We seek to be a *house of prayer* for the nations, because we know that human beings are designed to walk and talk with God, and to glorify him for ever.
2. *Creativity.* We seek to provide *studio space* for the arts, because God's creativity is worth celebrating with all the imagination and colour, flavour, and melody he has given us.

B. We seek to be *kind to others* through:
3. *Hospitality.* We seek to be an *open table* offering radical hospitality, because God has welcomed us into his family and calls us to make space for others sacrificially in our hearts and our homes.
4. *Justice and mercy.* We seek to be *centres for social justice* and mercy, because Jesus cares passionately about those on the edges of life, and he has sent us to be good news for the poor.

C. We seek to be *loyal to the gospel* through:
5. *Evangelism.* We seek to be *mission stations* for evangelism, because the gospel is good news for the salvation of every single person on the planet.
6. *Learning.* We seek to be *academies* for education because Jesus is still in the disciple-making business, calling us to lifelong learning and to train others in his ways.

We were astounded to discover the extent to which the early Methodists had outworked all six of these practices on Tabernacle Street.

A house of prayer. In Wesley's day the Foundery functioned as a house of prayer at the heart of the burgeoning British (and American) Awakening. It is hard to overstate the extent to which Methodism was founded and fuelled by persistent and expectant intercession. John Wesley, who had personally experienced the Moravian prayer meeting in Herrnhut, and had been baptised in the Spirit at an all-night prayer meeting nearby in Fetter Lane, organised and led daily prayer meetings at the Foundery. As if this wasn't enough, Wesley would also arise daily at 4 a.m. to intercede for four hours before the day began. In later life he might have relaxed this arduous daily regime, but instead he extended it, praying for up to eight hours a day. We can only guess what deals he struck with the Almighty during those many thousands of hours of prayer.

John Wesley rose at 4 a.m. daily to intercede for at least four hours before the day began, and increased this to eight hours in old age.

A place of creativity. The Foundery was a house of prayer but also a context for extraordinary creativity. Most notably, Charles Wesley wrote many of his hymns in this location. Tabernacle Street would often have resounded with voices singing one of his latest compositions. The composer George Frideric Handel lived on Brook Street, a twenty-minute ride from the Foundery, and may have invited John Wesley to attend a performance of his new oratorio *Messiah*. "There were some parts that were affecting," recorded the thirty-nine-year-old preacher of Handel's masterpiece, before unfortunately adding, "I doubt it has staying power."

Evidently, it was thanks to Charles Wesley's artistic sensibilities and not those of John that many of the most-loved songs in history found their first rendition at the Foundery—timeless hymns ranging from "And Can It Be?" to "Love Divine, All Loves Excelling." It is a tantalising possibility that on Christmas Day 1739, just a month after John Wesley's first sermon in the Foundery, the walls and cobbled stones of Tabernacle Street heard the very first public rendition of that greatest of carols, "Hark the Herald Angels Sing."

A home for hospitality. From the late 1740s, the Foundery served as an almshouse providing "accommodations to 9 widows, 1 blind woman, 2 poor children, and 2 upper servants, with a maid and a man." Wesley insisted that those who stayed as his guests should always dine with the occupants of these poorhouses, eating exactly the same food and sitting at the same tables. There was to be no hierarchy. The great and the good mingled with pilgrims and the poor as they flocked to this building from around the country. Wesley insisted, in the words of St. Benedict, that "all who arrive as guests are to be welcomed like Christ."[1]

A centre for justice and mercy. The Wesleyan revival was marked by irrepressible social enterprise. The Foundery offered a Friday clinic providing primary healthcare for the sick, a school for the poor, and one of the world's first lending banks for families in crisis. In its first year alone, the Foundery Bank issued micro-loans to 250 families. The Wesleys also operated a ministry to the inmates of nearby Newgate Prison, from which Charles would often accompany condemned prisoners to the gallows on Tyburn Hill, offering comfort and hearing their final prayers. John was compelled to go out begging for money, knocking on door after door in the neighbourhood

Wesley's final letter, just six days before his death, was to William Wilberforce exhorting him to abolish slavery.

requesting financial support for their work amongst the poor. In 1774, four years before the destruction of the Foundery, John penned *Thoughts upon Slavery*, an excoriating condemnation of human trafficking which he described as that "execrable sum of all villainies." His final letter, written on 28 February 1791, when he was eighty-eight years old and just six days before his death, was addressed to William

Wilberforce, urging the famous abolitionist to persevere in his fight to the end.

An academy of learning. The Foundery housed a library, a "band room" in which 300 people could be taught, and a school offering education to the local poor. It was also an auditorium for daily preaching, teaching, and theological education. Ideas mattered deeply here; there was no hint of anti-intellectualism in its corridors. On one occasion, a theological dispute provoked followers of George Whitefield to picket the Foundery. They handed out tracts condemning Wesley's teaching that anyone, anywhere can be saved. They believed that salvation is restricted to a preordained minority. John promptly stood up before the gathered congregation and demanded to know which ones of them had received one of these tracts upon entering. Sheepishly, people pulled the papers from their pockets, whereupon Wesley led them in tearing the tracts to shreds and ceremonially throwing the pieces aloft. Then, as the confetti fell like snow, they sang one of Charles Wesley's most adamantly Arminian hymns, declaring unequivocally that "for *all* he has the atonement made":

Arise, oh God, maintain Thy cause!
The fullness of the gentiles call;
Lift up the standard of Thy cross,
And all shall own Thou diedst for all!

A mission station for evangelism. The Foundery was preeminently a mission station in which—and from which—the gospel was preached. Lay evangelists were trained here and sent out to preach the good news of Jesus, establishing a national network of discipleship classes. It was from this evangelistic base that John Wesley rode more than 250,000 miles nurturing Methodist societies the length and breadth of the nation, planting churches, developing an arterial system of preaching circuits, and relentlessly proclaiming the gospel for the new urban masses of the Industrial Revolution.

• • •

Despite its many remarkable ministries, the Foundery remained a primitive venue. Buckets had to be deployed to catch the rainwater falling through the building's defective roof. Wesley was continually forced to fundraise until, in the end, the Foundery burned to the ground. Wesley moved up the road to build a grander chapel, and today's ugly office block was eventually built on the historic site.

Our supposedly radical ideas for Boiler Rooms as houses of prayer, mission, and justice, creativity, learning, and hospitality were clearly nothing new at all. These simple missional-monastic communities are, in fact, mini-versions of Wesley's great Foundery. And now, whether by life's strange symmetry or the direct intervention of God, we found ourselves on the actual site of the original prototype, with a vision to do the things that the Wesley brothers had done so brilliantly in this location, some 250 years earlier, in ways that had changed the destiny of entire nations. Phil and I stood there on this historic site on that particular day, humbled by the past and sobered as the sound of sirens in the streets overhead continued to call us to pray.

Seek the welfare of the city where I have sent you into exile,
and pray to the LORD on its behalf, for in its welfare you will
find your welfare.

JEREMIAH 29:7, NLT

• • •

Brian and Tracy Heasley were continuing their nocturnal rhythm, rescuing people in the Vomit Van, handing out their *Jesus Loves Ibiza* Bibles, ministering to long-term workers on the island, and praying through the night in shifts with the team at their 24-7 centre. For several years they had also been trying to build connections with the town's West African sex workers, but with little success. The women's pimps prowled around suspiciously nearby, and the women themselves were too busy making money, performing sex acts in darkened doorways and parking lots, to waste time with Christians. Some of them were just too nervous to talk. But then, one particular night, as the team in the prayer room was interceding for these women, there was an unusual surge of faith, a conviction that their prayers had finally "broken through." The girls on the team went out onto the streets that night with great expectancy, hoping to meet some of the women for whom they'd been praying. For the first time in years, the women responded warmly, opening themselves to conversation and even to prayer.

Friendships grew surprisingly quickly after this long-awaited breakthrough, and the Heasleys decided to establish a chaplaincy for the island's sex workers. Surprisingly, most of these women considered themselves Christians. They would nod enthusiastically whenever they were asked if they would like prayer or a personal relationship with Jesus. One of the women began to come to the Boiler Room meetings. She had the most beautiful voice and before long was helping to lead the worship. The sight and sound of this broken woman singing the song "Beautiful One" consistently reduced everyone to tears. But of course it was also troubling, and Brian called me one day to ask if it was OK to have a prostitute leading worship.

I paused. It wasn't a question I'd ever been asked before. I wondered why she couldn't just stop prostituting herself if she really wanted to follow Jesus.

Brian explained that it wasn't as simple as that. Of course they were trying to help her get free from the sex trade. But she had a madam to whom she owed massive debts. And she was on the island illegally, which meant that she couldn't just get a normal job.

As Brian talked, I realised anew just how messy and morally ambiguous discipleship can become on the front lines of mission. "It certainly sounds like a good problem to have," I said, as brightly as I could.

"Thanks for nothing," said Brian.

When Tracy and other female team members offered to pray with these broken women on the streets, some would immediately take a white handkerchief from their handbags and place it on their heads to receive the blessing. It always seemed such a quaint thing to do, utterly incongruous in the neon-lit streets of San Antonio. It could almost have been amusing if it hadn't been such a poignant indication that behind their current predicament there lay a half-forgotten, happier, churchgoing past.

The problem for many of these women was that they had been trafficked in one way or another. Some may have had drug addictions to feed, some were trying to pay off impossible "debts" owed to their traffickers, others lived in fear of their madam's "juju" curses, and many were diligently sending money home to their children, understandably pretending that they had good jobs in Europe. Every story was utterly heartbreaking.

Over the years, Brian and Tracy's primary prayer for all the ordinary partygoers, musicians, and promoters of Ibiza had been very simple: that they would come to know Jesus. Baptism services in the island's crystal-clear seas were always joyous occasions because they marked the start of a whole new life. But the normal principles of mission didn't seem to apply to these West African sex workers. If acknowledging your sins in prayer, apologising, and beginning a relationship with

The tendency of the rich is to spiritualise the gospel. But if you're hungry you need real bread before you will consider the heavenly variety.

Christ is all that it takes to become a Christian, these women would happily "get saved" every day of the week and twice on Sundays. Yet they didn't seem very safe or saved as a result. Salvation for them seemed far more practical and literal than it might for those whose lives are more privileged and free. They needed to be saved for sure, but it was not just from their own sins but also from the people and systems that controlled their choices, from the authorities trying to deport them, from the cruel powers driving them to prostitute themselves in the first place. Their problems, it seemed, were not primarily spiritual but financial, legal, and even political.

Brian and Tracy were starting to realise that if any one of these women should ever truly want to be free, it would probably be necessary to smuggle her off the island and set her up in a safe house on the Spanish mainland. She might need help getting free from addiction and the years of brutal trauma. If she should choose to stay in Europe, perhaps because her children back home would starve without their current levels of provision, she would need a safe job that could pay almost as much as prostitution. We would probably have to create these jobs for them, since most didn't have the papers to get work officially. Along the way we would also probably have to set up a savings scheme to help them reach the levels of financial stability which could ultimately enable them to return home to a new life with their children and their heads held high.

Such an illicit approach to redemption might well be questionable legally and even ethically, but the alternative course of action might have perpetrated an even greater injustice, either by ignoring their plight altogether, or by condemning them to deportation, social stigma, and extreme poverty back home. When God freed the Israelites from captivity in Egypt he did it literally—not just metaphorically. Similarly, when Jesus forgave the sins of the quadriplegic

The cross of Christ must be brought to bear on the systemic strongholds within societies, as well as the individual realities of sin.

man lowered through the roof he proceeded to heal him physically too. John Wesley and William Wilberforce understood that it wasn't enough just to help slaves believe in the right things, when their most urgent need was clearly to be freed from the physical bonds that controlled them. Down the ages, it has always been the tendency of the rich to reduce salvation to a purely spiritual experience. But if you're hungry you need real bread before you will consider the heavenly variety. If you're in chains you take the Bible verses about freedom very literally indeed.

As Brian and Tracy wrestled with the complex, practical implications of salvation for these West African sex workers, they realised more than ever that the consequences of the gospel are profoundly structural as well as spiritual. The cross of Christ must be brought to bear on the systemic strongholds of sin within societies, as well as the individual realities of personal repentance and morality.

Óscar Romero, the Archbishop of San Salvador who was assassinated for speaking out against injustice, warns us against an overly spiritualised and individualised approach to the gospel:

> It is very easy to be servants of the word without disturbing the world: a very spiritualized word, a word without any commitment to history, a word that can sound in any part of the world because it belongs to no part of the world. A word like that creates no problems, starts no conflicts. What starts conflicts and persecutions, what marks the genuine church, is the word that . . . accuses of sin those who oppose God's reign, so that they may tear that sin out of their hearts, out of their societies, out of their laws—out of the structures that oppress, that imprison, that violate the rights of God and humanity. This is the hard service of the word.[2]

● ● ●

The 7/7 attacks left a lasting scar on London; many of its victims would never fully recover. But eventually the national terror alerts were reduced from red to amber. It was becoming clear that God had placed us here, on the edge of London's financial district, not just to celebrate the glorious history of the Foundery, but also to respond to the worst financial crisis since the Great Depression of the 1930s. The world's markets were suddenly in free fall all around us. Invincible banking institutions were toppling, and systemic corruption was being exposed in our own new backyard. Finding ourselves in the middle of all this, we cried out as best we could for God to restore integrity, to bring down Mammon, to flood the boardrooms and trading floors of London and Wall Street, Tokyo, Hong Kong, and Frankfurt with his spirit of holiness, and to repopulate them with men and women of good conscience. We prayed for the peace and prosperity of the city for the sake of the poor.

Our prayers often seemed weak and even a little absurd in the face of such vast global events, and yet we knew beyond any shadow of a doubt that God had mandated us to partner with him in prayer and to do it here, in this particular place and time. Whenever we felt insignificant and naïve, the history of the Foundery would reassure us that simple prayers and quiet deeds can change the world.

Manenberg

As Phil Togwell continued to lead the charge in London, I tried to do the same elsewhere, talking as often as I could with leaders like Jon Petersen in America, Kelly in Mexico, Brian in Ibiza, and in South Africa, new friends Pete and Sarah Portal. Together they had galvanised a team to plant a community in Manenberg, an apartheid-era "coloured" township blasted by drugs, gang warfare, and one of the highest murder rates in the country.

"How are you guys doing?" I asked Pete one day, via Skype.

"Not so great. Rough day. How are you?"

"Me? Well, I guess I'm having a bad day too!" I'd argued a bit with Sammy and knew that I needed to apologise, the car was playing up, and emails were coming in faster than I could possibly reply.

"What's up?" he asked me kindly.

"You go first," I said. "Spill your guts."

Pete told me that open warfare was erupting once again between the gangs of Manenberg. In fact, he'd woken up that very morning to a stark warning: "Be careful today. There's been heavy shooting." I knew he wasn't exaggerating the dangers; I had visited Manenberg myself and seen a bullet that had come through his office window a few months earlier. Most of their prayer weeks had been punctuated by violence. But this latest battle, Pete said, was proving to be the worst one yet. For the first time ever they'd been wondering about shutting down the prayer room.

One of the people killed in the previous night's shootings had been Pete's friend Blinky, a crystal-meth user who'd approached him in the street wanting to be freed from his addiction. Pete had prayed with Blinky and had led him to Jesus. But he'd returned to his life with a gang called the Jesters, and now it was all too late. Blinky was gone.

"So, uh, yes, it's not been a great day so far." Pete's voice trailed off.

"I'm so sorry," I whispered.

I was far too ashamed to admit how trivial my problems were compared to his.

Two days later I called Pete again. I'd been praying for him and the community in Manenberg a lot, and I was anxious to hear how they were doing.

Jesus promises us "life to the full." We want this to mean a life full of joy, and it does. But it is also a life full of suffering, just like his.

"Oh, it's been a much better day," Pete told me cheerily. He'd been prayer-walking around the township with a friend, symbolically waving white flags, declaring peace over the troubled city in Jesus' name. Along the way they'd met an old man in a baseball cap with a weathered face, watery eyes, and a white beard. His name was Uncle Henry. He was sitting with a pair of crutches.

Uncle Henry had severely injured himself several months earlier by falling off a roof doing repairs. Pete offered to pray for him, and Uncle Henry was instantaneously, miraculously, completely healed. He leaped to his feet, yelping with delight, and began jumping, dancing, and waving his crutches in the air, grinning from ear to ear.

"Do you know who just healed you?" Pete asked him, laughing.

"No!" replied Uncle Henry, still dancing.

Pete told him about Jesus, and Uncle Henry whispered a prayer of surrender between great heaving sobs of thanksgiving. Picking up his crutches, Uncle Henry danced home rejoicing, to the amazement of everyone he knew.

It had been an eventful three days by anyone's standards. Pete had been dodging bullets on Monday, grieving the tragic loss of a friend, and on Wednesday he'd seen a crippled old man healed and saved. One minute in Manenberg Pete's heart was breaking, and the next it was bursting with joy. Several years earlier, when he had abandoned a good job as a researcher at the BBC after graduating with a top degree from Edinburgh University, there were probably a few well-meaning friends who thought he was throwing his life away for the sake of an impoverished community of no-hopers on the other side of the world. But in fact Pete had found life to the full (John 10:10), the kind that a television researcher can, well, only research. The kind of life that makes a difference in the world.

When he first arrived in South Africa, Pete had spent the best part of a year simply prayer-walking around Manenberg, allowing his heart to break for its evident pain. During that year of prayer, Pete led four people to Jesus, but three of them had fallen away and returned to their previous lives. But he'd also met Sarah, a beautiful Capetonian with blue eyes and brightly coloured feathers in her raven hair. They got married and spent her inheritance buying a house in Manenberg, a place where few white people dared to go, let alone live. "If you give me everything you've got," the Lord had told them, "I'll give you everything I've got."

Sarah set about making their new township home beautiful with brightly coloured walls, a garden of raised flower beds, a prayer room, and an entire section where men who want to get free from drugs and gangs can live in safety. It was a home worthy of the beautiful community Pete and Sarah were determined to grow with their friends in the streets of Manenberg.[3] Like Kelly in Boy's Town and Brian in Ibiza, they were experiencing remarkable breakthroughs as they sought to bring good news to the poor.

They were also beginning to ask important questions about the structures of injustice afflicting so many lives. Uncle Henry, for instance, had been dramatically healed and saved, but he wasn't interested in joining their community to receive further discipleship, so how was he ever going to truly change? It was becoming increasingly clear to Pete and Sarah that the answer for Manenberg was more complicated than just getting everyone healed and praying a prayer. Something was wrong with the place systemically, and it was only going to be changed by a profound cultural shift. Their acts of daily mercy on the ground would amount to little more than sticking plasters on the wound until God's healing was applied to Manenberg itself.

•   •   •

The broken people with whom we were increasingly dealing, in Ibiza, in Boy's Town, in Manenberg, and around the world, needed this kind of help—practical provision as well as spiritual truth, justice as well as charity, long-term hope as well as short-term help. If we were really serious about "justice for the poor," it was going to require more of us than just a little costly kindness and compassion. The Heasleys were learning this in Ibiza amongst the West African sex workers; the Portals were realising it too in the crossfire between Manenberg's gangs; and Kelly could see it in Boy's Town, where the mafia could make or break you and where each person she managed to rescue just seemed to be replaced by another victim. She knew that this weary flow of inhumanity would continue unabated until Boy's Town was properly regulated or, better still, knocked to the ground.

Kelly had invited me to visit her in Reynosa, and I was keen to go. I wanted to see the new Boiler Room complex she was building and to meet some of the wild characters she'd so often described. I suppose I'd expected Boy's Town to be dark, depressing, and ugly, and yet, within its concrete walls, I was about to experience a moment of luminous beauty.

SELAH

Do all the good you can,
By all the means you can
In all the ways you can,
In all the places you can,
At all the times you can,
To all the people you can,
As long as ever you can.
JOHN WESLEY

Thank you, Father, for the radical example of John Wesley. Raise
up such women and men again in this generation, to pray as
he prayed, to preach as he preached, and to fight injustice too.
Amen.

There is not a square inch of domain of our human existence
over which Christ, who is sovereign over all, does not cry: "It is
mine!"

ABRAHAM KUYPER, FORMER DUTCH PRIME MINISTER

13

DIRTY DANCING

MEXICO • UK

I should believe only in a God who understood how to dance.

FRIEDRICH NIETZSCHE, *THUS SPOKE ZARATHUSTRA*

One of the women walking towards us was wearing a white bikini top with jean shorts and smoking a fat Cuban cigar. The other one had pulled her grey T-shirt up to reveal her naked breasts. When they saw us coming they began to smile and wave.

"*Hola!*" the ladies screamed, throwing their arms around Kelly. "*Buenas tardes.*"

"Hey, let me introduce you," laughed Kelly. "Norah and Cubana, this is my pastor from America. His name is Roger Nix. And this is my friend Pete. He's from England."

I wasn't entirely sure how to greet a topless woman in a place like Boy's Town. For a moment I considered a handshake, but Cubana came in for a hug, smelling like smoke and pickled jalapenos. And then, with formalities dispensed, the three women were off, talking frenetically in Spanish as if they hadn't seen each other for years. Roger and I stood there a little awkwardly, grinning inanely, laughing at jokes we didn't understand. Norah paused to take a drag on her cigar and flashed a single gold tooth in my direction. I smiled back, trying desperately to maintain eye contact, trying not to let my gaze wander south.

Kelly had been hoping that we might bump into Norah and Cubana that night. "To know Cubana," she'd told us grandly, "is to know Boy's Town. No one knows how long she's been there, least of all Cubana! She's kind of a fixture of the place, a symbol of it all."

The three women linked arms happily, Kelly in the middle, Cubana still topless, Norah still puffing on that large cigar, and they set off walking. "Norah's invited us to her place," called Kelly over her shoulder.

How on earth did I ever get here? I wondered, feeling a very long way from home.

Norah welcomed us into her dilapidated room like a duchess receiving visitors to her castle. "*Bienvenido!*" she said, flicking the stub of her cigar out into the street and indicating a couple of white plastic chairs.

I sat down next to a deep-fat fryer as Norah busied herself making tea. Cubana had disappeared, but Roger folded his lanky frame into the other plastic chair and Kelly perched herself on the edge of the bed. Above us a fan on the ceiling lazily stirred the hot, heavy air. The room was lit by a single fluorescent tube. On the wall there was a colossal, incongruous mural depicting Santa Claus. And by the window I noticed a selection of confectionery for sale. Kelly had often seen people unconscious on the floor in here, so she knew it wasn't just candy.

Outside I could see women lining the dirt road in their underwear, haloed against brightly lit doorways like plastic mannequins in empty shop windows waiting to be dressed. Some were girls trying to look like women. Some were women trying to look like girls. Every minute or so a faceless predator would prowl slowly past in a growling pick-up or a car with tinted windows. It was all strangely sexless. I had wondered if I might feel angry on my first night in Boy's Town. I'd feared I might feel aroused. But in fact all I felt was a vast and overwhelming sadness.

A small, rounded man appeared at the door, blocking my view, holding a Spanish guitar. "A *mariachi!*" exclaimed Kelly with delight, immediately inviting him inside. "It's a Mexican tradition," she explained. "Folk music."

With a flourish, he strolled into the room, squeezing his portly frame between Roger's chair and mine, to station himself beside Kelly beneath Santa's cheery gaze. Then he threw back his head and began crooning like Julio Iglesias. Norah was handing tea to Roger, Kelly was reclining with Father Christmas, and we all just grinned and tried to sing along.

I glanced at Kelly's pastor, sitting in the other plastic chair. He was singing along with Julio at the top of his voice while Norah, our drug-dealing host, a semi-retired hooker in a white bikini, was trying to serve him tea. I had always liked Roger, but I was about to fall in love with the guy. Here he was paying a pastoral visit to a member of his flock, half a world away from Tulsa, Oklahoma, yet he seemed to be completely at ease. Roger's the kind of pastor who encourages everyone he meets. He's a lover of people, a faithful husband and fun-loving friend. Watching him now, singing his heart out in Norah's home, holding his tea aloft as if it was a flagon of German ale, I remembered the dramatic way he'd been called into church leadership, late one night alone in a 24-7 prayer room. It had been a holy thing, the details of which he rarely shares.

Slowly, deliberately, Roger stood up, put down his tea, and reached out a hand to touch Norah's shoulder. She winced and spun around to search his eyes for clues, expecting the inevitable assault. But Roger just smiled, completely unfazed. Carefully placing his other hand on her other arm, he politely invited her to dance, as if her bikini was a ball-gown and she was queen of the prom. Glancing at Kelly for reassurance, Norah relented. Seeing this, the *mariachi* strummed flamenco and sang even louder while the Tulsa pastor innocently took the former hooker in his arms, and began to guide her gently around her little room. Norah smiled, flashing that one gold tooth, enjoying for a moment the sense of dignity in the company of a man without any ulterior motive.

Outside in the street men were prowling, inflamed with lust, and women were selling themselves, too broken to care. But inside Norah's tiny house, that night, the *mariachi* sang, Norah danced, and I swear I sensed the Father smile. It was an exquisite picture of grace. One of the most beautiful dances I'll ever see.

• • •

Incarnation, if it means anything more than a "Once upon a time" story, means grace is carnal; healing comes through flesh.
SAM KEEN, *TO A DANCING GOD*

There are people, I suppose, who might question the judgment of a pastor who dances with a woman like Norah, in a depraved and dangerous place like Boy's Town. Their concerns are legitimate. The apostle Paul warns us starkly against the merest "hint of . . . immorality" (Ephesians 5:3). The evils of environments like Boy's Town must never be minimised, romanticised, or subtly condoned. Vulnerable people can sometimes be exploited, even by those with noble intentions.

But Jesus refused to play it safe. In Christ we find the name above every other name, the single key to eternal salvation, recklessly risking his reputation for the sake of love. He clearly didn't care about the opinions of the religious establishment, wasn't afraid of being corrupted by sinful company, didn't feel the need to protect his precious brand. Again and again, Jesus chose to plant his glory in the dirt.

On one occasion, when Jesus was dining at the house of Levi with "many tax-collectors and sinners," the watching Pharisees expressed alarm. Levi had a roadside tax-booth beside the lake, so it's likely that his business involved taxing the local fishing industry. Imagine how unpopular he must have been amongst Galilee's hard-working fishermen, including a number of Jesus' other disciples. These hardy men would stay out on the lake all night, in all weathers, their fingers numb and calloused from the water and the nets, returning in the morning cold and aching, smelling of stale sweat and fish, only to have Levi, a soft-skinned charlatan sitting comfortably in the shade of his booth, demand a cut of their toil. Levi was considered a parasite exploiting

The name above every other name recklessly risked it all for the sake of love. Jesus chose to plant his glory in the dirt.

everyone else's endeavours. To make matters worse, he was collecting their money on behalf of a pagan invader. Levi was an enemy collaborator, a brazen traitor, probably corrupt. Tax-collectors like Levi were the most hated figures in Jesus' world. In fact they were automatically excommunicated from worship in the synagogues, and excluded from testifying in Jewish courts of law. The very food Jesus was eating that day had probably been paid for by extortion and collaboration with an oppressive regime. As for his fellow diners, they must have been equally unscrupulous characters: pariahs, sycophants, and chancers.

No wonder the Pharisees muttered, "Why does he eat with tax collectors?" And yet Jesus responded to their challenge without the slightest hint of apology: "It is not the healthy who need a doctor," he said defiantly, "but those who are ill. I have not come to call the righteous, but sinners" (Mark 2:17).

Men like Levi and women like Norah tend to know that they are sick. They are rarely proud. Their problems are often on public display. If you've spent your life eating pizza and smoking twenty cigarettes a day and your doctor tells you you're at risk of a heart attack, you probably don't need much convincing. But if you've been highly disciplined all your life, meticulously watching your diet, diligently exercising at the gym, and priding yourself on your six-pack, you may doubt the doctor's counsel, or you may not visit him at all.

Jesus sought out those who knew they were sick, those who freely acknowledged their brokenness, those who were most aware of their sin. He knew that he could remain spiritually healthy whilst eating with tax-collectors and hanging out with sex workers, because holiness is a matter of the heart, not vulnerable to external corruption. "What goes into someone's mouth does not defile them," he told his disciples on one occasion. "Out of the heart come evil thoughts—murder, adultery, sexual immorality, theft, false testimony, slander. These are what defile a person" (Matthew 15:10, 19-20).

Kelly had moved to Boy's Town trusting that it is entirely possible to live a holy life in a dirty place. Brian had transplanted his family to Ibiza because he knows that "the one who is in you is greater than the one who is in the world" (1 John 4:4). Jon Petersen could sit in a caravan wallpapered with pornography, proclaiming the gospel to a drunk pirate, because he knew that the Holy Spirit in him was more contagious than the dirty spirit at work in his friend. And in Norah's room that night, watching a pastor from one of the most religious places in the Western world risking his reputation for a moment of grace with a single broken soul, I saw this same contagious holiness in action.

The Power of "With"

In their book *Living without Enemies* Samuel Wells and Marcia Owen outline four distinct approaches to Christian social engagement.

1. *Working for* the oppressed.
2. *Working with* the oppressed.
3. *Being for* the oppressed.
4. *Being with* the oppressed.

All four models are important, but the authors particularly encourage us to move beyond the remedial approach of "working for" those who are oppressed (fundraising, campaigning, advocacy, and so on), towards the more intimate posture of "being with" them instead.

> *Being with* is not fundamentally about finding solutions, but about companionship amid struggle and distress. Sometimes the obsession with finding solutions can get in the way of forming profound relationships . . . and sometimes those relationships are more significant than solutions.[1]

"Companionship amid struggle and distress" eloquently describes Kelly's model of engagement in Boy's Town, the Portals' relational response to oppression in Manenberg, and the Heasleys' incarnational activities in

Ibiza. Ultimately, it was the approach of Jesus himself, the Word who "became flesh and made his dwelling among us" (John 1:14).

Personal engagement tends to be slow, costly, and prosaic. Perhaps campaigning can feel heroic, sponsoring projects might assuage the conscience, lobbying governments can be strategic, naming injustices from the pulpit may appear noble. But befriending broken people is rarely any of these things. It's as unglamorous as inviting the lonely old lady in your street for dinner and when she says "no," taking the meal to her house instead. It might mean welcoming the disabled boy who screams and even undresses during the sermon, thanking his embarrassed father for coming,

Whenever a passion for justice loses its compassionate heart for individuals, it ceases to be truly Christian in its motivation and approach.

and asking how you can help them both to come again. Or it could mean befriending the most unpopular girl on your course, and persisting with kindness when she tries to push you away (as she probably will).

Even as I write, I'm recalling a man who started attending a new church that Sammy and I once planted. Sadly, he smelled so bad that we would often have to open the windows when he arrived, even in winter. I'm ashamed to admit that we started to joke a bit, behind his back, about the pungent smell.

Three young women invited this unfortunate man home for lunch. This in itself was a big thing to do. By spending time with him, they discovered that he couldn't afford a washing machine. They clubbed together and bought him the best washer they could afford.

It's way too easy to romanticise the poor, or to politicise social justice, or to categorise the struggle as something distant, exotic, and dramatic. The actions of those three women remind us that a truly Christian response to suffering is essentially personal. It may well be important to advocate for the poor politically, to fight against systems of oppression structurally, to shop ethically. But Jesus teaches us to earth such engagement in localised compassion. Resisting those who wanted him to take a far stronger political stance against Roman tyranny, Jesus changed the world by changing hearts.

When Jesus saw that the crowds "were harassed and helpless, like sheep without a shepherd," we are told that he "had compassion" on them (Matthew 9:36). (On another occasion we are told that he wept.) The word for "compassion" used in this verse comes from the Greek *splanxna*, which literally denotes the guts and vital organs, the seat of human emotion. Jesus was gutted by the plight of the masses, winded with grief, deeply upset by their despair.

It's one thing to oppose the prejudice of homophobia, but a deeper thing altogether when you sit and suffer with one of its victims as they show you the obscene threats being inexplicably posted through their door. It's one thing to sign an e-petition about the refugee crisis, and quite another to listen to the stories of a Syrian man who has lost his wife and children crossing the Mediterranean Sea. It's vital that we campaign against human trafficking, but it's another thing entirely to step into a place like Boy's Town and invite a lady like Norah to dance.

Mercy

Roger showed Norah mercy and gave her dignity because he himself has experienced Christ's mercy in his own life. We may not like to admit it (we may not be *able* to admit it), but each one of us is just as broken and needy as Norah. We have all done things, suffered things, and been to places so dark that we would surely rather hide them from his eyes. Our lives may appear more respectable and far less troubled, but when we stand before our Saviour, we do so like Norah in her white bikini, our poverty on display and our nakedness exposed.

> You see, at just the right time, when we were still powerless,
> Christ died for the ungodly . . . God demonstrates his own love
> for us in this: while we were still sinners, Christ died for us.
>
> ROMANS 5:6-8

If this verse means anything at all, it means this: that we were filthy and hopeless, trapped in our own equivalents of Norah's many prisons; we were wrestling with a tangled mess of inner compulsions strangling our souls; we were "still sinners" when Jesus looked at us and loved us and deemed us worth trading his life for our own. He arrived at the door, long before we'd fixed our hair or fixed our teeth, before we could put on a suit or put out our cigar, before we'd cleared our search history, kicked the drugs, or dried the tears. Jesus showed up before we had done anything at all to heal ourselves or save ourselves or make ourselves more deserving, when we were still just an unholy, seething mess. He stepped into our world "at just the right time" (which is to say, "just in the nick of time"). He saw us as we truly are, sat down in a plastic chair, and then, against all sensible expectations, stood with great dignity, faced us squarely in our shame, and with a smile invited us to dance.

> Perfection is not required of us. Honesty and the willingness
> to own up to what we are: this is what is required. When we
> finally receive this, when we outgrow our hankering after
> flawlessness and know that we are broken sinners, then we can
> discover the priceless joy of grace—we are accepted, accepted
> by that which is greater than us, however we name it. We are
> accepted. We are accepted. And that is all.
> DAVE TOMLINSON, *THE BAD CHRISTIAN'S MANIFESTO*

From Boy's Town I flew to Kansas City—my first visit since returning to England—and found the Boiler Room community thriving. In fact, to accommodate their growth they had moved into a super-cool, multistorey industrial unit on Main Street where they had installed a prayer room, a recording studio, space for local artists, classrooms for training, kitchens, and bedrooms for hospitality. All six of our Boiler Room values were evident in every corner of that building, and with its bare brick and exposed pipework, aluminium, and polished concrete, it was like wandering around a Foundery for the hipster generation.

From Kansas City I flew to England with a full heart, longing to tell Sammy about all the wonderful things God had been doing with our friends in America and Mexico in the months since we'd returned to the UK.

• • •

The kids had adjusted well to life back home in Chichester, the unlikely English city where the movement had begun. Their cute American accents were fading fast, and they'd settled into new schools. Sammy was doing better too; her tumour wasn't growing back, her seizures were becoming less frequent, and with our boys now at school, she was beginning to ask questions about the future.

"So what are you going to do?" I asked her one day, sitting at the kitchen table, warming my hands around a mug of steaming coffee. For years she'd been in and out of hospital, living on a knife edge, awaiting the next seizure or recovering from the last one. Her drugs left her exhausted and she'd often slept half the day. At times we'd not been sure if she would even have a future to discuss.

Sammy paused and took a sip of coffee. She opened her mouth to speak, but then just sighed. Addressing her coffee cup, she whispered, "No, it's impossible . . ."

"What? What's impossible? Any chance I can join the conversation here?"

She smiled coyly. "Well, when I was at school my dream was always to teach. I wanted to study English literature, but obviously that's impossible now."

I stared at her in amazement, wondering how it was possible to be married to someone for a decade, and still know so little about them. I couldn't recall Sammy ever having read a single serious piece of literature in all the years I'd known her. She'd never been to university—no one in her family had ever been to university. She had dropped out of school, moved to Chichester, landed a job, been promoted, joined a covers band, married me, had kids, got sick. That was her story. Never in all the years I'd known her had she ever mentioned this secret desire to teach.

"Look, I realise it's ridiculous," she said again, taking another sip of coffee. "And anyway, I don't suppose I'd ever be well enough to teach. And even if I could, I'd need a degree and I dropped out of school, so that's obviously never going to happen, and I'm just not academic or clever, so forget it, OK?"

A few months later Sammy bravely returned to school as a mature student to study alongside a bunch of seventeen-year-olds. She made a plan for how she'd cope if she had a seizure in class, or alone on the train. It was one of the most courageous things I'd ever seen. Then she began the intimidating process of applying to universities without any of the usual qualifications. We made sure that her application read like something from the movie *Dead Poets Society*: "I almost died and now I know that the only thing that matters in life is . . . English literature!" It was an exaggeration, of course, but it did the trick, and she received unconditional offers without any of the necessary grades. Suddenly my wife was sitting up in bed at night reading Jane Austen, Robert Frost, Kazuo Ishiguro, and John Keats.

Ode to My Nightingale

One of the difficult, shameful things that no one ever admits about the fallout from long-term illness within a marriage is the insidious way that romance can be poisoned merely by monotony. Without realising it, Sammy and I had been drifting apart. America had helped us recover, but there was an increasing dissonance between the worlds we inhabited. We sometimes ventured out for date nights, and I would tell her about all the exciting places I'd been and all the cool people I'd met. Sammy might respond by telling me that she'd managed to do a little housework, but it had wiped her out and she'd needed to sleep till the kids came home from school. I sensed that she was starting to resent my many adventures, and I'm ashamed to admit that, for my part, I was starting to find her restricted life a bit tedious and dull.

A few weeks into Sammy's course, we ventured out one night for a date, probably more out of duty than desire. We sat at a quiet table in a busy restaurant by candlelight, nursing our drinks. With a deep breath I asked her how she was doing. Slowly she told me that she'd been studying Keats's "Ode to a Nightingale." It's a dark meditation, she explained, on transcience and mortality in a world seeking ephemeral pleasure. Then she leaned forward, as if she was about to tell me a secret. Keats had written the poem as he grieved the death of his teenage brother from tuberculosis. His mother had died of the same disease when he was fourteen; his other brother was to die of it too. Keats himself probably contracted it in the very act of nursing his brother. Within twenty months of writing the ode, he would die of tuberculosis too.

No one ever admits that chronic illness within a marriage can poison romance merely with boredom.

It was a gloomy topic of conversation for a date night, but Sammy was telling me these things with a passion I'd not seen for a very long time, and I found myself drawn in and immersed. She understood the tragedy of Keats's story and the fragility of life better than most. And then, quietly, as if speaking from a place far away, she began to recite a section of the poem:

> The weariness, the fever, and the fret
> Here, where men sit and hear each other groan;
> Where palsy shakes a few, sad, last grey hairs,
> Where youth grows pale, and spectre-thin, and dies . . .

Her voice trailed away. She looked up and there were tears in her eyes, sparkling in the candlelight. I guess there were tears in my eyes too, because she smiled, touched my hand, and continued in a whisper:

Where but to think is to be full of sorrow
And leaden-eyed despairs;
Where beauty cannot keep her lustrous eyes,
Or new Love pine at them beyond to-morrow
Away! away! for I will fly to thee . . .

I was lost for words. The woman in front of me had always been beautiful, but here was something new. She was also becoming ardent, enigmatic, and wise. I was falling in love with my own wife all over again.

As her studies continued, Sammy came alive. Years of illness seemed to have given her an unusual depth of critical insight and a white-hot determination to prove to the entire world that her brain might have seen the light of day but it was just fine, thank you very much. I watched her grow in confidence, fighting occasional seizures and constant tiredness to attend lectures, read books, write essays, and meet deadlines. The woman who'd always considered herself non-academic was discovering that in fact she loved learning, and she was good at it. On the day that she graduated as the top student in her entire year, I was the proudest man alive. Illness had robbed her of so many precious moments: summer days she'd merely slept, memories of our children, adventures I'd undertaken alone. Now, at last, the Lord was redeeming her loss, repaying her for all the opportunities and memories the locusts had eaten (Joel 2:25).

God was clearly doing a new work in Sammy, and in our marriage too. We remembered Blue Camp 20 and sensed the Lord inviting us to pioneer together once again. Prayer rooms and Boiler Rooms were multiplying, new ministries were being born from them, young leaders were being trained. With so much activity spread across so many countries, we were sensing the need to establish some kind of hub for the movement—a 24-7 community that could serve and resource all these other amazing works. Sammy and I began to pray about where we should plant such a hub, sadly sensing that it was probably time to leave Chichester, where we'd first met, where 24-7 had begun, where our kids had been born. We drew up a short list of possible locations: a church we'd been offered in London, a farm in

Scotland, a place in Brighton. Somewhere near the bottom of our list was Guildford, where we'd launched 24-7 in Bojanglez nightclub under that big red moon.

Our old, wise friend Jon Petersen urged us to include our sons in this process of discernment. "It's important," he said, no doubt recalling his own kids growing up in Amsterdam, "that your children really feel that they're part of the team and that they learn to hear God's voice for themselves." It sounded good, but still seemed a little weird to share such a big decision with a four-year-old and a six-year-old, but we dutifully did it, praying every night at bedtime, asking God to show us where he wanted us to live.

• • •

Walking home from school one afternoon, Hudson turned to Sammy and said, "Mum, I can hear a voice in my head."

"Well, don't listen to it," Sammy snapped in alarm. Was he cracking up?

"But it's a nice voice," he insisted.

"Don't listen to it," she said again. "Nice ones can be the worst."

"But . . . Mum," he said firmly, "I think it might be God!"

Sammy stopped walking and stared at the little boy, riding on the buggy-board attached to the back of his little brother's pushchair. His enormous brown eyes were staring up at hers, unblinking. She reminded herself that we were supposed to believe in this kind of thing. The Bible talks about kids hearing voices. Maybe it didn't have to be a sign of mental illness after all. Maybe she should listen . . .

"OK, Huddy . . ." she said warily, "so what's the voice in your head saying?"

"Guildford," he said emphatically. "God's saying we're supposed to move to Guildford."

A few days later we took both boys for their favourite Chinese meal. I watched Hudson trying to use chopsticks. Danny was perched next to him on a cushion, his white-blond hair standing on end as if it had been electrostatically charged. "Danny," I said seriously, "your big brother thinks that God is telling us to move to Guildford. But you've been praying about it too. What do you think?"

Daniel looked at me earnestly, and placed his podgy little hands on the table. "I think," he said, speaking with as much gravitas as a six-year-old can muster, slowly screwing up his face and staring at the ceiling. But he said nothing else. Danny seemed to have fallen into a trance. Eventually Sammy whispered an encouraging "Yes, darling?"

He scanned our faces, clearly enjoying the undivided attention of his entire family for once. "I think God is saying that if we move to Guildford, can we please have a dog?"

We roared with laughter. Danny laughed too, though he didn't know why.

God speaks to his children in different ways, at different times. To some his voice comes supernaturally, through angelic messengers, prophetic dreams, or audible voices like the one that Hudson heard. But mostly he speaks with a still, small voice, through the Bible, common sense, or even the very sensible desire for a puppy!

After the Chinese meal, I phoned Jon Petersen. "We've been praying with the kids about relocation and, well, Daniel wants a dog."

I could hear Jon chuckling. "And Huddy?" he asked.

"How much weight," I asked, "should we put on a six-year-old hearing the audible voice of God?"

Jon laughed again. "You'd be nuts to move your entire family purely on the basis of a six-year-old hearing a voice," he said. "But you'd be nuts to ignore it, too."

Guildford unexpectedly jumped to the top of our list, and we started to realise why. There was already a Boiler Room community in town. It was where we'd originally launched 24-7. Local churches seemed keen for us to come. It's a thriving university city close to the centre of London, half an hour from the nation's two main airports and an hour from ferries to the European mainland. In fact, Guildford suddenly seemed such a sensible place for an international hub, we were a bit embarrassed that it had taken an audible voice from heaven to point it out.

● ● ●

While we were preparing to move to Guildford, Kelly was hunkering down for the long haul in Mexico. She had come to accept the many challenges of life in Reynosa and was busy building a centre on the outskirts of Boy's Town, preparing to become that wrinkly old lady she'd seen in her dream. She'd accepted that this was now where she would live the rest of her life and that she might never have much of a team or any money. She had even managed to accept the prospect of being single. It wasn't what she wanted, certainly not a "gift" she felt she had been given, but she just couldn't imagine any man wanting to share the life she now lived with people like gold-toothed Norah and topless Cubana in a dead-end border town.

She had decided to accept these things, and even to embrace them, because she wanted to live joyfully. She didn't want to become the kind of old missionary she'd sometimes encountered, who yells at comfortable Americans back home. She wanted to be content.

Her new centre was being constructed predominantly by visiting teams of fit young American men who came to give a week or more to help move the project along. Kelly was seriously considering a vow of celibacy, until one of these volunteers caught her eye. When Zach Tietsort returned to Tulsa, she was alarmed to find herself missing him, and even more alarmed at the happiness she felt when he started to call. Sixteen months later, Kelly and Zach were married and living in Reynosa.

Within a month of their return to Mexico, the border slammed shut behind them. Rival cartels in Reynosa were now openly at war. A group of hired assassins called the Zetes had broken away from the Gulf Cartel in an attempt to take control of the city's drug trade. They worshipped Santa Muerte, the goddess of death. Meanwhile another gang, the Sinaloa Cartel, was trying to muscle in for a piece of the lucrative action. Local and federal police had been mobilised in Reynosa; even the Mexican military had been sent in. It was like the Wild West. There were open shoot-outs in the streets between the warring gangs, the police and the army. Sixty people were killed at the local supermarket alone.

Kelly and Zach's first child was born, after ten months of married life, into this civil war. The maternity ward was massively understaffed, with everyone trying to get out of town. The city was under curfew because it had become too dangerous to leave home after dark. With all the usual protective instincts of new parents, Kelly and Zach checked Hazel out of the hospital when she was eleven days old and drove her carefully back to their little home near Boy's Town. That first night there were loud explosions, grenades going off all around them, killing everywhere, and Hazel just screaming in the middle of it all. It wasn't a safe place for a baby. It wasn't a safe place for anyone. Yet Kelly and Zach were determined to stick it out. People like Norah and Cubana couldn't just run away when the shooting started. Their friends in Boy's Town needed support more than ever.

But gradually even Boy's Town began to close down. Many of the women went into hiding. Some of them urged Kelly to take her baby and get out quick. But she still wasn't sure. Hadn't God sent them here?

Then one day Kelly was at home with Hazel and the front door was open because the day was so hot. She was trying to hang a picture when suddenly the shooting outside got louder. A man with a semi-automatic rifle appeared at the door. Kelly wanted to scream. Her eyes raced involuntarily to the baby's stroller. "O God," she said. The man with the gun looked at her, then moved down the street.

Kelly's heart was racing. Now she knew for sure that they were not immune to the danger and that they had no divine right to gamble with the safety of the little girl God had given them. She called Zach, and they grabbed Hazel, locked the doors of the new centre, and fled across the border, thanking God for their American passports.

The war in Reynosa raged on for weeks and months. The population halved. The place became completely lawless. Meanwhile, far away in Tulsa, Kelly's prayers turned continually to her many friends in Boy's Town. Anxiously she thought of Cubana and of Norah's little room with the Santa Claus mural, wondering how they both were, if they'd even survived the violence, often feeling guilty at having abandoned them and all her other friends in Reynosa. Sometimes she wondered whether all her hard work, all her years of prayer and love, had come to nothing, trampled under the hobnail boots of the cartels and the demonic blood-lust of Santa Muerte.

Liliana

Then one day Kelly received a message from an old friend in Reynosa about an American couple who had met a woman selling pastries on the Hidalgo Bridge. She introduced herself as Liliana and willingly recounted a tragic tale of stomach cancer and heavy drugs in a place called Boy's Town. She interspersed her story with the strangest phrase: "Jesus loves Kelly." Again and again: "Jesus loves Kelly."

"Who is this Kelly?" they asked.

"I had cancer, but now I am healed because Jesus loves Kelly," said Liliana. "I was addicted to drugs, but now I am clean because Jesus loves Kelly. I was in Boy's Town, but now I have my own place to live. It's all because of Miss Kelly. She asked Jesus for these things, and he gave them to her for me because—Jesus loves Kelly!"

"I had cancer, but now I am healed. I was addicted to drugs, but now I am clean because Jesus loves Kelly!"

Kelly began to weep. In Boy's Town Liliana had gone by another name. Liliana was none other than Cubana, the topless lady we'd met that night with Norah. Cubana, of whom it was said "to know her is to know Boy's Town." Cubana, who'd been fighting stomach cancer and had often asked Kelly for prayer. Cubana, who'd been addicted to the strongest drugs for longer than anyone could remember. Liliana (or Lily), whose name means "purity." Somehow Cubana had survived the war. She was out of Boy's Town, free from drugs. And she had even, it seemed, been healed. It was almost too much to absorb. Kelly's heart erupted with great sobs of joy, thanking God for sending word that her prayers and her tears and her years in Boy's Town had not been wasted after all.

• • •

The works of God are eternal. "My word that goes out from my mouth," he says, "will not return to me empty, but will accomplish what I desire and achieve the purpose for which I sent it" (Isaiah 55:11). Nothing we sow for the Lord is ever wasted—no prayer, no kindness, no sacrifice. The seed may be buried for a while, but it will come to fruition in due season. Kelly now knew that the tiny seeds she had sown in Boy's Town had not been wasted. They had been buried, for sure. They had apparently died. But now, it seemed, there were inklings of a harvest still to come.

The book of Revelation describes twenty-four elders in heaven holding bowls full of the prayers of God's people, ready to be poured out at the end of the age (Revelation 5:8, 16; 21:4). It's a powerful reassurance that whenever a prayer seems to have gone unanswered or a seed seems to have died in the ground, it has in fact been cherished by God and now awaits a fulfilment to come greater than any permutation we can possibly currently imagine.

SELAH

The four living creatures and the twenty-four elders fell down before the Lamb. Each one had a harp and they were holding golden bowls full of incense, which are the prayers of God's people. And they sang a new song, saying: "You are worthy . . ."
REVELATION 5:8-9

I give you back today the prayers I've prayed that are not answered—yet. The seeds I've sown that haven't borne a harvest—yet. The dreams I've buried, that haven't risen—yet. Restore the years, the prayers, the trust that the locusts have eaten. Remember me, Lord, redeem my life, and answer my oldest, truest prayers. Amen.

JOY

GOD'S PRESENCE IN US

I will give them joy in my house of prayer.

ISAIAH 56:7

The Holy Spirit turns to joy whatever he touches.

ST. SERAPHIM OF SAROV, 1754–1833

14
LET US BEGIN
ENGLAND · AUSTRIA · EVERYWHERE ELSE

Brothers, let us begin, for until now we have done little or nothing.

FRANCIS OF ASSISI

My phone buzzed. A text message from a friend: "If you keep prioritising the poor," it said, "the Lord is going to give you the palaces too."

We didn't know anyone with a spare palace. Palaces weren't really on
our prayer list. That bit was obviously just a metaphor; an encouragement to keep loving people like Cubana in Boy's Town, scraping drunks
off the street in San Antonio, dignifying drug abusers in Vancouver's
Downtown East Side, loving gangsters on the Cape Flats, putting
shoes on the feet of Roma children in Macedonia, campaigning against
human trafficking around the world. Prayer and the poor: that's us.
Palaces? Not so much.

Then, just a few days after the prophecy, I received a phone call.

"Hello. Is this Pete Greig?" A foreign accent. Unknown number.

"Yep, this is me."

"Pete, I am calling on behalf of Cardinal Schönborn, the Archbishop
of Vienna."

"Um, wow . . . hello Vienna!"

I'd met the cardinal a couple of times. He's one of the most important church leaders in the world, having edited the *Catechism of the Catholic Church*, and even having helped to elect Pope Francis.

"The cardinal would like to extend a formal invitation to you—to the 24-7 prayer movement—to come to Austria next year. I think it is your fifteenth birthday, no?"

"Um, yes. That's right."

"Well, the cardinal would like you to come here to Vienna to celebrate in his cathedral."

"Wow!" I said again, struggling to process what I was hearing. It's not every day that a Catholic cardinal cold-calls a maverick prayer movement, offering the keys to his cathedral. As for Vienna, it ranks as one of the coolest places on earth. It's the city of Strauss, Freud, and Einstein, with St. Stephen's as its iconic central edifice.

But I needed to think. The towering Stephansdom would be a very long way indeed from the quiet back-street warehouse where we'd begun, even further from Bojanglez, the semi-derelict nightclub in which we'd kicked things off under the biggest, fattest red moon you ever saw.

"That's incredibly generous of the cardinal," I said. "Please thank him. Sincerely. It's very kind. But it's just not us. We tend to meet in nightclubs with sticky floors, not world heritage sites. I'm worried that we won't, um, fit in or be true to ourselves in such magnificent surroundings."

I detected a slight chuckle from Vienna. "Well, if you really don't want to use the cardinal's palace, it's completely up to you."

The word *palace* hit me like a jet of icy water. Could it be God on the phone from Vienna? Was I about to slam a door in his face?

The thought of celebrating our fifteenth birthday in a grand palace and a Catholic cathedral was frankly terrifying. It would be messy, complicated, and disruptive. But if the previous years had taught us anything at all, it was simply to say yes to God and work out the details along the way.

• • •

It was a mild October evening, and in the gathering darkness, tourists in horse-drawn carriages and crowds on foot marvelled at Vienna's fairytale cathedral. Its magnificent Gothic spires seemed to erupt from the Stephansplatz like stalagmites from the floor of a cave. Inside the cathedral, I looked around at thousands of expectant worshippers and drew a deep breath, trying not to show my nerves. The stakes were far higher than most of the crowd realised. They were understandably excited about letting rip in such a cool building and looking forward to the after-party later that night across the street in the palace. But I knew that, in almost a thousand years of this cathedral's history, there had only ever been three other services involving non-Catholics. At the first one, quite recently, worshippers had actually stormed out, physically shaking with rage at the mere inclusion of Protestant believers.

On the other side of the ecclesiastical fence, I knew that some Free Church pastors were boycotting our event because it was taking place in a Catholic cathedral. Here we were, gathered just 350 miles south of Wittenberg, where Martin Luther nailed his ninety-five theses to the church door 500 years ago, and the wounds of division were still unhealed.

I scanned the faces in the crowd, looking for a little reassurance. Most were chatting, grinning enthusiastically; a few were earnestly already praying. A nun was talking to a guy in horn-rimmed spectacles whose arm, covered in tattoos, hung round the neck of a girl with hair bleached white. I noticed a Catholic bishop standing quietly by a pillar observing the scene, and wondered what he was thinking.

The sensitivities of the night seemed daunting, but a conviction began to take hold of me, quite forcefully, that we had no right to consider ourselves a prayer movement unless we participated actively, not just notionally, in Christ's great unanswered prayer for "complete unity" (John 17:23). What if Christian reconciliation is more than just a naïve ideal for religious hippies? What if it is a burning necessity and a strategic priority? What if our Lord is as passionate about the unity of his family today as he is about worship, justice for the poor, and the fulfilment of his Great Commission? "By this," he says unambiguously, "everyone will know that you are my disciples, if you love one another" (John 13:35). Isn't it time we obeyed? That was surely the opportunity of the evening, the desire of the Spirit, the reason he'd prompted the cardinal to set this whole thing up in the first place.

Family Values

There is ultimately only one church, one family, one house of prayer. The burning desire of our Father in heaven is that we as his children should become a true family—a reconciled community in which "there is neither Jew nor Gentile, neither slave nor free, nor is there male and female, for you are all one in Christ Jesus" (Galatians 3:28). We are different in culture, geography, psychology, and even theology, of course, but that's what makes it fun! Surely we could learn to look at each other generously and, instead of wondering, "What's *wrong* with them?" we could ask, "What's *right* with them? What can I learn from them? How can I season my current convictions with a little more humility?"[1] The apostle John warns us starkly against hypocrisy in this area: "If someone says, 'I love God,' but hates a Christian brother or sister, that person is a liar" (1 John 4:20, NLT).

> Jesus is as passionate about the unity of his family as he is about worship, justice for the poor, and the fulfilment of his Great Commission.

Of course no one admits to "hating" his Christian brother or sister outright. But in my own life I admit that I have sometimes been competitive and judgmental towards other parts of God's family. I have secretly resented the success of others and been critical of viewpoints I haven't taken the time to comprehend. It's easy to do. On one occasion I was reading a newspaper report about a terrible child abuse scandal in a particular denomination and realised that my gut feeling had been relief that it was "them and not us." Yet in Christ there can only ever be "us."

It's disturbingly easy to disguise a critical spirit. To criticise mega-churches for consumerism, small churches for poor leadership, Pentecostal churches for dualism, traditional churches for dead religion, prosperity churches for exploiing the poor, Reformed churches for reductionism, inclusive churches for syncretism, conservative churches for bigotry. With each new prejudice, we diminish the body of Christ a little more into our own flawed likeness. But you can't change the church until you love her, and true love accepts imperfections, it forgives hurts, it isn't conditional upon perfection.

It is entirely possible to think rigorously and pursue our convictions passionately, while holding them lightly.

One of the most effective antidotes I've ever discovered against the arrogance of a sectarian spirit in my own life is to pray this Jesuit "Litany of Humility" from the heart:

From the desire of being praised, deliver me, O Jesus.
From the desire of being preferred to others, deliver me, O Jesus.
From the desire of being consulted, deliver me, O Jesus.
From the desire of being approved, deliver me, O Jesus.

That others may be esteemed more than I, Jesus, grant me the grace to desire it.
That, in the opinion of the world, others may increase and I may decrease, Jesus, grant me the grace to desire it.
That others may be chosen and I set aside, Jesus, grant me the grace to desire it.
That others may be preferred to me in everything, Jesus, grant me the grace to desire it.[2]

When we begin to prefer other Christians and churches with the radical attitude desired in this prayer, the result is reconciliation, cooperation, and mutual blessing. The church of Jesus takes a few more steps towards greater unity. This may sound a little utopian, but I am not advocating for one moment a movement towards structural unity in which the church loses its many beautiful differences under a single hierarchy with a global monopoly on the gospel. That would be a regressive step for many obvious reasons. Unity is not uniformity. It is organic, not mechanistic—a family full of differences yet one in blood.

Simple, Bare Necessities

It is entirely possible to think rigorously and pursue our convictions passionately, while holding them lightly, recognising that we cannot always be 100 per cent right in everything we think. The English puritan Richard Baxter popularised the famous maxim "In essentials unity; in non-essentials liberty; in all things love." He was advocating a posture of gracious, generous orthodoxy that keeps things simple, refusing to obsess about peripheral matters, and recognising that our current opinions about non-essentials are unlikely to be universally important and absolutely correct.

The essentials of Christian belief are clearly listed in the Nicene Creed, which was formulated in the year AD 325. All Christians ever since, whether they are Roman Catholic, Eastern Orthodox, Anglican, Protestant, or Free Church, have agreed on the central doctrinal statements expressed in this particular statement of faith.

These, then, are the "essentials" around which we can all unite and beyond which we must grant liberty for differing opinions about issues relating to the future of Israel, or the chronology of the end times, or the nature of the priesthood, or the practice of the gifts of the Spirit, or church governance, or even (dare I say it?) impassioned perspectives about marriage and human sexuality. Such topics are all extremely important. We should think about them very carefully indeed and form opinions. But since they do not feature in the creed, they must

"In essentials unity; in non-essentials liberty; in all things love."

—RICHARD BAXTER

never be allowed to define orthodoxy or divide the church. The Nicene Creed provides us with a common language for loving conversation within the family of God. And having mastered its language, there is much for us to discuss!

• • •

In St. Stephen's, the crowd hushed reluctantly as a choir near the altar began to chant, "*Veni, creator Spiritus, mentes tuorum visita.*" Some of the 24-7 old-timers were looking perturbed. *Latin?* I could hear them thinking. No one had expected our fifteenth birthday party to kick off in Latin. People had travelled from more than forty nations for this. A man in the front row actually started scowling.

"What's happening?" Sammy whispered, a little nervously.

"It's OK," I grinned and squeezed her hand. "We're just asking the Holy Spirit to come like we always do. Trust me. It's a hit worship song. It's just, um, quite old."

"Well, I'm really not sure about it," she sighed.

"You'd love it if you lived in the ninth century!"

Sammy smiled. The chanting subsided and the worship leader, Tim Hughes, stepped forward with a more familiar song. The cathedral erupted with celebration.

In every corner, through every vast arch, down every aisle, there were people singing. A big-bearded Orthodox priest in long black robes stood with hands aloft beside a hipster in skinny jeans whose beard was even bigger. A Salvation Army officer punched the air. An Asian girl closed her eyes and when she opened them again, they were glistening with tears. A child on her daddy's shoulders gazed up in awe at the shadows dancing on the vast, vaulted stone ceiling. The Catholic bishop who had looked mildly terrified at the start of the service now raised his hands in worship. Tourists came in from the streets, blinking in amazement to find the cathedral packed with thousands of young people, all worshipping Jesus, dancing, and interceding together for the poor.

"Mein Führer"

As we worshipped in the cathedral that night, we could not forget the misery of more than a million refugees, many of them huddled nearby in makeshift camps throughout Austria and elsewhere across Europe, fleeing the tragedies of their homelands in Syria, Libya, Iraq, and Afghanistan. It was the greatest humanitarian crisis on earth at that time, and many world leaders had decided to convene that very day in Vienna—of all places—to formulate an international response.

We prayed for their meetings, just a few streets away, with particular faith and passion. We also gave clothes and money for one of the nearby camps. It was a strange symmetry, I reflected. By prioritising the poor we had been given a palace, as the prophet had predicted. And yet, by coming to this palace we had actually been placed back amongst the poor, right at the epicentre of one of the gravest humanitarian disasters in the world.

Earlier that day I had studied a disturbing painting of the crucified Christ, hanging in the cardinal's palace. Set in an ornate gilt frame, the canvas was ripped and torn. The damage had been done, I learned, back in 1938 when the Archbishop of Vienna was trying to appease the rising Nazi party. A group of young people urged him to defy fascism and nail his colours to the mast as a follower of Jesus. Challenged by their words, the archbishop had stood in the cathedral where we were now worshipping and issued a brave declaration: "Jesus is Lord! There is no *Führer* but Jesus Christ!" Enraged by this public diminishment of their own exalted leader, Hitler's followers vented their fury upon this painting. It hangs there to this day, deliberately unrepaired—a poignant reminder that Christ's body remains broken and despised in our world.

The ideologies and idolatries of every generation are ultimately dethroned by the death and resurrection of Jesus.

In the cathedral that night, however, Christ's body seemed a little less broken. Everywhere I looked, his resurrection seemed to be breaking in.

Hitler and his minions are long gone, but Jesus is alive! The ideologies and idolatries of every generation are ultimately dethroned by his death and resurrection. People may vent their fury on pictures, on material things, and even on humanity itself for a while, but their power cannot last. The kingdom of Christ is advancing, his church is being built, and he is soon to return. We have every reason to rejoice and to hope, even amidst suffering. We are called to dispense joy.

Implanted Happiness

When the prophet Isaiah first coined the phrase "house of prayer" and envisaged nations flocking to worship at the temple, God promised that he would "give them joy in my house of prayer" (Isaiah 56:7). True houses of prayer are to be marked by joy. They will erupt frequently with laughter, celebration, singing, and exclamations of delight. "The Holy Spirit turns to joy whatever he touches," says Seraphim of Sarov, the revered Russian hermit.[3] Another great saint, St. Gregory of Palamas, described the Holy Spirit as "the eternal joy . . . where the Three delight in each other."[4] To be filled with this Spirit is to overflow with the joy that effervesces at the heart of the Trinity.

Healthy children laugh 300 times on average per day, but boring old adults laugh just five times.[5] Jesus calls us to be like children: to find delight in life continually, to trust easily, to understand simply, to receive freely, to imagine extravagantly, to play readily, to learn humbly, and to laugh a lot at the sheer absurdity and wonder of it all. As Teresa of Ávila once prayed, "From silly devotions and sour-faced saints, good Lord, deliver us."

In the early days of the 24-7 movement we once posted a link to a website depicting Bible stories in Lego. We did this simply because we thought it was amusing. Then we began to receive emails from anxious people asking about the underlying prophetic significance of the Lego. Others seemed to think it was irreverent. Christians can often be overly earnest.

When Jesus finally launched his public ministry, after an extraordinarily long time merely making tables, he had just three years left to save the planet. It was a tight schedule, and yet he still made time for parties, picnics, and fishing trips. Isn't it ironic that so many pastors today are too busy for such frivolity? As Christian leaders we can often be busier and far less fun than Jesus.

The surprising aim of Jesus' teaching was, he said, "that my joy may be in you, and that your joy may be complete" (John 15:11). When

Jesus had just three years to save the planet, and yet he still made time for parties, picnics, and fishing trips.

he prayed for his disciples he asked that they "may have the full measure of my joy within them" (John 17:13). The life of faith is not meant to be miserable and overly earnest. It is intended to be "filled with an inexpressible and glorious joy" (1 Peter 1:8). Perhaps Origen was thinking of such delightful verses when he concluded that

Christ's mission on earth was "to implant in us the happiness which comes from knowing him."[6]

The joy of Jesus is easily forgotten, partly because it is so seldom depicted in any artistic form. In painting after painting, in sculpture and in stained glass too, he is presented as an unsmiling, intense, tragic figure. The nearest Jesus ever gets to smiling is an occasional look of mild constipation.

It's such a shame that so few preachers, painters, and sculptors have reflected on the opening chapter of the book of Hebrews, in which we read that the Father anointed Jesus with more joy than any other being in the universe (Hebrews 1:9). The writer John Piper, whose Reformed theological tradition isn't known for its joy, argues from this particular Scripture that

the glory and grace of Jesus is that he is, and always will be, indestructibly happy. I say it is his glory, because gloom is not glorious. And I say it is his grace, because the best thing he has to give us is his joy . . . Jesus Christ is the happiest being in the universe.[7]

The apostle Paul commands us unequivocally to nurture and cultivate Christ's joy in our lives. "Rejoice in the Lord always," he says. "I will say it again: rejoice!" (Philippians 4:4). Paul is not advocating here the kind of horrible, fake optimism of the motivational speaking circuit. There is an important place, as we have seen in this book, for lament. Sometimes it is impossible to rejoice in our circumstances, but we can always rejoice "in the Lord." Sometimes this will be in the midst of suffering and in spite of our circumstances. The theologian Karl Barth describes this kind of belligerent joy as "a defiant 'Nevertheless!'" to the culture.[8]

Pain is inevitable in life. Joy is not. Pursue joy. Laugh a lot. Listen well. Celebrate the ordinary.

Suffering is sadly inevitable in life, but joy is not. We must therefore pursue joy relentlessly, by creating space for celebration and disciplining ourselves rigorously to have fun. This may sound obvious, but some Christians go through their whole lives with an undiluted sadness, deferring happiness and denying themselves pleasure. They may even secretly consider misery more holy than laughter. The root of such unhealthy asceticism may be religious—a complete misunderstanding of God's goodness; or it may be clinical—a depression draining the colour from life and requiring medication; or it may be psychiatric—a deep-seated self-hatred. We all go through seasons of sadness, but the prevailing Christian attitude is not gloom but gladness. We have a delightful duty to nurture joy by pursuing the people, places, and things that help us to "rejoice in the Lord." On Judgment Day, according to one old Hebrew adage, we shall be required to give an account for every good thing we refused to enjoy!

• • •

Joy was certainly erupting in St. Stephen's Cathedral that night as we celebrated a decade and a half of adventuring with Jesus. It was obvious in the smiling faces, in the exuberant worship, the frequent bursts of laughter, and the prospect of the party we had planned for the palace after the service.

Suddenly the music died down as screens around the cathedral flickered to life to broadcast a special birthday message from the Archbishop of Canterbury. At one point he threatened to sing us "Happy Birthday," and everyone laughed. Next Cardinal Schönborn spoke live from the Vatican in Rome, with a personal greeting for the 24-7 movement from the Pope, followed by a request from the Pope for our prayers. There was a simultaneous gasp of amazement.

How on earth did we get here? I wondered. All we ever did was hide ourselves away to pray in a back-street warehouse in a nowhere town. We didn't know anyone famous, didn't have any money, didn't have a plan, weren't even trying to start a movement. And yet here we were, fifteen years later, thousands of us, gathered from many nations, getting photobombed by the Archbishop of Canterbury and the Pope.

The impetus behind 24-7 Prayer has been, I think, the word *yes*. For fifteen years we have simply been saying yes to Jesus. Again and again, even when it didn't make sense. Even when it hurt. He told us to pray night and day, and we said yes. He sent us to Sodom and Gomorrah, and we said yes. He told us to trust him for money, and we said yes. We kept saying yes even when the zeroes multiplied. He invited us to start missional and monastic communities, and we said yes. He sent Jon and Mindy Petersen to Amsterdam, and Brian and Tracy Heasley to Ibiza, and Kelly Tietsort to Boy's Town, and us to Kansas City, and we all just said yes. He told us to prioritise the poor and promised us palaces, and we said yes.

Fifteen years of non-stop prayer had taught me that saying no to the Holy Spirit is far more dangerous than the alternative.

That's how it happened. Our roadmap to Vienna had been nothing more complicated than fifteen years of saying yes, OK, and amen.

We tend to assume that the greatest risks in life await those zealots who pick up their crosses, pack their bags, and abandon themselves to the call of the wild. But the previous fifteen years had taught me something else: Saying no to the Holy Spirit is far more dangerous than the alternative. By saying no to God's leadership in your life you will miss out on the actual reason for which you were born. You will quietly live a second-rate life, sometimes sensing the missed opportunities, feeling unfulfilled like an actor waiting to perform, without knowing why. When you become a Christian you take your first step out of futility and into your destiny. When you keep surrendering your life, your plans and preferences, again and again, to the Lordship of Jesus, saying yes to whatever he says, you look around one day blinking in amazement at the ways he has deployed you, the places he has taken you, the person he is enabling you to become.

"Do whatever he tells you," said Mary to the servants at a wedding party in Cana. It was good advice. By obeying Jesus in a mundane way, they stepped into the pages of Scripture and participated unwittingly in his first recorded miracle. Whenever we say yes to God, we reverse the effects of Adam and Eve's first no. That's why acts of obedience are often contested so fiercely and blessed so wonderfully.

If God is asking you to change your career, or to end an unhealthy relationship, or to stop and take a holiday, or to befriend someone in your street, or to quit your job, or to start a prayer room, or to accept singleness, or to admit a problem, or to go to another place, the wisest, safest thing you can possibly do is to say yes. He knows you perfectly and only ever wants the best for you. Life to the full awaits your yes. Hell is an eternal no to his love.

In the Beginning

Francis of Assisi first said yes to God in the semi-derelict church of San Damiano when a supernatural voice emanated from the cross commanding him to "rebuild my church." In response to that commission, Francis gave up everything he owned and never stopped saying yes. In doing so he became one of the most joyful saints the church has ever known.

Twenty years later, near the end of his short life, Francis of Assisi gathered his followers and gave them a call to arms. By that stage the Franciscans had returned to the gospel with such a force that they'd altered the course of European history: reviving the medieval church, caring radically for the poor, preaching the gospel (even to the Muslim sultan of Egypt), pioneering a new environmentalism, and impacting millions of lives with a fresh revelation of Jesus. The Franciscans could easily have looked around at such achievements and been content. But instead, towards the end of his remarkable life, Francis exhorted his friends with these words: "Brothers," he said, "let us begin, for until now we have done little or nothing."[9] Against all odds, they had changed the world—and now Francis was near his own death, but he wasn't remotely satisfied. It was time, he said, to begin.

The most dangerous thing that any of us could have done in the cathedral that night would have been to look around and think, even for a single second, *This will do.* There is work to be done when the vast majority of our peers do not yet know Jesus. There is work to be done when hundreds of thousands of faceless children are being trafficked as slaves, many to be raped again and again in the back streets of Bangkok and Mumbai, Amsterdam and New York City. There is work to be done when terrorists are still regularly destroying innocent lives in the name of God and drones are still dropping bombs on innocent families in retaliation. There is work to be done when millions of displaced people have nowhere to call home and elected officials are busy building walls to keep them out. There is work to be done when the church of Jesus Christ stands divided and riddled with scandal. We can't afford to be complacent or content. It's time to roll up our sleeves and get our hands dirty. There is work to be done.

God help us if we think that a few thousand people singing songs in a pretty cathedral is even the beginning of an effective response to the scale of human need. Vienna was invigorating, it was inspiring and encouraging, but it will not be our epitaph. It will not become our Blue Camp 20. We are called to Santa Fe.

The really exciting thing that night was not the sense of celebration looking back, but the sense of consecration looking forward. "If God could do all this in the last fifteen years," we kept saying, "what might he do next?" Where might we be fifteen years from now if we just keep saying yes to the Holy Spirit? Our world needs prayer, mission, and justice more than ever. It's been a great pregnancy, but now it's time to be born.

We never sought palaces or papal blessings. We sought God, and he did the other stuff as well. Let's not be impressed by the trappings of obedience. Instead let's be impressed by the thirteen-year-old who is talking to God right now in a prayer room when none of her friends even believe he exists. Let's be impressed by the eighteen-year-old spending his summer and all his savings being puked on and worse, rescuing girls from rape and showing them a little dignity. He is the hope of the world. Let's be impressed by young families choosing to live in the darkest places on earth so that they can shine a little light, while their peers climb the career ladder. No one ever said that saying yes would be easy, but it is the ride of our lives.

There is much hard work still to be done when the majority of people in our generation are turning their backs on Jesus.

Prisons

Scanning the crowd, I notice Brian and Tracy Heasley laughing in amazement at the message from the Pope. These days Brian's beard is flecked with grey, there are a few more laughter lines around his eyes, but he's still the same guy I sat with in Skies, overlooking Kansas City, the night we agreed to keep pioneering. Brian's journey has been remarkable by anyone's standards, and yet I know that he's already beginning to dream of new adventures. God has taken him from prison into pastoring, and from a safe church in rural Norfolk to a mission field in a contemporary Sodom and Gomorrah. He and Tracy have recently returned from Ibiza to England, where remarkable doors are opening for Brian to minister to prisoners.

On their first night "inside," new inmates are more likely to attempt suicide than at any other time in their lives. Brian is longing to reach those in such despair before they do anything stupid. He wants to let them know that they are not alone in that cell, that there is a God of grace who specialises in forgiveness and fresh starts. And so he has developed a simple resource to help prisoners pray. Wouldn't it be amazing, we've been thinking, if the world's prisons could become houses of prayer for the nations? Inmates might not be able to travel anywhere as missionaries, but wouldn't it be just like God to use those who have messed up their lives the most to bless the nations the most? And wouldn't it also be just like God to take Brian's own story of criminality and turn it into a redemption song that touches thousands of others around the world? It's time for Brian and Tracy to begin.

Ibiza

Back in Ibiza, a new team is benefiting from Brian and Tracy's legacy of pioneering. They have inherited an enviable reputation on the island and a full schedule of mission teams every summer. The 24-7 Centre, slap-bang in the heart of San Antonio, is decked out with computers, a decent coffee machine, crates of the much-loved *Jesus Loves Ibiza* Bibles and, of course, the famous Vomit Van parked outside. Their mission is also spreading to other Mediterranean islands, impacting refugees on the Greek island of Samos and party animals in Magaluf, Majorca. The new team is beginning to achieve things that Brian and Tracy barely imagined. They are "prioritising the poor," serving Ibiza's ostracised Romany community, visiting those in prison on the island, delivering people to hospital and safely back to their hotels, night after night. For the new team in Ibiza, it's time to begin.

Japan

Remembering Jon Petersen's experiences with mavericks like Porky the Pirate, and his lifelong vision for a new Jesus Movement, I invite him to come and pray a blessing over the crowd in the cathedral. He stands there close to tears, quoting great chunks of Scripture from memory, imparting the wisdom refined by so many years saying yes to Jesus.

On Friday, 11 March 2011, one of the biggest earthquakes ever recorded threw a tsunami more than forty metres high at the Japanese mainland, shifting the earth's axis by about twenty-five centimetres and generating soundwaves detectable by satellites in space. More than 15,000 people died, and countless others lost their homes that day.

As we prayed for Japan at that time, God spoke: "It's time to set Jon apart and recommission him to the land of his birth." This we did, laying hands upon him and asking the Lord to open closed doors. Within minutes of that prayer, Jon received an unsolicited email from Japan inviting him to return. This was the first formal invitation to minister in Japan that Jon had received in almost forty years of asking. You can imagine his joy. From that moment Jon began taking teams to pray and to work in the worst-affected exclusion zone near the damaged Fukushima nuclear plant. Now, at the time of writing, after so many years of waiting and praying, Jon Petersen is beginning to mobilise an army of indigenous young church-planters throughout Japan. Give it another fifteen years, and Jon will, I guess, be an old man. But I'm pretty sure there'll be hundreds of Japanese faces in the crowd, all because of the way Jon just keeps saying yes to Jesus. After a lifetime of prayer for the land of his birth, Jon senses more than ever that it's at last time to begin.

Prayer Spaces in Schools

Phil Togwell is standing near the front of the crowd with his wife and three daughters. He still reminds me of Mr. Tumnus, although he's shaved off the wiry goatee. It seems such a long time ago that he and I sat outside Wesley's Foundery on the terrible day that suicide bombers destroyed so many lives in London. These days Phil is developing a new ministry called Prayer Spaces in Schools, turning school classrooms into prayer rooms, enabling students to pray as part of their normal day, even during class time, at normal, secular schools.

This simple idea has been welcomed by head teachers in the UK, and even applauded by the regulatory bodies as "cross-curricular, experiential learning." Children climb into tents to pray, or dissolve their "sins" in clear water using effervescent tablets, or tie luggage tags to the branches of imported trees. The most moving prayers are often the simplest ones, posted anonymously on a blizzard of Post-It notes stuck to classroom walls:

- "Is my dad going to be OK? Please say yes."
- "God, why did you make me ugly?"
- "Are you real? I'd like to know."
- "I'm sorry for arguing with my parents and lying to make things OK."

Phil Togwell has found himself once again surfing this latest wave of the 24-7 prayer movement as it spreads out from the UK to schools in Malta, Germany, and Austria. Looking around at the massive opportunities to reach a generation of schoolkids, and the profound challenges they are facing growing up at a time like this, Phil Togwell knows for sure that it's time to begin.

Manenberg

On the other side of the cathedral I can just make out Pete and Sarah Portal. They continue to prioritise the poor in Manenberg, having establised their home in a place with the second-highest murder rate in South Africa. Pete and Sarah and the Tree of Life community just won't stop saying yes to Jesus. They've helped their first few friends get free from drugs and out of gangs, but there are thousands more to reach, an entire community to rebuild. They know that in Manenberg tonight, it's time to begin.

Near the Portals, I see Ralf Neumann with his big beard, shaved head, and pierced eyebrow, the German skater kid who first trained with us in Kansas City and continues faithfully and prayerfully to serve the poorest, most Godless postcode in Germany. Neubrandenberg is a former stronghold of the Stasi, the brutal East German security services from the communist era, and to this day the majority of Ralf's neighbours are atheists. There are very few churches. It's tough soil for the gospel, but Ralf's committed to this place and these people for the long haul. Polylux, their little Boiler Room community, is changing the lives of local kids. Ralf and his wife, Katharina, can see for sure that there is much more to be done in their city. After all these years, they feel like they're just getting started. They know that it's time to begin.

I glance at Tim Hughes standing at the front of the cathedral under a vast suspended crucifix, singing his heart out. He and his wife, Rachel, have just planted a new church in Birmingham, England's second-largest, least-evangelised city. He could so easily be taking it easy, making albums, living from royalties, touring conferences. But the gospel is compelling him to pioneer something new.

Boy's Town

Far away in Reynosa, Mexico, the gang warfare has subsided to manageable levels, and we are preparing to plant another team from Tulsa back into Boy's Town to pick up the important ministry that Kelly Tietsort was forced to abandon. A number of the women she befriended back then continue to live in freedom, but the new team is being trained to help many more people suffering the trauma of violence, addiction, and sexual abuse. Kelly and Zach now have three children, but she cannot wait to return. "It's weird," laughs Zach, "but sometimes when I smell sewage and disinfectant I am transported back to Boy's Town and I just miss it like crazy." All those years ago, Kelly dreamed that she would one day be an old, wrinkly lady wandering around the streets of Boy's Town. For a while she had to give up that dream, but now, as the work is preparing to relaunch, she knows that, once again, it's time to begin.

Vancouver, Thun, and Kansas City

Near the front of the cathedral, I see Aaron White, leader of the Boiler Room in the poorest part of Vancouver, Canada. Next to him stands Susanna Rychiger, the Swiss prayer warrior who once received thousands of bank notes in her kitchen cupboard and still trusts God for financial provision. I look behind me and see Adam Cox, the blue-eyed Bible teacher we first met with Floyd the night our firstborn children nearly died. Adam heads up the Boiler Room community in Kansas City with his wife, Julie. It's now ten years old, growing fast, and they're just about to launch out in a major new direction under a new name, Navah, which means "to bring home and make beautiful." They're making it their mission to welcome people home and to beautify ugly places and broken lives. Adam knows that, for the sake of the many lost souls in downtown Kansas City, it's time to begin.

Guildford

Sammy catches my eye, and I notice that there are tears in hers. The last fifteen years have been the most wonderful and yet the most terrifying of our lives. She has endured things that no young woman should ever have to face, and yet she is still standing, still worshipping, still serving by my side. Back home they've demolished Bojanglez nightclub, where the 24-7 movement was launched, but our 24-7 community in Guildford is growing fast. We are busy pastoring, hosting a steady stream of visitors, training leaders, and preparing to plant more communities throughout Europe. We are determined to play our part in turning the tide back to Jesus in our time.

Our children, who were babies when all of this began, are teenagers and will soon leave home. But we aren't settling down. In fact, we've just been offered a large tract of land in a remarkable location to build a modern-day monastic community—a little Herrnhut—as a Mother House for the whole 24-7 movement. It'll require a miracle to get planning consent, and it'll cost millions we haven't got, but we sense that perhaps the Spirit is speaking, and we've learned to fasten our seat belts and say yes. It's been a wild fifteen years, but now, at last, it's time for us to begin.

Mother House

Many years ago, when the Roman Empire was falling across Europe, long before buildings like St. Stephen's Cathedral in Vienna and the Foundery in London, the darkness of the era was illuminated by a surprising proliferation of monastic communities. These houses of prayer, mission, and justice sustained and cultivated the gospel, laying foundations for Europe as the great, global crucible of Christian faith for most of the second millennium.

> **"We are waiting not for a Godot, but for another—doubtless very different—St Benedict."**
>
> —ALASDAIR MACINTYRE

Remembering these monasteries, the philosopher Alasdair MacIntyre concludes his landmark work *After Virtue* by comparing those so-called "Dark Ages" of European history with the era in which we now live.

A crucial turning point in that earlier history occurred when men and women of good will turned aside from the task of shoring up the Roman imperium and ceased to identify the continuation of civility and moral community with the maintenance of that imperium. What they set themselves to achieve instead—often not recognising fully what they were doing—was the construction of new forms of community within which the moral life could be sustained so that both morality and civility might survive the coming ages of barbarism and darkness. We have reached that turning point.

What matters at this stage is the construction of local forms of community within which civility and the intellectual and moral life can be sustained through the new dark ages which are already upon us. And if the tradition of the virtues was able to survive the horrors of the last dark ages, we are not entirely without grounds for hope. This time however the barbarians are not waiting beyond the frontiers; they have already been governing us for quite some time. And it is our lack of consciousness of this that constitutes part of our predicament. We are waiting not for a Godot, but for another—doubtless very different—St Benedict.[10]

MacIntyre's comments ring with prophetic resonance for a time like our own. Houses of prayer (Benedictine and otherwise) are beginning to multiply in the darkening landscape, and maybe they can help cultivate and propagate the light of the gospel once again, in "the new dark ages which are already upon us."

So we are beginning to dream of a Mother House—a place of encounter, education, and enterprise—sustained by a religious order with a fixed rule of life.[11] The heartbeat of the Mother House will be prayer and worship—the joy of God's presence. It will also be a house of hospitality for pilgrims, a centre of practical mercy and justice for the poor, a place of creativity with recording studio, collaborative workspace, art studio, and kitchens, a hub for training, and a mission station for the evangelisation of nations.

The nights are getting darker, but the lights are getting brighter.

At a time when others are pushing forward into the culture, planting congregations, starting businesses, engaging politically, fighting injustice, making the gospel relevant, establishing a monastery feels to us like the most peculiar and subversive thing we could possibly do. We truly don't know for sure if it's going to be possible. Right now, all we have is some land and some faith. People may read these words one day and hold them against us if this dream has failed to materialise. In fact, we've already been told, in no uncertain terms by one professional, that it's impossible. But then again, that's often where the fun begins. Maybe we won't make it to Santa Fe, but we're at least going to try.

• • •

We established that first prayer room with the simplest of desires for more of the presence and power of God. Gradually we learned to encounter Jesus in prayer, in the lost, and in the poor. But after all these years we have come full circle, back to the place where we began, longing for more of Jesus in our lives, in our churches, and in our world. My friend Jason Mandryk sums it up beautifully:

> Each and every prayer is a tiny piece of a great cosmic puzzle, which when fitted together will allow for the completion of the grand picture of the Almighty Lord's plan for humanity and the universe. We do not merely pray about [things], we pray toward something, and that something is magnificent, the fulfilment of the Father's purposes and His Kingdom come. In keeping with all we see of God's character and commands, we long for poverty's end, for justice toward the oppressed, for the blind to see and the lame to walk, for widows and orphans to be looked after, for those in chains to be set at liberty, for the earth to be rightly stewarded, for wars to cease, for those at enmity with each other to be reconciled and for those who are lost to be found by Jesus and the salvation He brings . . .
>
> In the end, such a vision will never completely come to pass without Jesus returning to assume the Kingship of this world. It is this that is the ultimate purpose of the Great

Commission; even the evangelization of the entire world is not an end in itself. Our mission is to see vibrant, growing, mature churches planted and multiplied among every people, and so fulfil our Lord's mandate. But this is only the preparation and completion of the Bride; her Heavenly Bridegroom awaits her readiness. Too often we immerse ourselves in the task but lose sight of its ultimate purpose—the glory of God.[12]

•   •   •

In St. Stephen's Cathedral I studied the sea of faces: prayer warriors, freedom fighters, old friends. Was this the army I'd seen at Cape St. Vincent, all those years ago? An involuntary shiver ran down my spine with the thought. But then I blinked, and saw something else. Not a distant memory, not an imaginary army, but an actual, visible family, a physical community with dirty hands and dirty knees, flawed friends, luminous in the darkness, a story about to begin.

We have this treasure in jars of clay to show that this all-surpassing power is from God and not from us . . . For our light and momentary troubles are achieving for us an eternal glory that far outweighs them all. So we fix our eyes not on what is seen, but on what is unseen, since what is seen is temporary, but what is unseen is eternal.

2 CORINTHIANS 4:7, 17-18

Selah.

STUDY GUIDE

FOR SMALL GROUPS AND FURTHER REFLECTION

— Hannah Heather —

1—Punk Messiah

God's story from beginning to end describes glory getting dirty and dirt getting blessed. The Creator made humanity out of the dust and if, on that day, we left a little dirt behind in the creases of his hands, it was surely a sign of things to come . . .

Scripture Reflection: John 1:14; Hebrews 2:14-18

1. John 1:14 contains the shocking truth of the incarnation: that Jesus was both gloriously divine and scandalously human. Pete talks in this chapter about the offensive impact this would have had for both Greeks (who despised the body) and Jews (who had a deep reverence for the holiness of God). What aspect of Jesus' incarnation do you find shocking or difficult to comprehend?

2. Looking at the depths of Jesus' humanity, Pete says: "We believe in omnipotence surrendering to incontinence. . . . We believe that God's eternal Word once squealed like a baby, and when eventually he learned to speak, it was with a regional accent. The Creator of the cosmos made tables, and presumably he made them badly at first. The Holy One of Israel got dirt in the creases of his hands." How does it feel to imagine these deeply human aspects of Jesus? How does this change your view of God? Reflecting on Hebrews 2:14-18, knowing that Jesus suffered and overcame human temptations, how does that change the way you approach the trials you are facing today?

3. "We believe in the Word made flesh who dwelt among us as a kind of prayer, and sends us out to speak the 'Amen' in every dark corner of his creation." Where could God be sending you today to speak "Amen" and bring incarnation in the darkness? What unlikely place could you transform into a place of prayer? Is there any area of your life where you might be more afraid or proud to get your hands dirty than Jesus was?

Prayer

Jesus, thank you for your miraculous, scandalous incarnation. Thank you that you put on skin and bones. That you cried, that you felt tired. That you got dirt underneath your fingernails. And that you walked through everything I will experience in this life, meaning that I am never alone, even in the depths of suffering. Would you send me into the dark corners of this world to bring your light? Amen.

2—The Time of Our Lives

We were discovering that prayer didn't have to be boring and benign, the gentle pursuit of sweet ladies in their autumn years. It could be militant, defiant, catalytic, even violent.

Scripture Reflection: Exodus 33:15-16; John 14:13-14

1. In this chapter, Pete describes his personal journey of growing dissatisfied and discontent in his faith, becoming "increasingly hungry for a truer Christian experience." Have you ever felt the kind of spiritual hunger he is describing? What do you do when you feel this hunger?

2. John 14:13-14 contains a bold promise from Jesus concerning our prayer lives. The journey of 24-7 is that prayer can be powerful, exciting, and subversive, and yet, as Pete says, often we are guilty of talking more *about* Jesus in public than we ever talk *with* him in private. How is your personal prayer life? Do you think there are times when you are guilty of talking more about Jesus than with him? What practical steps could you take to grow in prayer?

3. Between his vision of the army of young people and the disaster of 9/11, Cape St. Vincent became an important holy place, a "Bethel location" for Pete. Do you have any significant Bethel moments, Scriptures, or locations where you have encountered the presence of God? Reflect on the importance of these in your Christian journey.

4. "That was, I guess, what our non-stop prayer room was all about: a busy church finally exhaling; making a little space for God. And much to our surprise, when we eventually did make that space, he accepted the invitation almost immediately." Where might your busyness have overtaken your pursuit of God's presence? How could you, and your church community, make some space for God to walk into the room?

Prayer

"Put salt in our mouths that we may thirst for you." Amen.

PRAYER OF ST. AUGUSTINE

3—Encounter Culture

The point of prayer, the entire impetus behind the 24-7 movement, is not the power that it releases but the person it reveals.

Scripture Reflection: Psalm 27; John 2:13-17; Jeremiah 29:12-13; Hebrews 12:1-2

1. In this chapter, Pete argues that "the focus for any true house of prayer should never be prayer itself, but rather the Father himself at its heart." How does this description of prayer, defined by the importance of seeking the presence of God, affect your view of prayer and the way you engage with it? Reflect on the prayer of David in Psalm 27:4. Are you challenged by David's plea in these verses? How might you recalibrate your focus in prayer?

2. What do you think of Pete's statement "It might be healthier if we all just stopped being Christians for a bit—a week, a month, or even a year"? What might it look like for Jesus to "hack your system" and refresh your perspective of who he is and what he is calling you to do? How might you pursue wonder this week?

3. Pete says in this chapter that Satan's number one aim is simply to divert your attention away from Jesus. He lists just some of the ways this happens, including sin, busyness, shame, pain, religion, *Candy Crush Saga* (!), obsessive relationships, a golf handicap, a pay rise, and illness. What do you currently find are your biggest obstacles to prayer? How might you overcome these things?

4. Based on the "house of prayer" texts, Pete identifies five clues to Christ's priorities for his church: presence, prayer, mission, justice, and joy. How do you see these priorities outworked in your church community? Are there any ways in which you could help to increase these individually or with friends?

Prayer

God, my desire is to encounter your presence. Would you help me to fix my eyes on you, that I may dwell in the house of the Lord all the days of my life, to gaze on your beauty and seek your face? Would you lead me in the way of wonder today? Amen.

4—The Presence Paradigm

The most important discovery you will ever make is the love the Father has for you. Your power in prayer will flow from the certainty that the One who made you likes you, he is not scowling at you, he is on your side. All the other messages of this book lose their meaning without the infilling presence of God the Father.

Scripture Reflection: Psalm 84; Acts 2:1-12; Romans 8:15

1. "The hour you spend in the prayer room is when you refocus, re-centre on Jesus, becoming fully aware of his presence once again. When this happens, you can carry God's presence with you into the other twenty-three hours of the day, knowing all the time that he is with you, he is for you. . . . When problems arise you'll pray in real time, right then and there. . . . In fact, your life will become that moment: a continual conversation with God." What did you think of Brennan Manning's description of prayer? Does this change anything about your approach to your quiet time?

2. What did you think of the challenging statement from Madeleine L'Engle that "to be a witness is to be a living mystery. It means to live in such a way that one's life would not make sense if God did not exist"? Reflect on the witness of your own life. What areas of your life right now don't make sense to your non-Christian friends, and where in your life could you be challenged to live more counter-culturally?

3. Pete argues in this chapter that our primary calling as a house of prayer for the nations is to celebrate and demonstrate God's presence on earth. How important do you think this "presence paradigm" is? What does this look like for you and your church community? What practical measures could you put in place to increase your celebration and demonstration of God's presence in your community?

Prayer

"How lovely is your dwelling-place, LORD Almighty! My soul yearns, even faints, for the courts of the LORD; my heart and my flesh cry out for the living God." Thank you, God, that you have made me a temple of your Holy Spirit and that I can encounter your presence in my life every day. Help me today to carry your infectious, joyful presence to everyone I meet. Amen.

5—All Hell

The truth is this: There are terrible evils that will only be restrained, and wonderful blessings that will only be unlocked, by our prayers. "You do not have," says the apostle James very simply, "because you do not ask God" (James 4:2). The Lord's purposes are contingent upon our prayers because he has chosen to work in partnership with our free wills.

Scripture Reflection: Ephesians 6:10-20; Job 9:10

1. In this chapter Pete talks about the authority we have as Christians in the spiritual realm. He identifies two opposing problems we often have in this area: overplaying our own significance, and underestimating the authority we have as children of God. Which of these do you identify more strongly with? What might God want to teach you today about the role your prayers play in the spiritual realm?

2. Have you ever experienced God performing miracles in your life or the life of your friends? How did these "mountaintop" moments affect your relationship with God?

3. Reflect on the armour of God found in Ephesians. In which of the areas below do you want to grow more, and what practical steps could you put in place this week to do that? The armour of God: the belt of *truth*, the breastplate of *righteousness*, the shoes of the *gospel of peace*, the shield of *faith*, the helmet of *salvation*, the sword of the *Spirit which is the Word of God* (Ephesians 6:10-20).

Prayer

God, thank you that you provide for our needs and even our desires each and every day. Thank you that sometimes you work in wondrous miracles and sometimes in the beautiful creativity of the normal. Please help me to understand and take hold of my authority in the spiritual realm, that I might partner with you in the coming of your kingdom. Amen.

6—Super Bowl

The King of Kings requests your presence "at the very seat of government." He offers you a place on his executive so that you can influence his actions on behalf of the people. . . . The Bible is clear that our opinions and choices really can shape history; that our prayers really do make a difference in the world.

Scripture Reflection: 2 Chronicles 7:1-14; Luke 18:1-8; 2 Corinthians 1:20

1. Pete talks about intercessors actively laying hold of the promises of God with "violent insistence." Have you ever experienced prayer like this? Reflecting on the parable of the persistent widow (Luke 18), how important do you think this kind of intense and intentional intercession is, and how might

you grow in this area? What prayers might God be calling you to keep praying and not give up?

2. Pete makes a challenging statement when he says: "I suspect that many of our prayer meetings today are less effective than they could be because we merely ask but we don't expect." In your church community, what is the level of expectancy when you pray? Do you expect God to move in nations or major stadium events like the Super Bowl story when you pray for them? How can we raise the faith level in our prayer times?

3. In this chapter Pete argues that far more of our prayers are consistently being answered than we will ever realise, but that we are blind to the goodness of God all around. The solution, he says, is this: "Our eyes can only be opened to see the world as it truly, objectively is by nurturing a daily attitude of gratitude." How might you begin to nurture gratitude more on a daily basis? Pause and reflect on the blessings that God has given you this week and the way he has been present with you every day.

Prayer

God, I thank you that the wild and radical truth of the Bible is that the rusty hinge of human history turns out to be the bended knee. Thank you that in the place of prayer you invite us in to partner with you in your work in the world. Would you increase my expectancy and faith? May my prayers be an "Amen" to your desires today. Amen.

7—Blue Camp 20

Secretly I was struggling profoundly with the same temptations to stop pioneering, to settle down for an easier life. . . . Somehow the world I'd been trying to change had begun changing me. I'd always had a thirst for adventure, but it had been the craziest five years imaginable; it had been heaven, but it had sometimes also hurt, and I simply wasn't sure I could face any more pioneering.

Scripture Reflection: Hebrews 11:1-10; Ephesians 4:1

1. Pete describes in this chapter the encounter he had with God which challenged his temptation to settle down and pushed him back into pioneering for the vision which had once fired his soul: "It's perfectly possible to settle for our current level of spiritual experience, but we are given the opportunity to strike out again into the wilderness seeking a deeper place of relationship with God than ever before." Where have you experienced this temptation to stop chasing after your dreams and visions? Or to settle for a smaller, more sedate version of what God has called you to do?

2. Abraham pressed on into the calling of God rather than settling as his father had done before him. Pete argues in this chapter that often the pain and grief we walk through in life causes us to re-evaluate the vision and calling we have and can make us settle in the place of our pain. Is there any disappointment or pain that has caused you to doubt and bury your God-given dreams, or to redefine your relationship with God and the calling he has for you? How could your friends and church community support you in this?

3. In this chapter, Pete describes Brian as an *anam cara*, a "soul friend," and together they supported and pushed one another into the frontiers to which God was calling them. Do you have anyone you would describe as a "soul friend" in this way? How might you encourage them this week to keep pressing into the visions and dreams God has given them?

Prayer

"Disturb us, Lord, when we are too well pleased with ourselves; when our dreams have come true because we have dreamed too little; when we arrived safely because we have sailed too close to shore. Disturb us, Lord, when with the abundance

of the things we possess, we have lost our thirst for the water
of life. Stir us, Lord, to dare more boldly, to venture on wider
seas, where storms will show your mastery; where losing sight
of land, we shall find the stars. We ask you to push back
the horizons of our hopes and to push us into the future in
strength, courage, hope and love. Amen."

AUTHOR UNKNOWN

8—Strange Angels

The church is a prayer-fuelled missionary movement,
continually discomfited by the consequences of its own gospel.

Scripture Reflection: Acts 10:9-15; Isaiah 6:8; Mark 2:13-17

1. In this chapter Pete argues that true prayer provokes and
   propels us out of our "holy places" to engage with the
   unchurched and overcome any religious prejudice. In this
   way, many 24-7 prayer rooms have spilled out into radical
   missional expressions all over the world. In what ways are you
   and your church community being commissioned out from
   the place of prayer into mission in your local context? How
   might you increase in missional prayer (praying for the lost in
   your community and beyond) and prayerful mission (stepping
   outside the church walls and reaching the lost)?
2. Pete describes Brian's faith journey and the incredible, unique way
   in which he was positioned to pioneer the work in Ibiza. Think
   about your own journey of faith and the experiences and lessons
   God has taught you along the way. How might recognising God's
   hand in your testimony help lead you to step into your destiny?
3. "To reach the unchurched we will have to leave the church to
   visit places and people we might previously have considered
   'unclean.'" What do you think of this statement? Reflecting on
   the witness of Jesus to the "unclean" people of his day, who do

you think is culturally "unclean" in your neighbourhood? How could you reach out to these people?

Prayer

"Take, Lord, and receive all my liberty, my memory, my understanding and my entire will, all I have and call my own. You have given all to me. To you, Lord, I return it. Everything is yours; do with it what you will. Give me only your love and your grace; that is enough for me."

PRAYER OF ST. IGNATIUS OF LOYOLA

9—Porky the Pirate

Those who pray continually without engaging missionally are simply missing the point. If we claim to have our eyes fixed on Jesus and yet fail to focus on the profound needs that break his heart, we are hypocrites.

Scripture Reflection: Mark 11:15-18; Romans 15:20-21; Hebrews 12:1-3; Isaiah 56:4-8; Hebrews 10:19-23

1. Pete talks in this chapter about the two axes of the Christian life: the vertical axis of coming to God in prayer and worship, and the horizontal axis of going out into all the world to make disciples. Which of these two do you find comes most easily to you and your church community? How might you grow in both of these aspects to increase your intimacy with God and your mission to your neighbourhood?

2. Reflect on Mark 11:15-18. As well as the fact that the people were being *exploited*, Pete argues that Jesus was angry that people were being *excluded* from the house of God: "His message was unequivocal: A house of prayer that is inaccessible, unwelcoming, and disengaged from the lost is failing to be a true house of prayer." Are there any areas of your church

community where you could be more focused on including, welcoming, and engaging outsiders? How could you develop a culture of welcome and inclusion in your church that goes beyond offering a cup of coffee on a Sunday morning and shaking their hand on their way out?

3. Pete shared some of the stories of radical mission pioneering which inspired the 24-7 prayer movement to continue to step outside the prayer room and define itself by the fact that "the majority of people in our generation are turning their backs on Jesus." What stories of mission have most inspired you? What impact have these had on your expectation of what the Christian life looks like?

Prayer

Jesus, we love encountering your presence in the place of prayer and worship. Thank you that you could not be contained by the Holy of Holies, but continue to break through into our lives every day with your presence. Please give us your heart for the lost, unsettle our cosiness and our comfort, and send us out to go and carry your presence like light bulbs to every lost and excluded corner of this planet. Amen.

10—Word on the Street

The flow of the gospel is this . . . "I was hugged . . . until I cried, held so close that the excrement wiped off me onto his white robes, listened to until I had no more lies inside me, accepted until I was changed."

Scripture Reflection: Acts 17:16-34; Luke 23:32-43; Luke 15:11-24

1. Reflect on the examples of mission explored in this chapter, from Hudson Taylor with his ponytail, to the *Jesus Loves Ibiza* Bible, to the apostle Paul evangelising with the use of an idol. What would mission which recognises and celebrates what

is good in culture look like in some of the "weird and dark" places of your neighbourhood? Where might you have heard the whisper of God emanating from unlikely people this week?

2. "We were discovering, I think, that prayer is more than a preliminary to evangelism—it can also be an effective form of missional engagement in its own right. People who don't want to be preached at almost always still want to be prayed for." What did you think of this idea of prayer as a form of missional engagement? Have you ever tried it? What were your experiences like? And would you ever consider exploring this within your community and neighbourhood?

3. What did you think of Pete's argument that the traditional idea that we must first articulate a coherent confession in order to activate Christ's forgiveness may well be unbiblical? How does it change the nature and style of our evangelism if we approach people as those who have already been forgiven by Jesus? In what practical ways could you put that into place this week?

Prayer

> *Christ with me, Christ before me, Christ behind me,*
> *Christ in me, Christ beneath me, Christ above me,*
> *Christ on my right, Christ on my left,*
> *Christ where I lie, Christ where I sit, Christ where I arise,*
> *Christ in the heart of everyone who thinks of me,*
> *Christ in the mouth of every one who speaks to me,*
> *Christ in every eye that sees me,*
> *Christ in every ear that hears me.*
> *Salvation is of the Lord.*
> *Salvation is of the Christ.*
> *May your salvation, Lord, be ever with us. Amen.*

PRAYER BY ST. PATRICK

11—Boy's Town

The simple key to fighting injustice and unlocking your highest destiny is the word *yes* addressed to God. Perhaps he is waiting for you in a prayer room somewhere even now, or speaking to you through this book, inviting you to seek his face and to allow your heart to be broken with his deep concerns. Perhaps he is wanting to wreck your life for good; longing to give you the commission for which you were born.

Scripture Reflection: Isaiah 58:1-12; Luke 4:14-21; Amos 5:21-24

1. "'No!' she wanted to cry. 'We can't just ignore a place like that. Surely that's why we're here. Not to play religious games. Jesus wouldn't have ignored Boy's Town, and neither should we.'" Has God ever broken your heart like this for a particular place or people? How might your sung worship and prayer spill over into acts of justice and care for the poor in your community this week?
2. Kelly's compassion and calling to the people of Boy's Town resulted in many personal sacrifices being made in order to reorder her life around the broken, the hurting, and the lost. Are there any sacrifices (for example, your time or your finances) that God might be calling you to make as you serve those that he has placed on your heart? How could you support one another in this pursuit within your church community?
3. "The church, at its best, has always been radically committed to a gospel that is revolutionary both socially and spiritually." What do you think of this statement? What might it look like for the kingdom of God to radically transform both the spiritual and practical needs of your community?

Prayer

I am no longer my own but yours.
Put me to what you will, rank me with whom you will;

put me to doing, put me to suffering;
let me be employed for you, or laid aside for you,
exalted for you, or brought low for you;
let me be full, let me be empty,
let me have all things, let me have nothing:
I freely and wholeheartedly yield all things
to your pleasure and disposal.
And now, glorious and blessed God, Father, Son and Holy Spirit,
you are mine and I am yours.
And the covenant now made on earth, let it be ratified in heaven.
    Amen.

PRAYER BY JOHN WESLEY

12—The Foundery

The consequences of the gospel are profoundly structural as well as spiritual. The cross of Christ must be brought to bear on the systemic strongholds of sin within societies, as well as the individual realities of personal repentance and morality.

Scripture Reflection: Luke 18:18-29; Luke 10:25-37; Proverbs 21:15

1. When faced with the injustices in our world or when terrible disasters take place, it can be challenging to truly intercede for God's intervention. Pete lists four reasons why he suggests we struggle with this: *a limited worldview, a low self-esteem, doubts about prayer, practical questions about how to pray.* Do you identify with any of these? Is there anything else you would add to the list?

2. Do you find Pete's "three Ps" helpful in beginning to pray for global justice? *(1) People afflicted: comfort. (2) Pastors: courage. (3) Peacemakers: clarity.* Often it is easy to overlook or forget justice issues in our prayer lives. What creative measures could you put in place to help you remember the three Ps and

intercede for justice when you see suffering in your community or on the news or social media?

3. If "justice is what love looks like in public" (Dr. Cornel West), in what practical ways could you love your neighbourhood this week? What systems of oppression or dark pockets of suffering exist, and where could you "pick a fight" with injustice both globally and locally?

Prayer

Jesus, thank you that through prayer and action in the world, we can live our lives as an "Amen" to your heart for justice. Help us to dismantle the systems and structures that are creating pain in our world. Teach us how to show love and justice in our communities. And may we always love you, love our neighbours, and take the gospel to the nations. Amen.

13—Dirty Dancing

In Christ we find the name above every other name, the single key to eternal salvation, recklessly risking his reputation for the sake of love. He clearly didn't care about the opinions of the religious establishment, wasn't afraid of being corrupted by sinful company, didn't feel the need to protect his precious brand. Again and again, Jesus chose to plant his glory in the dirt.

Scripture Reflection: John 1:14; John 8:1-11; Revelation 5:8-10

1. "In Norah's room that night, watching a pastor from one of the most religious places in the Western world risking his reputation for a moment of grace with a single broken soul, I saw this same contagious holiness in action." In describing that beautiful dance between Kelly's pastor and a retired prostitute, Pete reminds us that our calling as Christians is not to shy away

from the "dirt" but to carry with us "contagious holiness" and bring grace wherever we go. How could you pursue contagious holiness this week? Is there any area where you might value your reputation more than the opportunity to show grace and kindness to people around you?

2. What do you think of the following statement from Pete? "It may well be important to advocate for the poor politically, to fight against systems of oppression structurally, to shop ethically. But Jesus teaches us to earth such engagement in localised compassion. Resisting those who wanted him to take a far stronger political stance against Roman tyranny, Jesus changed the world by changing individual hearts." Does this challenge the role that justice and mercy play in your day-to-day life? What about the life of your church community?

3. True justice begins at home with simple acts of kindness. What tangible act of kindness could you do this week that would show grace to brokenness and contagious holiness to those in your neighbourhood? Try committing to at least one relational, incarnational act of kindness this week.

Prayer

Jesus, thank you that again and again, you chose to plant your glory in the dirt. Thank you that you showed up before we had done anything at all to heal ourselves or save ourselves or make ourselves more deserving, when we were still just an unholy, seething mess. Thank you that you stood with great dignity, faced us squarely in our shame and, with a smile, invited us to dance. Please help us to live with small and great acts of kindness to the broken people around us, that we might live with contagious holiness and incarnate your grace to everyone we meet. Amen.

14—Let Us Begin

When you become a Christian you take your first step out of
futility and into your destiny. When you keep surrendering
your life, your plans and preferences, again and again, to the
Lordship of Jesus, saying yes to whatever he says, you look
around one day blinking in amazement at the ways he has
deployed you, the places he has taken you, the person he is
enabling you to become.

Scripture Reflection: Ephesians 3:20-21; John 17:20-26

1. Reflect on the Jesuit "Litany of Humility." Which aspects
    of this do you find hardest to pray? How might it affect
    unity within your church community and across all the
    denominations in your city if Christians everywhere were
    committed to unity and living this level of humility?

O Jesus, meek and humble of heart, hear me.
From the desire of being esteemed, deliver me, O Jesus.
From the desire of being loved, deliver me, O Jesus.
From the desire of being extolled, deliver me, O Jesus.
From the desire of being honoured, deliver me, O Jesus.
From the desire of being praised, deliver me, O Jesus.
From the desire of being preferred to others, deliver me, O Jesus.
From the desire of being consulted, deliver me, O Jesus.
From the desire of being approved, deliver me, O Jesus.

From the fear of being humiliated, deliver me, O Jesus.

From the fear of being despised, deliver me, O Jesus.
From the fear of suffering rebukes, deliver me, O Jesus.
From the fear of being calumniated [slandered], deliver me, O Jesus.
From the fear of being forgotten, deliver me, O Jesus.

From the fear of being ridiculed, deliver me, O Jesus.
From the fear of being wronged, deliver me, O Jesus.
From the fear of being suspected, deliver me, O Jesus.

That others may be loved more than I,
Jesus, grant me the grace to desire it.
That others may be esteemed more than I,
Jesus, grant me the grace to desire it.
That, in the opinion of the world, others may increase and I may
    decrease,
Jesus, grant me the grace to desire it.
That others may be chosen and I set aside,
Jesus, grant me the grace to desire it.
That others may be praised and I go unnoticed,
Jesus, grant me the grace to desire it.
That others may be preferred to me in everything,
Jesus, grant me the grace to desire it.
That others may become holier than I, provided that I may become as
    holy as I should,
Jesus, grant me the grace to desire it.

2. "If the previous years had taught us anything at all, it was
   simply to say yes to God and work out the details along the
   way." As this book draws to a close, is there anything you feel
   God calling you to say yes to?
3. What would "Blue Camp 20" look like in your life? And what
   is your "Santa Fe"? If, as Pete says, we have only just begun,
   what are you going to do to make sure you keep pressing
   on after God rather than settling where it feels comfortable?
   In reading this book, have you heard any divine whispers of
   kingdom mischief he might be calling you to create?

Prayer

Sovereign God. We would be a people consumed by your glory.
Set alight by the fire of God. Help us to live in the radical
simplicity of saying yes, OK, and amen to your divine whispers
. . . the plans that you have for us. And may we continually,
just like Jesus, give of ourselves to the lost, the broken, and the
needy. Spreading contagious hope and holiness . . . that your
will would be done and your kingdom come in every corner of
the earth as it is in heaven. Amen.

DISCLAIMER ABOUT MIRACLES

There are three riders I would like to place upon all the miracle stories recounted in *Dirty Glory*.

1. Miracles are rarer than they seem in this book

Don't forget that a full decade of actual living has been condensed into these pages—and I've deliberately picked out the exciting bits because, well, you would want your money back if I'd told you all the boring stuff instead. I want you to know that my life isn't an unending stream of supernatural occurrences, partly so that you don't get disillusioned with just how boring I can be if we ever actually meet, but also so that you don't get a downer on the normality of your own daily experiences (give it a decade, and you'll be surprised what happens). C. S. Lewis says: "The very conception of a common, and therefore stable, world demands that [miracles] should be extremely rare."[1] He's right, of course, but then again . . .

2. Miracles aren't as rare as you may think

"I believe in miracles," sang the soul band Hot Chocolate, before continuing, slightly less helpfully, "Since you came along, you sexy thing." We believe in miracles, we believe in the power of prayer, because Jesus is alive and he promised to answer us. You don't have to kiss your brains goodbye to believe this stuff. My last book, *God on Mute*, was honest about unanswered prayer, and a lot of people ended up reading it. I'm so glad they did. I hope I can now talk with equal honesty about miracles. No one becomes a Christian because God *doesn't* answer prayer! There are 222 prayers recorded in the Bible, excluding the Psalms, and only six of these are unanswered. That ratio sounds about right to me: thirty-six answered prayers to every one that isn't. There are far more blessings in our lives than we sometimes realise. Amazing things happen; and it's important to remember and recount these encouragements, because that's how we grow in faith. In fact, it's how half the Bible got written. If you only have one miracle story, tell it again and again until you have another one. And feel free to steal a few of ours.

3. Miracles aren't really miracles

The Hebrew mindset recognised that God is intertwined with normality, disguised in the mundane, caught up in the physical realm as well as the spiritual one. He heals supernaturally, but also through medicine. He speaks through angels, but also through donkeys. You can worship him at church, but also riding your bike down a steep hill at top speed and screaming for your life. The miracle stories in this book are classified as such merely because they are hard to explain scientifically. But there are endless things that science *can* explain which are still infused with God's mystery and presence. Like a starfield at night, or a human iris, or a baby born with its own unique fingerprints. If you feel like you don't see many miracles, try celebrating God's presence in the normal stuff, thanking him for every coincidence, and yes, cheesy as it may sound, counting your blessings. As you thank God for all the really understandable stuff, you will one day soon—sooner than you might think—find yourself thanking God for a few things that those nice people in white coats (shrinks and scientists alike) can't fully explain. When that happens, you might like to try recording your experiences in a journal, and then you could one day draw the threads together and help me write the next book in this series of Red Moon Chronicles.

A NOTE TO MY AMERICAN FRIENDS

(WITH GLOSSARY)

Dear cousins,

My publishers in Colorado have kindly, carefully weeded from
the pages of this book many of my trickier, more befuddling
English expressions, whilst attempting to retain the "quirky"
old-world weirdness of the way I spell. Of course, this may well
have been a terrible mistake. As the Irish playwright George
Bernard Shaw observed, "England and America are two nations
divided by a common language."

    When we lived on the great Midwestern plains, we
certainly encountered endless subtle, occasionally hilarious,
cultural and linguistic differences between your version of
English and ours. For instance, when you say *pants* we hear
underwear. This can be unsettling when you think the school
receptionist is publicly admiring your smalls. Similarly, when
you talk about your *purse* we picture a wallet, and when you
say *football* we assume you mean a game involving a foot as
well as a ball. Your chips are our crisps, and our chips are
your fries. Our state schools are your public schools, and
your public schools are our most exclusive private schools.

We call a vest a waistcoat and an undershirt a vest. Your train tracks are our braces, our braces are your suspenders, and your suspenders are an intimate item of lingerie for English ladies. We have absolutely no idea what you mean when you say words like *duplex*, *faucet*, *zucchini*, and *rutabaga*. You say "tom-ay-to" and we say "tom-ah-to."

What else? Well, when you talk about falling on your fanny or introduce yourself as Randy we hear something very, very different. I'd rather not explain. Unfortunately we also refer to pitchers as "jugs." No one warned me about this until an unfortunate conversation one Sunday breakfast with a pastor's wife at a megachurch in Florida. I'll leave the embarrassment to your imagination.

We are indebted to you, America, for so many reasons. You have given us Disney, Robert Frost, Elvis, and *West Wing*. For these we are grateful. In return we offer you Shakespeare, the Beatles, C. S. Lewis, and *Downton Abbey*. We appreciate the fact that God has blessed you with Silicon Valley, perfect dentistry, and Chuck E. Cheese, whilst giving us the lesser-known delights of haggis, cricket, and the ultimate ability to make a decent cup of tea.

Here in the Old World, the word *route* does not rhyme with *doubt* but with *boot*, *toot*, *fruit*, *shoot*, and *loot* (blame the French). You'll have noticed that we also spell things differently, like *aluminium* (notice that extra *i*), *colour*, and *honour*—for most of these offences you can also blame the French. We call diapers *nappies*, baby strollers are actually *prams*, sidewalks are *pavements*, the trunk of your car is the *boot* of ours, a truck is really a *lorry*, and a highway is a *motorway*.

And while we're on the subject of driving, we do it on the left for a very good reason: to ensure that our sword hands are free to attack approaching knights (you are, as a nation, currently in grave danger from oncoming knights).

God bless America! God save the Queen! God help us communicate!

Pete

P.S. If you are Canadian, South African, Australian, or from New Zealand, this list (like so many things) only half-applies to you.

UK ENGLISH	US ENGLISH
Accident & Emergency	Emergency Room
Ambulance	Emergency vehicle
Aubergine	Eggplant
Biscuit	Cookie
Bonnet (car)	Hood
Boot (car)	Trunk
Braces	Train-tracks
Braces	Suspenders
Candyfloss	Cotton candy
Car park	Parking lot
Caravan	Trailer
Cashpoint	ATM
Chemist	Drugstore
Chips	Fries
Crisps	Chips
Cinema	Movie theatre
Cupboard	Closet
Dustbin	Trash can
Fag (*sl.*)	Cigarette
Flat	Apartment
Fly (*sl.*)	Zipper

UK ENGLISH	US ENGLISH
Football	Soccer
Garden	Yard
Handbag	Purse
Holiday	Vacation
Houses of Parliament	Congress
Housing estate	Housing development
Jumper	Sweater
Lift	Elevator
Lorry	Truck
Motorway	Highway / Freeway
Mobile	Cell phone
Mum / mummy	Mom / mommy
Number plate	License plate
Off licence	Liquor store
Pants	Underwear
Pavement	Sidewalk
Polo neck	Turtleneck
Porridge	Oatmeal
Postcode	Zip code
Purse	Wallet
Pushchair	Stroller
Sweets	Candy
Queue	Line
Tap	Faucet
Tartan	Plaid
Tights	Pantyhose
Toilet	Rest room
Trainers	Sneakers
Trolley (shopping)	Cart (shopping)
Trousers	Pants
Undergound	Subway
Vicar	Anglican church pastor
Wardrobe	Closet
Windscreen	Windshield
Zed	Zee

NOTES

INTRODUCTION

1. M. M. Poloma and G. H. Gallup Jr., *Varieties of Prayer: A Survey Report* (Harrisburg, PA: Trinity Press International, 1991).
2. General Social Survey 2008; C. Bader, K. Dougherty, P. Froese, B. Johnson, F. C. Mencken, J. Park, et al., *American Piety in the 21st Century: New Insights to the Depth and Complexity of Religion in the US: Selected Findings from the Baylor Religion Survey* (Waco, TX: Baylor Institute for Studies of Religion, 2006).
3. *The Times*, Sunday, January 17, 2016, reporting on a 2015 YouGov poll of British beliefs.
4. Hugh Stuart Boyd, *Select Passages of the Writings of St. Chrysostom, St. Gregory Nazianzen and St. Basil* (Whitefish, MT: Kessinger Publishing, 2006), 32–33.
5. Boiler Room communities are explained in chapter 12.

CHAPTER 1: PUNK MESSIAH

1. The word translated "flesh" in English (in John 1:14) was originally the Greek σάρξ (*sarx*), a descriptor of flesh which predominantly carried the same sense of carnality that was later expressed in the Latin *caro*.
2. Within sixty years of Christ's resurrection, the gospel had spread throughout Asia Minor to the extent that there may have been as many as 100,000 Greek-speaking Christians— most of them Gentile—to every Hebrew- or Aramaic-speaking believer.
3. William Barclay, *The Gospel of John*, vol. 1 (Edinburgh: Saint Andrew Press, 1975).
4. Gerard Manley Hopkins, "The Blessed Virgin Compared to the Air We Breathe" (1883).
5. Joel Green, *The Gospel of Luke* (Grand Rapids, MI: Eerdmans, 1997), 310.
6. Mary is mentioned no fewer than twelve times in the Gospels, more than most of the male apostles. In his third-century commentary on Song of Songs, Hippolytus of Rome described Mary Magdalene as *apostolarum apostola* (apostle to the apostles).

CHAPTER 2: THE TIME OF OUR LIVES

1. Augustine's *Confessions*, book III, trans. Henry Chadwick (Oxford World Classics, 2008), 35.
2. Quincy Jones, quoted in Joy T. Bennett, "Michael: The Thrill Is Back," *Ebony*, December 2007, 90.

CHAPTER 3: ENCOUNTER CULTURE

1. *Rolling Stone* magazine commissioned journalist Kimberley Sevcik to write the 5,000-word feature which focused particularly on 24-7's innovative approach to mission in Ibiza. Its release was delayed by coverage of the presidential election. The article, entitled "Christian Party Animals," was ultimately published in December 2004 by Salon.com. Accessed June 1, 2016, at http://www.salon.com/2004/12/10/evangelicals_10/.
2. The Boiler Room network is a worldwide family of missional and monastic communities committed to a shared life of prayer, mission, and justice.
3. Robert L. Wilken, *The Spirit of Early Christian Thought* (New Haven, CN: Yale University Press, 2005).
4. Andy Crouch, "No Jesus, No Justice," January 9, 2014, Andy-Crouch.com.
5. Mother Teresa, quoted in Brian Kolodiejchuk, M.C., ed., *Mother Teresa: Come Be My Light: The Private Writings of the Saint of Calcutta* (New York: Doubleday, 2007), 41.
6. Mother Teresa, Nobel lecture, December 11, 1979, http://www.nobelprize.org /nobel_prizes/peace/laureates/1979/teresa-lecture.html.
7. Wilken, *The Spirit of Early Christian Thought*, 108.

CHAPTER 4: THE PRESENCE PARADIGM

1. Duncan Campbell, *Principles that Govern a Spiritual Quickening* (Faith Mission Recordings, n.d.).
2. Carol Arnott, "The Purpose of Soaking in His Love," *Revival Magazine*, February 28, 2001.
3. Paul Vallely, *Pope Francis: Untying the Knots* (New York: Bloomsbury Continuum, 2013), 144.
4. Madeleine L'Engle, citing *Priests among Men*, by Cardinal Emmanuel Célestin Suhard, who served as Archbishop of Paris from 1940 until his death in 1949, a period that included the German invasion and occupation of France.
5. Henri J. M. Nouwen, *In the Name of Jesus: Reflections on Christian Leadership* (New York: Crossroad, 1989), 37.
6. Augustine's *Confessions* (Lib 1,1–2,2.5,5: CSEL 33,1–5).
7. This is the famous opening confession of the Westminster Shorter Catechism of 1647.

CHAPTER 5: ALL HELL

1. Barry K. Ray, Manuel C. Vallejo, Mitchell D. Creinin, et al., "Amniotic Fluid Embolism with Second Trimester Pregnancy Termination: A Case Report," *Canadian Journal of Anaesthesia*, vol. 51, February 2004, 139–144.
2. The story of Misha McClung's healing is told, and explored, in greater detail in chapter 5 of my *God on Mute: Engaging the Silence of Unanswered Prayer* (Grand Rapids, MI: Baker, 2012).
3. Karl Barth, *Prayer*, 50th anniversary ed. (Louisville, KY: Westminster John Knox, 2002), 13.

4. Martin Luther, *Luther's Works*, vol. 54 (Minneapolis: Fortress, 1967), 94.

5. Blaise Pascal, *Pensées* (CreateSpace, 2011), 63.

6. Gordon Kaufman, cited in Melanie C. Ross, *Evangelical versus Liturgical* (Grand Rapids, MI: Eerdmans, 2014), 50.

7. J. R. R. Tolkien, *The Fellowship of the Ring* (New York: Mariner Books, 2012), 68.

CHAPTER 6: SUPER BOWL

1. Deb and Jack Welch continue to mobilise prayer through Lite the Fire Ministries.

2. Origen, *Contra Celsus*, 1.65-66.

3. Karl Barth, *Church Dogmatics*, vol. 3, The Doctrine of Creation, part 3 (London: Bloomsbury T & T Clark, 1960), 288.

4. P. T. Forsyth, *The Soul of Prayer* (Rough Draft Printing, 2012), 94.

5. Hugh Black, *Revival—Personal Encounters* (New Dawn, 1993), 77.

6. Arthur Wallis, *In the Day of Thy Power* (Washington, PA: CLC Publications, 1956).

7. John Donne, *The Works of John Donne* (Amazon Digital Services, 2013), 423.

8. Charles Finney, *Lectures on Revival of Religion* (Belding, MI: Alethea In Heart, 2005), 35.

9. Lettie B. Cowman, *Streams in the Desert* (Grand Rapids, MI: Zondervan, 1999), 244.

CHAPTER 7: BLUE CAMP 20

1. William G. Johnston, *Overland to California* (Oakland, CA: Biobooks, 1948).

2. I pose this idea about the naming of Haran (the place: הָרָן) after Terah's son (הָרָן) very tentatively. Although the names are the same in the English transliteration, they are different in the original Hebrew. The point should therefore be taken more allegorically than exegetically, as a device illustrating the human tendency to "camp out" in our grief.

3. Coretta Scott King, foreword to *Standing in the Need of Prayer* (New York: The Free Press, 2008).

CHAPTER 8: STRANGE ANGELS

1. Stephen Spencer, *Christ in All Things: William Temple and His Writings* (Norwich: Canterbury Press, 2015).

CHAPTER 9: PORKY THE PIRATE

1. Ernest Hemingway, *Ernest Hemingway: Selected Letters 1917–61*, ed. Carlos Baker (New York: Simon & Schuster, 2003), 88.

2. John Telford, *The Life of John Wesley* (London: Epworth Press, 1929), 394.

3. Eugene Peterson, *Where Your Treasure Is* (Grand Rapids, MI: Eerdmans, 1993), 65.

4. Donald Miller, *A Million Miles in a Thousand Years* (Thomas Nelson, 2009).

CHAPTER 10: WORD ON THE STREET

1. William Hogarth's famous etching *Gin Lane* depicts a sign over one of the taverns reading: "Drunk for a penny / Dead drunk for two / Clean straw for nothing."

2. Vincent J. Donovan, *Christianity Rediscovered: An Epistle from the Masai* (London: SCM Press, 1982), preface.

3. The church in question was Hope Missionary Church in Bluffton, Indiana, led by Pastor Gary Aupperle. Names in this story have been changed.

4. Craig L. Blomberg, *Contagious Holiness: Jesus' Meals with Sinners* (Downers Grove, IL: IVP Academic, 2005), 128, 167.

5. Ibid.
6. Ibid., cf. Romans 5:8.
7. Ambassador Charles Malik's speech at the dedication of the Billy Graham Center at Wheaton College, September 1980, cited in Billy Graham, *Just As I Am* (New York: HarperCollins, 2007), 647.
8. To find out more about the Princeton Pledge and the history of God's work on America's campuses see Trent Sheppard, *God on Campus: Sacred Causes and Global Effects* (Downers Grove, IL: InterVarsity Press, 2010).
9. The Campus America initiative filled the year 2007 with continuous intercession on US university and college campuses. Mobile "Wilder" teams also toured campuses, stirring up the flames of intercession amongst students, inspired by Robert Wilder's historic 1886–1887 tour. As part of this initiative, Trent Sheppard released his brilliant summary of American student mission, *God on Campus*. Universities continue to be a primary strategic focus for the 24-7 movement in America and around the world.

CHAPTER 11: BOY'S TOWN

1. The Divine Comedy, "Eye of the Needle," from the album *Regeneration* (Parlophone EMI, 2001).
2. W. C. Wright, trans., "Julian the Apostate: Letter to Arsacius, High Priest of Galatia, AD 362," in *Works*, vol. 3, accessed June 6, 2016, at http://www.tertullian.org/fathers/julian_apostate_letters_1_trans.htm.
3. See Tim Chester, *Good News to the Poor* (Wheaton, IL: Crossway, 2013), 14, 37.
4. The Stockbridge Boiler Room: http://www.stockbridgeboilerroom.org.
5. The businessman, Clark Milspaugh, served on the board of 24-7 Prayer USA and established The Harvest, a church and a market in West Tulsa. See www.WestSideHarvest.com.

CHAPTER 12: THE FOUNDERY

1. Rule of St. Benedict, 53:1, trans. Abbot Parry, OSB (Leominster, UK: Gracewing, 1990), 83.
2. Óscar Romero, *The Violence of Love* (Maryknoll, NY: Orbis, 1988), 18.
3. Pete and Sarah's community is called The Tree of Life, Manenberg. See https://vimeo.com/111198014.

CHAPTER 13: DIRTY DANCING

1. Samuel Wells and Marcia A. Owen, *Living without Enemies: Being Present in the Midst of Violence* (Downers Grove, IL: InterVarsity Press, 2011), 30. Italics in original.

CHAPTER 14: LET US BEGIN

1. This idea of Christian unity comes from Nicky Gumbel.
2. For the unabridged version of this prayer, see "Litany of Humility" by Cardinal Rafael Merry del Val, secretary of state to Pope Saint Pius X, from the *Prayer Book for Jesuits* (1963).
3. Seraphim of Sarov, quoted in Harry Boosalis, *The Joy of the Holy* (Waymart, PA: St. Tikhon's Seminary Press, 1993), 82.
4. Gregory of Palamas, quoted in Paul Evdokimov, *The Art of the Icon: A Theology of Beauty* (London: Oakwood Publishers, 2011), 3.

5. Heather King, *Words of Wisdom for Every New Mom* (New York: Avon Books, 1994).
6. Origen, quoted in Robert L. Wilken, *The Spirit of Early Christian Thought* (New Haven, CT: Yale University Press, 2005), 22.
7. John Piper, *Seeing and Savoring Jesus Christ* (Wheaton, IL: Crossway, 2004), 35–36.
8. Karl Barth, *The Epistle to the Philippians* (Louisville, KY: Westminster John Knox, 2002), 15.
9. St Francis, quoted in *Francis and Clare: The Complete Works*, ed. Regis J. Armstrong and Ignatius C. Brady (New York: Paulist Press, 1982), xii.
10. Alasdair MacIntyre, *After Virtue: A Study in Moral Theory* (London: Bloomsbury Academic, 2011), 305.
11. The Order of the Mustard Seed (OMS)—find out more at http://24-7prayer.com.
12. Jason Mandryk, *Operation World: The Definitive Prayer Guide to Every Nation* (Downers Grove, IL: InterVarsity, 2010), xxiii.

DISCLAIMER ABOUT MIRACLES

1. C. S. Lewis, *The Problem of Pain* (New York: HarperCollins, 2001), 25.

INDEX OF BIBLE REFERENCES

ABOUT THE AUTHOR

PETE GREIG is one of the bewildered founders of the the 24-7 Prayer movement, the Senior Pastor of Emmaus Rd in Guildford, England, and a vice-president of the NGO Tearfund. He has written or co-written a number of books and resources, available in various languages, including the following:

>
> *Red Moon Rising: How Prayer Is Awakening a Generation*
> (David C. Cook, 2003, 2015)
> *The Vision and the Vow: A Call to Discipleship*
> (David C. Cook, 2004)
> *God on Mute: Engaging the Silence of Unanswered Prayer*
> (Baker Books/David C. Cook, 2007)
> *The Prayer Course: A Six-Part Video Series for Small Groups*
> *Exploring the Lord's Prayer* (Alpha International, 2013)

Information about all Pete's books, as well as his latest writing projects, can be found at http://www.petegreig.info, where you will also find additional information, photographs and perhaps the odd video relating to the contents of this particular book. Information about the 24-7 prayer movement can be found at http://24-7prayer.com.

ACKNOWLEDGMENTS

I am indebted to those who allowed me to tell their stories in this book. It has truly been an honour to do so.

A number of people took time to make the manuscript considerably better than it would otherwise have been: Brian Heasley, Carla Harding, Gill Greig-Allen, Hannah Heather (who also wrote the study guide), Ian Nicholson, Jon Petersen, Jonny Hughes, Kelly Tietsort, Mark Knight, Phil Togwell, Roger Nix, and Roy Goble. Special thanks are due to Gill and Peter, Nick and Jane, for providing cloistered space in which I was able to hide away and write.

Don Pape and David Zimmerman at NavPress and Katherine Venn at Hodder have been incredible. Your encouragement, patience, prayers, and forensic advice have stretched far beyond the bounds of normal editorial duty. Thank you.

I am also indebted to the leadership teams at both Emmaus Rd and 24-7 International for putting up with my absences, to Ben Connolly from Angel & Anchor for the illustrations, and to Holly Dobson for her unstinting thoughtfulness, support, and patience.

Finally, thank you to Sammy, Hudson, and Danny. This story is our story. I love you more than words can say.

WANT TO BE IN THE NEXT BOOK IN THE SERIES?

You've read the story, now help us write the next chapter.

JOIN THE MOVEMENT AT 24-7PRAYER.COM

PRAY WITH US

Run a 24-7 prayer room where you live /PRAYERROOMS	Host a Kingdom Come event /KINGDOMCOME	Watch our award-winning podcasts /PODCASTS

TRAIN WITH US

Run The Prayer Course /PRAYERCOURSE	Enrol on The Vision Course /VISIONCOURSE	Come to our next conference /EVENTS

FIGHT WITH US

Add your voice to a justice campaign /PICKAFIGHT	Join an international mission team /MISSIONTEAMS	Support us with a gift /DONATE

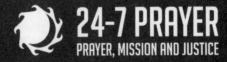

24-7 PRAYER

PRAYER, MISSION AND JUSTICE

CP1173